Life's Little Parables
and
Other Lessons Along the Way

Life's Little Parables
and
Other Lessons Along the Way

A Year of Daily Devotionals

by
Patricia Harper Cummings

E-BookTime, LLC
Montgomery, Alabama

Life's Little Parables and Other Lessons Along the Way
A Year of Daily Devotionals

ISBN: 978-1-60862-255-9

Second Edition
Published January 2011
E-BookTime, LLC
6598 Pumpkin Road
Montgomery, AL 36108
www.e-booktime.com

First edition published by Xulon Press, 2005

Also by Patricia Harper Cummings
Published by E-BookTime, LLC:

Making Room for Jesus: The Secret Life of Prayer, 2007

Through the Valleys with Jesus, 2008

Help for Clergy Wives, How to Please Without Being a Pleaser, 2009

Dedication

In memory and honor of:

All those whom the Lord has used to teach me along the way — my ancestors, my parents, my husband, my sons, Michael and Daniel, their wives, Karen and Becki, my granddaughter, Kaylee, my nieces, Laura and Nancy, my nephew, Steve, my extended family, my faithful friends, my pastors and my many spiritual mentors.

Introduction

O God, you have taught me from my earliest childhood, and I constantly tell others about the wonderful things you do. Psalm 71:17 (NLT)

Through the years the Lord Has taught me many things. I've written about these lessons over a period of more than 30 years so that I could share what I've learned with you, my dear readers! I've found that the Holy Spirit speaks to us all in many different ways — through the Bible, dreams, visions, music, Christian authors, family members, pastors, spiritual mentors, counselors, friends, enemies, through sad times, through joyful times, and through His marvelous creation, to name some. In one sense, this book will never be finished; there is always more to learn and more to share. I'm reminded of what the Apostle John wrote at the end of his gospel: *Jesus also did many other things. If they were all written down, I suppose the whole world could not contain the books that would be written.* John 21:25 (NLT)

JANUARY

January 1

A New Beginning

When our son, Michael, was about four years old, he was all excited about the winter holidays. His hazel eyes were larger than usual, his little feet running around, checking out the food, and awaiting with anticipation the arrival of the guests for the New Year's Eve party at our home. Soon the house was swarming with people laughing, talking and eating. In his usual friendly manner, he was getting right into the swing of it all. He plopped himself down on a sofa beside one of the guests and with an original and enthusiastic blend of Christmas and New Year's greetings, blurted out: "Well, merry endings!" All of us who were within hearing range burst out laughing.

He got it right! We were in the midst of saying good-bye to the old year and why should the endings not be merry?

But just think of this: The New Year is a clean slate, a clear calendar before us. We don't know what it will bring for the world or for us. As someone said long ago, "We don't know what the future holds but we do know who holds the future." So simple. So true. Let us trust in God for our future, including this New Year. Putting our faith in Him is the only place it really belongs!

Trust in the LORD with all your heart; do not depend on your own understanding. Seek his will in all you do, and he will direct your paths. Proverbs 3:5, 6 (NLT)

Well Lord, here I am. I made it through the Christmas season and into a brand new year. Now I trust you completely with the coming days. I hope for opportunities to believe you more, learn new lessons, recall old wisdom, and find ways in which to serve you and others day-by-day, moment-by-moment. Amen.

January 2

The Prayer of Faith

Did you hear about the little boy who, before he went to bed, came into the living room where his parents and their guests were sitting and said, "I'm going to say my prayers now; does anyone want anything?" That's it! I believe that's the way to go to the Father in prayer. When our hearts have become transformed by gazing on the glory of His presence, we will see God more clearly and recognize what He is doing in our lives and in the lives of those around us, and realize anew that He wants to give good gifts to His children. So we can ask our good Father for good gifts!

Once when I was at a World Vision staff meeting in the early 1960s, Bob Pierce, the founder, said, "When you have the ear of the King, ask for everything in sight." Again, that's it! Do you have the ear of the King? Are you willing to wait until you get it? It will happen. Don't give up. God is there to hear and answer all of our heart-felt prayers, offered up in faith.

> *Let the little children alone, and do not stop them from coming to me; for it is to such as these that the kingdom of Heaven belongs.* Matthew. 19:14 (The New Jerusalem Bible, © 1985 by Darton, Langman & Todd, Ltd. and Doubleday & Company, Inc.)

Father in Heaven, whatever the answers we receive from you, *yes*, *no*, or *wait*, help us to remember and believe that you are the good Parent and on our side, and that you give us grace sufficient for every day even when our desires are not granted. Amen.

January 3

Angels on the Wind

Throughout my life I have had strange moments of sensing something mysteriously special around me. I don't *see* anything, but all of a sudden, there is a freshness, a peace in the air; there is love and holiness standing by me; there is a sweet after-the-rain scent all about me. It can happen any time, and almost anywhere.

The last time I experienced it, I was not feeling well. I went outside and sat in our patio to read. Suddenly I felt the unmistakable visitation of this almost palpable beauty around me. It lasted only a few seconds, but for those sweet moments, I was reminded that I am never alone. It was as though a sweet scent in the air had been borne on the wings of a gentle breeze. Perhaps what I've sensed at such times is the presence of an angelic being just passing by to offer a gift of silent love from the Father's hand.

If you ever feel this kind of touch too, why not say *thank you* to the Father of Lights who has sent a bearer of a little piece of light into the world to warm your heart on a cold winter's day.

> *Every good gift and every perfect gift is from above, and comes down from the Father of Lights, with whom there is no variation or shadow of turning.* James 1:17 (NKJV)

Dear Heavenly Father, thank you for the good gifts you send to us like the touch of angels' wings when most needed. Amen.

January 4

A Choice of Winds

As children, we used to call them "whirl winds" — what appear to be miniature tornadoes that swirled around the school yard, scooping up dust and moving it somewhere else, disappearing and then reappearing again.

In the Arizona desert they call them "dust devils." They can whip up the dry earth at any time and whirl through your yard, making a mess and then disappearing the next moment. They are well named for that is just like the devil, isn't it — making trouble here and there, and then disappearing so we can't even point a finger!

But what about us? We too can become a little devil whirlwind and stir up things and then leave and watch from a distance, as someone may struggle with what we have left behind. That is why we need to watch our words as well as our actions. It's so easy to say, "But I didn't *do* anything," when it isn't what we did, but what we *said* that caused the problem! We do have a choice. We, as a born again people, have within us the Holy Spirit, the winsome wonder, whom Jesus described as being like the wind. We can be like that too — quietly, like a gentle breeze, touching those around us with a warm smile, a word of praise, an encouraging comment, a gentle touch on a shoulder, doing what the Spirit of God within us is telling us to do! I want to be like that, don't you?

> *The wind blows where it wants to and you hear the sound of it, but you don't know where the wind comes from or where it is going. It is the same with every person who is born from the Spirit.* John 3:8 (NCV)

Lord God, help me to be like a gentle wind that comes and goes, leaving behind that which is a blessing to those around me. Amen.

January 5

Hiding Places

Today I was driving behind a black Ford Bronco. On it was a bumper sticker that read: "The last best hiding place: Lincoln, Montana." I did not know at the time that this was an allusion to the hideout of the Unabomber, Ted Kaczynski. I said to myself *No, not the last and not the best either, no matter how safe a get-a-way that might be.* I thought about the Garden of Eden and how Adam and Eve, after sinning, hid from God (as though that were possible). He called to them in the cool of the evening, "Where are you?" Isn't it ironic that God, from whom we originally wanted so desperately to hide, is the One who offers us what really is the *last best hiding place*?

Do you ever feel like David who said, *"Hide me under the shadow of Your wings,"* (Ps. 17:8) and *"He shall hide me in His pavilion; in the secret place of His tabernacle He shall hide me..."* (Ps. 27:5). God offers a refuge like no other, not in a place, but in a person — in Himself, not only from spiritual danger, but in Himself as Savior *from* Himself as judge. He hides His face from our sins that we might not have to hide ourselves from Him, but can rather flee *to* Him — not just in the day of trouble, but always, any time, and forevermore. God doesn't call me asking, "Where are you?" He knows where I am — I'm hidden in Him.

> *You are my hiding place; You protect me from trouble. You surround me with songs of victory.* Psalm 32:7 (NLT)

Oh, my Lord, I thank you for giving my spirit this safe refuge. Let me never remove myself from it, but stay there in the hollow of Your hand. Amen.

January 6

False Authority and True

One church consultant that we met while Don was a pastor in Goodyear, AZ was so sure that she knew everything there was to know about church procedure and policy that on occasions when her authority should have been questioned, it was not. Her rules and regulations became legalistic and brought a bondage that scripture warns us against.

Some have an innate charismatic aura of authority and when we are searching for someone to look up to, it's easy to follow one who presents such a confident air. We may believe we can find easy answers as we seek this authority figure to which we can turn. It is this same false, but convincing, authority that cult leaders possess, bringing to themselves needy, but unwise, followers.

One of the most priceless things we as Christians have is the authority of the Bible that we know to be inspired by the Holy Spirit. It is that which gives us all the knowledge we need to live life fully now, here on Earth, and into Eternity as well. So with this source of divine wisdom, we have a plumb line by which to judge all the other information that is "out there."

> *All Scripture is given by God and is useful for teaching, for showing people what is wrong in their lives, for correcting faults, and for teaching how to live right. Using the Scriptures, the person who serves God will be capable, having all that is needed to do every good work.* 2 Timothy 3:16, 17 (NCV)

Dear Father, thank you for inspiring the writers of the Bible so that we have a book to which we can turn for the answers to our deepest questions about life. You have done your part; now help me to do mine — in reading and listening to what you speak to me through your word, the Bible. Amen.

January 7

Bibliophobia

As I was growing up I had a fear of books. With the dread of books, came the fear of learning, because as I read, I discovered how little I knew. It meant I had to face my own ignorance, and there was something in me that feared that ignorance being exposed. The way one would expose ignorance is to ask questions. So I didn't ask. I was afraid to ask questions even in classes at school where it would be, of course, most useful and most expected. I thought I had to know it all, even before I read the text or attended a single classroom lecture.

Then I met Carol. Carol unabashedly asked questions any time she felt like it, which, much to my astonishment was often. There was, of course, as with us all, an amazing amount of things that she did not know, but she was not in the least ashamed to let other people discover her lack of knowledge. Furthermore, after she asked, I noted, she then had acquired valuable and satisfying information, and all this was done without shame! I'm thankful for Carol's friendship in my life and I'm thankful that because of her example I was finally able to admit what I didn't know about the value of asking questions. I learned something wonderful from her — that it was OK to be openly curious, that no one thinks less of one for the asking, and I've been learning how to do it ever since.

I've also found that it's possible to ask God for answers and that He does not belittle us for doing so. The Holy Spirit is our teacher and the Bible, of course, is our textbook, what some call "the owner's manual." Through the years, many of the questions I've had about life and salvation, morality and meaning have been answered, though new questions have arisen. Also, as I've prayed, I've found that when there is truly something I need to know, in time, the Holy Spirit will reveal it to me through one source or another.

If you need wisdom—if you want to know what God wants you to do—ask him, and he will gladly tell you. He will not resent your asking. But when you ask him, be sure that you really expect him to answer, for a doubtful mind is as unsettled as a wave of the sea that is driven and tossed by the wind. James 1:5, 6(NLT)

Dear Father, I thank you for friends in my life who have taught me simple things. I pray that I will grow and learn by continuing to ask without embarrassment. Give me holy curiosity about life and love and Godly wisdom and then, lead me into the truth about these things. Amen.

January 8

Bill's Hill

Bill is a friend who has a special hobby — a hill. He has owned the property with a small hill for a backyard for many years. During that time he has planted, and weeded, sowed and reaped. His vision was to make the hill accessible to all, so he started at the bottom, as any good workman would do, cleared away brush and wild vegetation and began to build a stone wall and a red brick switch-back trail up to the top. His great joy was in the process of the building and, over the years, he, stone-by-stone, brick-by-brick, with steadfast patience, built the wall and laid the path all the way to the top. And what awaits the hiker at the end of the journey? Well, there's a stone and brass sundial, a hammock in which to rest, and a radio fastened to a tree so that one may listen to music or a Dodger baseball game. Or one just might rest and read in the midst of this verdant hillside, lush with ferns, oleander bushes and pine trees, mocking birds and doves, and a cool breeze from the not-too-distant Pacific Ocean. That is where you will find Bill on a Sunday afternoon — enjoying his hill at its topmost to his utmost! It was created that he might enjoy it to the fullest.

And so God works on us. You've no doubt seen the bumper sticker, "Be patient with me. God hasn't finished with me yet." Our Heavenly Father allows life to work on us, weeding and planting, trimming and pruning, so that He can enjoy us, not only now in our imperfection, but to the fullest when the work is finished! And He will finish what he's started. We can count on it.

God began doing a good work in you, and I am sure he will
continue it until it is finished when Jesus Christ comes again.
Philippians 1:6 (NCV)

Dear Lord, thank you for being my patient care giver — the one who carefully allows me to go through some joyful times and some painful times so that I may flourish and become the person you want me to be — a new creation in Christ. Amen.

January 9

The Courageous Follower

I watched her from the car, the swallow flying toward the north. But there was a wind blowing from the direction in which she was headed, and at exactly the same speed at which she was flying. She appeared to hang in the air motionless, but her sights were on her destination and so she did not give up. I watched as long as I could, and she had made no progress, but, of course, eventually that wind would die down and she would be free to go home to the nest where she would find her young ones waiting for her.

That is how I feel sometimes, trying so hard to get somewhere, and all the time feeling that I am on a treadmill, "Going no place fast." But I know the key is the same as for that little mother — to keep my eyes on the destination! And what is that destination for all those who follow Jesus? It is: To do the will of God by living justly, showing mercy to others and following Him, thereby proving that we love Him with our entire being.

He has shown you, O man, what is good; And what does the Lord require of you But to do justly, to love mercy, and to walk humbly with your God. Micah 6:8 (NKJV)

Dear Shepherd, sometimes I feel as though we walk hand-in-hand. At other times, I feel that you have gone on far ahead of me. Help me, just like that swallow, not to give up. Please, remind me that should I become lost you will come back for me and meanwhile, help me to keep you ever before me so that I may continue on the path that you have forged ahead for me. Amen.

January 10

The Blue Bottle

The blue glass was returned to me! This time it took the form of a bottle. Don and I were treated to dinner one evening at a fine restaurant, and I ordered mineral water. It came in a beautiful, blue glass bottle — all the way from Wales. It struck me as apropos because John Roberts, the gentleman who was treating us to this special meal, was from Wales himself and would be on his way back there the very next morning. Yet there we were, sitting in a restaurant in Avondale, Arizona! I asked the waiter if I could have the bottle and he said, "Yes, that's why I left it on the table, in case you should ask."

What the bottle reminds me of is my first (and only) physical altercation at some unknown but young age. I was not at fault at first of course, but I will admit that Suzy B. just might have seen the piece of cobalt blue almost hidden in the dust at our feet, before I did. However, it was on my folk's property, so, it rightfully belonged to me, didn't it? We fought physically. I think that this was the first time I expressed anger openly. But there was, you see, the *principle* of the thing. In the end, she won, and took the silly, little piece of broken blue glass home with her, claiming self-righteously, "It belongs to my mother." She lied, of course, just once again, like always. And I saw somewhere in my heart that wrong should not win like that, though I didn't know the word "justice" yet. The old, deeply ingrained inner voice was saying loudly, "It's not fair!" The blue glass belonged to me. So I lost.

Or did I? Here it is fifty years later and there the cobalt blue glass in the form of a bottle, somehow rightfully mine, sits on a stand beside my computer, looking stately and beautiful. It is a reminder to me that God restores to us what we have lost. He keeps track and, in some time, or perhaps some eternity, we will receive it back from His generous hand, a hand that never stops giving.

> *I will restore to you the years that the swarming locust has eaten...* Joel 2:25 (NKJV)

Dear Heavenly Father, there are things in life that were wrongfully taken from my loved ones or from me. I pray that anything that has been stolen from us, and that we truly need, will be returned to us by your generous hand. Those things that do not come back to me, whether dreams or heartbreaks, spiritual or material, I freely give to you, to hold or to restore, according to your perfect will, in this life or the next. Amen.

January 11

The Unruly Tongue

Gossip is one of the things that God despises. In the sixth chapter of Proverbs it says that there are seven things that the Lord hates: Among these things are: "a lying tongue" and "a false witness who speaks lies and one who sows discord among brethren." When my husband and I lived in a small community in Arizona, we had the experience of meeting someone who gossiped about others and, later on, about us. I think we should have talked with this individual early on as we, as Christians, are called to correct and rebuke the unruly and she had an unruly tongue, but we underestimated the damage that can be done by just one person. She passed on just a tale or two, a bit of distortion here, just sowing a little doubt there, and then watched as the pot stirred itself. These few words spoken to a few key people in the church could have destroyed Don's ministry. It could have destroyed the church. There was an answer, but it was far more drastic than it needed to be: This person had to be exposed. It was a grueling and painful experience for her and for us, and she continued even in the midst of this controversy to strike out at my husband with more lies rather than accepting correction. Ultimately, there was a way in which it destroyed her place in the church.

God allowed this to happen. I hope that a warning will suffice: A little gossip can break a heart, kill someone's reputation, and destroy someone's credibility in his or her profession. It doesn't take much. We are told in scripture to keep guard over our tongues. Perhaps the importance of this admonition is greatly underestimated. Be careful, dear friends, you and I are accountable for every word our tongues speak.

I tell you, on the day of judgment you will have to give an account for every careless word you utter, for by your words you will be justified, and by your words you will be condemned. Matthew 12:36, 37 (NRSV)

Dear Holy Spirit, please help me guard my tongue. Help my words to uplift and encourage and correct in love but never do personal or spiritual damage. Amen.

January 12

Soap Bubbles

Is there anything quite so marvelous as a soap bubble? It is delicate, beautiful, an orbed rainbow! When my brother, Preston, and I were little children, a friend of my mother's, Bea, used to blow bubbles for us when we bathed together. Oh, not just little bubbles — really big, long, balloon-like bubbles, and they would last forever! We thought she had some magical ability. She blew with intense concentration and lots of steady, patient, long breaths and those bubbles were a wonder to us.

There is something almost spiritual about bubbles, isn't there? They are like something between the seen and the unseen world because they are transient and unpredictable — here one second, *poof!* — Gone the next. They are as soft as the presence of the Holy Spirit and as fragile. Do you know that if you resist the Holy Spirit, He will back off immediately? He will never press for His own way, unless you give Him permission. We hate to get our feelings hurt, our "bubbles burst," but we can hurt the feelings of the Holy Spirit, wound Him or grieve Him, if we do not follow His sweet, gentle, leadings. I do that sometimes, and I hate the feeling of hurting someone I love, the Spirit of my Lord. What sweet, soft thing is the Holy Spirit whispering to you, whispering to me today? Let's take time to listen so that we might not hurt this Precious One who dwells within us.

And do not bring sorrow to God's Holy Spirit by the way you live. Remember, he is the one who has identified you as his own, guaranteeing that you will be saved on the day of redemption. Ephesians 4:30 (NLT)

Dear Holy Spirit, I want to sit here right now in your presence and listen to you. Is there something you have been trying to say to me that I have been ignoring? I now await your answer. Amen.

January 13

On Cats and Projections

Our friend, Patricia, had an enormous tabby cat named Buster. Once, when she and Buster lived near a wooded area in Virginia, she had to leave on a work-related trip for a few days. A neighbor came by regularly to feed him, but Buster missed Pat terribly. When she returned home she found, lined up in perfectly neat rows, several birds and rodents — an offering to her. After all, in the cat's mind, what could be a better gift? In psycho-babble that would be called a "projection" on the cat's part — in this case, imagining that what it wants is what Pat would want — the ultimate of all gifts: one rat, five field mice, and assorted feathered friends!

I know I'm guilty of this kind of projection. Someone is suffering and I assume I know what they are feeling, what they are going through. Something in me wants to "fix" them so I come up with my version of solutions, or perhaps a whole collection of scripture verses; they are wonderful in and of themselves, but can become distorted in my mouth if I have an unloving spirit or I am just trying to get someone straightened out!

I've found that the more I pray about what someone needs from me, the more likely I am able to be truly helpful (not just project my own needs or wants onto them). Usually the answer is simple — for instance, just saying, "I'm sorry," or holding someone's hand. A smile. A card. A potted plant. Jesus will lead us to do a simple, loving thing that will touch that hurting person just where they need comfort.

> *Why worry about a speck in your friend's eye when you have a log in your own? How can you think of saying, 'Friend, let me help you get rid of that speck in your eye,' when you can't see past the log in your own eye? Hypocrite! First get rid of the log from your own eye; then perhaps you will see well*

enough to deal with the speck in your friend's eye. Luke 6:42, 43 (NLT)

Dear Lord, help me to fix myself so I won't be always trying to fix others. Amen.

January 14

God's Champion

In June of 1997, sports fans the world over were shocked to see Mike Tyson bite off a piece of the ear of Evander Holyfield. A few days later, on "Larry King Live," Holyfield was asked about the incident. How did he feel at the time? Holyfield described the pain and explained that if he had done what he felt like doing, he would have gotten even, but instead, he prayed. Yes! He prayed and what happened? He continued on, but without the vengeance that most people would have seen as justifiable, only to be bitten once again! Mr. King asked him if he had forgiven Mike Tyson and he said, "Yes."

Now that's a man after God's heart. I am so thankful that there is a well-known sports figure with integrity and a will to do what is pleasing in God's sight, so that those looking for that rare commodity, a real hero, could see one in this godly man. May God bless Evander Holyfield and may he have a great ministry as a witness for Jesus Christ.

> *But I say to you, love your enemies. Pray for those who hurt you. If you do this, you will be true children of your Father in heaven. He causes the sun to rise on good people and on evil people, and he sends rain to those who do right and to those who do wrong.* Matthew 5:44, 45(NCV)

Dear Father in Heaven, it is hard to forgive those who hurt us, but you have taught us through your son, not only to forgive, but to bless and do good to our enemies. Help me to prove that I believe this by acting on it. Amen.

January 15

Comfortable Ruts

When I first moved to our home in Arizona in 1997, I kept finding myself turning to the left to throw something into the trash and turning to the right to get a spoon when I should have done just the opposite. Everything was reversed. Changes! I prefer nice safe, comfortable ruts. I like things with a boring kind of sameness; that's for me. Even my morning quiet time with God should be the same — all spaced out in reading a Psalm, a section from this devotional, a page from that one, and then going through a list of prayer requests, neatly arranged, so that I can pray for one thing at a time, checking each off in my mind.

But, of course, as you've no doubt guessed already, God, the Father of variety has other ideas. So, if I flow with His Spirit, though I may stick to the same time every day, He will not allow me to monotonously walk through this discipline without, in some way each day, interrupting me with an unexpected twist or turn — prompting me into reading further, for instance, than the assigned passage for the day! Or having me (Can you believe it?) pray for someone not even on my prayer list!

Then throughout the day, there He is reminding me that when I leave my quiet time, I don't leave *Him*. He's right here with me. He may urge me to do a good deed, call a friend, write a note, or just sit and do nothing for a while, changing my plans all around. These changes along the way of my day can be distressing and yet make life such an adventure, that in spite of myself, I thank Him, that He — unlike me, is not afraid of change and yet, is somehow mysteriously the One who never changes. What a wonder!

I am the LORD, and I do not change. Malachi 3:6 (NLT)

Dear Father, please teach me how to accept change graciously. Amen.

January 16

Created in God's Image

I read recently about the child who kept asking her parents if she could be in the room alone with her newborn brother. They were reluctant at first, fearing that she might harm the child out of jealousy. Finally they decided that they could monitor the meeting by using the speaker system that was in the nursery. The little girl went in and leaned over the crib and whispered, "Hurry up and tell me what God looks like; I'm starting to forget."

Why does this story warm and touch us so? Is it because we once knew what God "looked" like? Perhaps so, in the sense that we are created in God's image and there is a longing in all of us that can only be satisfied by a living bond with Him. There is one sure way to be in such a relationship and it's a person and His name is Jesus. If we believe on His name from our heart we are to go tell someone that we do. That's all that is needed.

> *...He has put eternity in their hearts...* (Ecclesiastes 3:11b)

> *...If you confess with your mouth the Lord Jesus and believe in your heart that God has raised Him from the dead, you will be saved.* Romans 10:9 (NKJV)

Lord, thank you that you have provided a Way for us to become one with You. Amen.

January 17

Dreams of the Future

My husband and I stood together, leaning against the chain-link fence and watched the F-16 swoop down just over our heads and make a perfect landing, swift and smooth. We were living close to Luke Air Force Base in Arizona and this was one of our morning treats — before the temperature soared. Something about the freedom, the stark beauty, the incredible power, the roar of the jet as it came over us was electrifying. I wanted to be there, in that plane, feeling what it must be like to make those turns and climb hundreds of feet into the heavens in just a few seconds.

That's my fantasy anyway. But do I really want that? Of course not. To be free to soar, yes, but the responsibility, the danger, the fear of failure, lives at stake — no, I don't want that. It's easy to imagine what we think we want. The reality, however, is almost always different. On the movie screen we see things silvery, and mere humans luminescent. They are larger than life, in slow motion, or stop action, with a full musical score behind every scene to give us the sense of romance or danger, suspense or beauty. And all of this, not reality, but a flat one-dimensional world into which we escape, our own lives put on hold, while the condensed lives of others speed by in a total of two hours!

But what about our ideal of Heaven? Jesus promised to prepare a place for us; it is not a place that we can see in our mind's eye. It's better than any happy-ending movie you ever saw, better than retirement, better than a Thomas Kinkade painting — this spiritual reality of the Kingdom of God by His miracle of grace toward us. What an incredible wonder! That which is in store for us is beyond what our finite minds are even capable of imagining. Praise and honor be to Jesus Christ who shares His glory, His Kingdom, His majesty with us — starting now and continuing on into Eternity!

> *There are many rooms in my Father's house; I would not tell you this if it were not true. I am going there to prepare a place for you. After I go and prepare a place for you, I will come back and take you to be with me so that you may be where I am.* John 14:2, 3 (NCV)

Dear Lord Jesus, we believe that you have gone ahead of us and that you are preparing a place of ineffable beauty for us. We wait and long for the time when we can be in your blessed and holy presence and see you face to face. Amen.

January 18

Choices and Service

Sometimes we don't have choices about the things that happen to us. But we always have a choice about the way that we respond to what happens to us. I once worked for a woman who was a complete and utter perfectionist. As I typed her documents over and over, they were never right for the first seven or so drafts. Finally they were right but by that time, I was already so discouraged, her compliments came too late.

So, to combat this negative mind-set, I just did the best I could every day and dedicated my work to the Lord. It made all the difference in the world. I did what was required of me by the Lord and no more. I was no longer enslaved. I was no longer discouraged. I worked for my own approval, yes, but mostly for the Lord's approval and no one else's. She would never know this, but I knew, that at 5:00 p.m., the Lord would say to me, "Well done, good and faithful, servant." Now, that was worth waiting and working for. And at the end of the day, it was all that mattered.[1]

And at the end of our lifetime of days, that's all that matters. Did we do our best for the Master? Did we do all as unto him, or as people pleasers? Were we servants of the Most High God, or did we choose to please others — for praise and honor, thereby robbing the Lord of Hosts from what is due Him?

Slaves, obey your earthly masters with fear and trembling, in singleness of heart, as you obey Christ; not only while being watched, and in order to please them, but as slaves of Christ, doing the will of God from the heart. Render service with enthusiasm, as to the Lord and not to men and women, knowing that whatever good we do, we will receive the same

---

[1] I want to share that I didn't hold this against my employer. I know this for certain because twelve years later I ran into her at a consignment shop in Pasadena and I had nothing but friendly feelings toward her and she seemed sincerely happy to see me again.

again from the Lord, whether we are slaves or free.
Ephesians 6:5-8 (NRSV)

Dear Lord, I admit that I care far too much what other people think. Help me to bring you to the forefront of my day-to-day service in life, so that I will do what I do, first of all, for you and for your glory, and then out of my love for others. Amen.

January 19

Cleaning Time

The old, faded red Volkswagen van sat in the parking lot at the water's edge in Seal Beach, California. On the back window someone had spelled out in the dust, the appropriate message: "Clean Me." I thought about how visibly and obviously the old van needed just that. Then I thought about people — how we often look so clean and great on the outside, all dressed up in our Sunday best, for instance, going to church and sitting primly in the pew. And yet, with unforgiven sin, God sees a sign over us that clearly announces our greatest need: "Clean me."

There is only One to whom we can ask this with any hope of having the work done. As the line from the old hymn says, "Wash me and I shall be whiter than snow" (Psalm 51:7). And something else — we don't need to worry that we don't know what our daily sins are, because there are those errors that only God knows we have committed, as well as the deeds we have *omitted.* That's why the Psalmist says, *Who can understand his errors? Cleanse me from secret faults* (Psalm 19:12). Our sins are not hidden from God, but they can be hidden from us! We need to ask forgiveness by saying, "Lord, clean me," every day even if the "dirt" of guilt isn't as obvious as the dust on that old van.

As far as the east is from the west, So far has He removed our transgressions from us. Psalm 103:12 (NKJV)

Lord, you know far better than I all the places in which I am not clean. I ask you to cleanse me of all my sins, not just those of which I am aware. I praise and thank you for your grace that makes this possible. Amen.

January 20

Co-Yoked: The Dance

In 1995 Olympic skater, Sergei Mikhailovish Brinkov, collapsed and died from a massive heart attack while rehearsing on ice with his wife, Ekaterina. Later, even though she was overwhelmed with grief, she decided to do a solo performance to Mahler's Symphony No. 5 as a tribute to him. She knew it would be incredibly difficult to skate alone. She says in her book, "My Sergei: A Love Story," that as she skated she felt that when she would start a movement it seemed that Sergei would finish it for her.

I don't know if God allows such miracles to happen. Perhaps He does. But what it reminded me of this: When we take a chance — begin to do something by faith — even though in ourselves we feel this is an impossible venture, we then find that the Lord is doing it with us and through us. We take the first step and He is there with us for the next step, and the next, not following, but leading. It becomes easy because He is giving us strength and power and love each step of the way. Our life in Him, with Him, by Him is as good as the faith we have received from Him, to believe it is! It is the two of us together in the dance of life.

> *I was put to death on the cross with Christ, and I do not live anymore—it is Christ who lives in me. I still live in my body, but I live by faith in the Son of God who loved me and gave himself to save me. By saying these things I am not going against God's grace. Just the opposite, if the law could make us right with God, then Christ's death would be useless.*
> Galatians 2:20, 21 (NCV)

Dear Lord, give me courage to step out and do what I believe you are calling me to do — to dance the dance in which you are guiding me, not the other way around. I know you are inviting me to step right in and I choose to join you and follow your lead. Amen.

January 21

Colors

All the colors of the rainbow — they range from the visible red (on the other side of that is infrared) to violet (on the other side of that is ultraviolet). We are surrounded with color and each has its own wavelength, absorbing some rays and reflecting others.

For years I lived in a desert neighborhood where the predominant color was beige — it was in the buildings, the roof tiles and the pebbled landscapes. This sameness, while properly within the homeowners' association's building and landscape guidelines, was not the most pleasant place for me to take my daily walks. However, much to my delight, I found, less than a mile away, a little park with a small man-made lake. There I discovered palm, orange and pine trees, grass and clover, coots, geese and mallards. The trees that line the streets were in a variety of shades of green, and homes were of different styles and colors, all creating the contrasts that I find stimulating. So I drove a little way in the morning to take my morning walk.

How thankful I am for the variety in God's world, colors enough for everyone, even me with my unique color needs. We are all unique and each of us has different and legitimate needs. The Lord knew my need for certain colors, as small a thing as that may seem, and He helped me to find the perfect place where I could have that need met!

You comprehend my path and my lying down, and are acquainted with all my ways. Psalm 139:3b (NKJV)

Dear Heavenly Father, it is a wonder to me that you know all the little things about each of us. We trust you to supply our every need, even the small things in our everyday life. Amen.

January 22

The Continuing Savior

"**H**ow ignorant she is," I thought, as I would pass by Grandma while she listened to her old-fashioned Christian radio program, *The Haven of Rest* with First Mate Bob. I, on the other hand, feeling superior and broad-minded, sought for religious truth by attending the Vedanta place of worship, a combination of many belief systems (Christian, Hindu and Buddhism). It was there that, when comparing Jesus Christ to other great religious leaders of the world, the Vedanta Priest spoke these words that pierced me to the heart with light: "Now, we take Jesus Christ — He was the Son of God and that was something special." I nearly fell off the pew bench. That was it then, what I was searching for! I knew at that moment what I desired more than anything else in the world — to be a Christian. I determined, on my own, that the way to do that was to think nothing bad, say nothing bad and do nothing bad. I tried it — for a week. Then, I gave up. I was disappointed to the core. At last I knew what I wanted and it was impossible to achieve. I called Millie, a Christian friend of my mother's.

"Hello, Millie," I said, "This is Patty."

"Oh, my goodness, do you know that my husband and I were just now talking about you?" This gave me a strange, miracles-are-possible feeling. It also gave me courage to get to the point.

"Millie, I've been trying to become a Christian."

"Oh, my dear, you don't *try* to become a Christian. You just get down on your knees, ask Jesus to forgive you for your sins and ask Him to come into your heart."

"Oh." My ego sank. My pride rose. I did not want to do *that* — anything else, but not but that! "Well, uh, thank you, Millie. I'll — I'll think about it."

I hung up. I sat down. I thought. I had to make a decision. Something in me sensed that this was vitally important. I waited. There was a strange silence in the room. Angels were waiting. Jesus was waiting.

I decided. I would do it. I knelt down by my bed.

"Dear Lord Jesus, forgive me for my sins and come into my heart."

There! It was done. I stood up. I didn't feel any differently. Had anything happened? I'd have to wait and see. If this were real, I would know soon enough. Of course, something had happened. Angels rejoiced (They always do when someone comes to the Savior.) The Spirit of Jesus did come into my heart (He always does when invited.).

In the days that followed I slowly saw that there was a change in me. I didn't feel the haunting fear that had always been with me. I didn't feel alone anymore; there was Someone with me, Someone who knew *all* about me, Someone who loved me. And, when I read the Bible it was not the same book. Now it was neither boring nor totally mysterious; I was beginning to understand it.

That was more than fifty years ago. Though He is the same Lord, in whom is no shadow of turning, I am not the same person. He has continued faithfully to heal me in area after area of my wounded spirit. He is transforming me, patiently, lovingly. He is teaching me obedience to the perfecting work that He accomplishes by His Spirit through the circumstances of my life. He is the author and finisher of my faith and He's not finished yet, but oh! — Such a walk we've had. How could I have come so far without Him? He has been there for me in all the terrors and griefs of life and there in all the joys and celebrations of life. He has promised to never leave me. And to the future? Though there will be times I cannot *feel* his presence, I know He will be there, whether in the darkness, through the forest, in the desert, on the mountain top, or in the valley — whatever, wherever, He will be there, the captive Spirit within, having committed Himself to me, I know He will not leave. And I am in awe. What a wonderful day-by-day Savior He is.

Most assuredly, I say to you, unless one is born again, he cannot see the kingdom of God. John 3:3 (NKJV)

Dear Jesus, thank you for responding to our heart-felt confessions and coming into our lives and hearts when we ask. Amen.

January 23

Courage

When I was a child my grandmother, three-quarter Cherokee, told me about the courage of my great-grandmother, Sarah Hicks Stephens. This is that story:

> *One evening she heard what were known as "Pin Indians" outside her home, making a disturbance. They were all wearing masks. She recognized their voices and went out and walked right up to one and pulled his mask off, called him by name and demanded that he leave their property with his friends. They did so, and speedily!*

I'm proud to have had such a brave great grandmother. I was also proud of my own mother who exhibited that same kind of courage. When I was in my teens, we lived in an old house that had a sunroom that had been converted into a closet, jutting out over a portion of the roof. It was directly off my bedroom and had very large windows, which in my young imagination would make it easy for someone to break in. One morning I awoke and heard a noise inside the closet. I was sure someone was going to get me. I ran to tell Mama whose immediate response was not fear, but anger. She hesitated for not one second, went directly to the closet door and opened it, revealing nothing out of the ordinary. I was relieved, but amazed at her courage. I had the hope that it must run in families and perhaps I would someday be like that too. Unfortunately I cannot claim such an attribute, but the Lord still asks this of us all, so, with His help, I know that it is possible.

Be of good courage. Numbers 13:20 (NKJV)

Thank you, Lord, for applauding my heart for doing brave, little invisible acts of courage. Give me more of your overcoming power, day by day. Amen.

January 24

On Wings of the Morning

I was feeling down that morning. I needed some little uplift to my spirit so my husband and I, with Lucy our dog, went on a morning drive to get a glimpse of the F-16s at nearby Luke Air Force Base. On the way I looked out of the car window and saw a large white bird flying a few yards away from us over the farm fields to our left. We watched it, amazed at the size and beauty of this great egret. She landed for a short time and then took off again. She lifted off gracefully, effortlessly, flying northward. Her beauty and grace were captivating, even awe-inspiring. We were not disappointed that the F-16s were not flying that morning, for how much more beautiful and graceful and uplifting to our spirits was this lovely silent creature of the Lord's making. It was just the touch of beauty our souls longed for, and there she was, a gift of love from God, on wings of the morning.

> *Rise up, my love, my fair one, And come away.* Song of Solomon 2:10 (NKJV)

Dear Lover of my soul, I believe that you offer us these special moments as thoughtful, precious gifts. You know where we will be at any moment, and you can appoint lovely surprises along the way for all of us. Make us just as focused, brave and beautiful as that snowy egret, as we extend our spiritual wings to fly wherever you would have us go. Help us take off and overcome the psychological gravity that would hold us down. We want to soar and, in our spirits, go with your Spirit. Amen.

January 25

The Words of Love

As we grew up, I knew somewhere inside that Mama loved me, but we were not a hugging, kissing family and the words, "I love you" were never spoken that I recall. After she had several strokes when in her late 70s and was confined to bed, I would visit her at the convalescent hospital where she stayed for her last years. I tried to get her to tell me that she loved me by example. I would just say, "Mom, I love you." I had hoped she would say, "I love you too," but the words were not forthcoming. Then one day I asked her, "Don't you love me?" She was annoyed with me. "Well, of course I do," she grumbled. That was not quite what I had in mind. Finally, however, over the months, when I would say, "I love you," she learned to respond with "I love you too." However, this voicing of her heart was not something ideally meant that a child should teach the mother.

Then almost precisely one year from the date of Mama's death, I had a dream in which I was told by a voice from an invisible source to walk "up" somewhere on a large staircase. I obeyed and then looked up to see my mother "coming down" the staircase. She was young looking, perhaps in her thirties. Her hair, which had been gray and sparse, was now dark and thick. She walked to me and reached out her arms. I reached out mine. She had come to tell me something. She said as she embraced me, "I want you to know that I always loved you." And I replied, "Yes, I know." There it was, the desire of my heart, finally spoken from mother to daughter. Perhaps it was more than a dream. That's what I believe, but whether wish fulfillment dream or real, it is good to be reminded to speak out our love when we are still able to do so, isn't it?

A new commandment I give to you, that you love one another, as I have loved you, that you also love one another. John 13:34 (NKJV

Now the purpose of the command is love from a pure heart, from a good conscience, and from sincere faith... 1 Timothy 1:5 (NKJV)

Dear Lord Jesus, Give us the courage to not only act out our love but to speak it out to those you have given us to love so that their hearts may be encouraged. Amen.

January 26

God's Timing in Death

A friend told me that once she had seen an obituary for an elderly woman that reported: "She died of nothing serious." I burst out laughing. However, I would really like to die that way — just go and be with the Lord because it's time. I've not known anyone to have so chosen their time of departure, but there does seem to be a small amount of choice involved in the time of a persons' death. One hospital nurse was reported to have gone around to her dying patients, telling them in a threatening voice, "Don't you dare die on my shift." As the story goes, they waited! When the year 2000 came around, I read that there were a record number of deaths in January. It was speculated that many people just wanted to wait around long enough to see in the new millennium.

I once heard the great man of God and teacher, the Rev. Jack Hayford, share on a TBN program of how, in seeing his mother suffer, he asked God to take her. The Lord spoke to him and, in essence, told him that was not his affair, that a person's date and time of death are in His hands alone! Now there's something to remember when you wonder why God doesn't take the loved one you see suffering and still breathing and you are asking "Why?" — It's essentially none of your business! In 1997 James Mitchner took himself off life-support systems so that he could die; it was a matter of, at the age of 90, deciding to do nothing more to keep himself alive. Then there are those who, in fear of being out of control of their own life span, choose to take their own lives, but I do not believe that this is in accordance with God's plan. There is a last lesson learned at the last moment of life that such persons forfeit when they take things into their own hands. Our days are numbered and no one knows that number but the Lord himself. It is arrogant to try to foresee it or change it, just for the sake of being in control so that we will not have to depend on faith to help us through our last days and hours on earth.

My times are in Your hand. Psalm 31:15a (NKJV)

Dear Lord of the future, you know the number of my days. I do not. You are God. I am not. I entrust the day and time of my death completely to you. Amen.

January 27

Lost in the Magic Kingdom

It happened at Disneyland in Anaheim, California. Don, my husband, and Michael, our son (who was 30 years old at the time), and I all went out for a day of play. They wanted to go on a new water ride that I was too afraid to try, so I waited for them. It was hot, and getting hotter by the minute. We thought the ride would take about 20 minutes. I watched for them at the ride's exit. I waited. And waited. They didn't come out. After waiting for 45 minutes, much to my chagrin, I discovered I was waiting at the wrong gate! I was at the Haunted House exit. I had missed them. But where were they?

At once, I was a little girl, lost and afraid, not a woman in her fifties. I decided to go where lost children go and wait for their parents. They were not there. Then I remembered the rule, "Go back to where you last saw the person you lost." I was on my way back when I spotted my tall, handsome son coming toward me. How wonderful it was! I was found. No longer lost. Not only that but, "Oh, Mom," he said, "poor Mom. It's OK. I'll tell you what, let's go to the restaurant at the Pirates of the Caribbean and have lunch. Dad said he would meet us there. I'll treat." He put his arm around me and led me back to where Don waited.

Now don't I have just the most wonderful son in the world? Could I have been happier and more contented than I was that day as we sat in the blue bayou ambiance eating Monte Cristo sandwiches, watching those little fake fireflies sparkling all around us?

Do you see it? — The lesson here of how, when we get lost, the Lord really does go out of His way to find us — and then He wants to treat us to something special, never holding a grudge, never pouting, only desirous that his children are feeling safe and happy? What a wonderful God, what a kind friend.

Rejoice with me for I have found my sheep which was lost.
Luke 15:6b (NKJV)

Dear Shepherd of my soul, sometimes I *feel* so lost and unsure of myself. I am so thankful that to you I am not lost, and that no matter where I may wander off in an unsafe spiritual place, you will find me and bring me back to yourself. Amen.

January 28

Hearts United in Devastation

When the Space Shuttle Challenger went down on this day in 1986, 73 seconds after lift-off due to a faulty rocket booster seal, U.S. citizens went into a collective state of shock. I will never forgot where I was — standing beside my desk at work when I heard. Out of my pain I wrote the following, and still each January 28 I remember.

To the Challenger

We had come to think of you as the Space Titanic, hadn't we? Somehow, along the way we had forgotten that you were part of an imperfect world, a world where both victories and tragedies exist. You were our Disneyland in the Sky — someday we might even have a chance to go ourselves, or our children, on the ultimate vacation to the cosmos.

On Tuesday we cheered as you carried seven of us with you. And we trusted you to bring them back, but you failed us. Or did we fail you? In that smoke and in those ashes that we watched in horror and disbelief drift sadly down into the sea, we watched our hero, our false god and our fantasies fall as well. You who had become our symbol of national pride, of triumph and of adventure, perhaps you were meant to be something else.

We will search to find that now — your true identity — for we will now search with hearts united in devastation. Perhaps then you will be resurrected in our wounded spirits into that which you were destined to be: a reminder of our finitude, a call to try again, and an invitation to a new mission with our sights fixed even Higher next time.

Do you know the laws of the sky and understand their rule over the earth? Job 38:33 (NCV)

Lord, with all our knowing, we confess that we know so little. Amen.

January 29

A Blessing of Doves

One morning while my husband and I were still living in Arizona, two mourning doves sat atop a neighbor's mailbox across the street in the cool of the afternoon. The next day the same doves were sitting on the mailbox of our neighbor to the east of us. I told my husband, "They are making their way around the cul-de-sac, and tomorrow they will be at our house." Then the next day, after we returned home from a drive, we found two doves sitting atop our mailbox, just as I had jokingly predicted! They flirted with each other and cooed at us. "You were right," Don said as we drove into our driveway.

I once heard that visiting doves are a sign of blessing on a home, so I decided the doves were blessing our little neighborhood and our home and I received it as from the Lord. What sweet surprises our Father gives us sometimes. How easily special touches from His hand might be missed! Let's make a point to look for these kinds of gifts from His hand and thank Him for them as they come so unexpectedly to us, like these birds came to us on a warm winter afternoon.

When you search for me, you will find me; if you seek me with all your heart... Jeremiah 29:13 (NRSV)

Lord, I want to learn how to truly find you in some way every single day. I know that if I seek You from my heart, I will find You, because you have promised. Amen.

January 30

Lost and Found

At the time it happened, Don and I were at an Episcopalian retreat in Santa Barbara, California. It was Friday night and everyone decided to go to a nearby restaurant — *The Angel and the Scythe*. Once there, it was noisy and I was tired so I wanted to go back to our dorm but I didn't know the way. Another lady said she'd like to go back too and she assured me she knew how to get there, so we decided to return together. Once on our way, however, we were suddenly aware that there were no lights along the path and no moonlight; we were literally in the dark. We began wandering the grounds, would begin to go up a road and find that it was a private driveway, and eventually realized that we were walking in circles. We finally admitted we were completely lost. I was really frightened. The grounds were acres of woods and fields with an occasional residence. Where in the world were we? Then a little dog appeared. It reminded me of Frazier's "Wishbone" on TV. I told my friend, "Let's just follow the dog." She agreed; after all, what could we lose? We followed and he led us right up to the entryway of the campus.

When we realized we were "home," I looked around for the dog. He was gone. That's when it occurred to me that maybe it wasn't a dog at all; maybe, just maybe, it was an angel sent to help us find our way back. Or it could have been a dog to which God gave some instructions. Who knows? But whatever the explanation for our guide, we felt without a doubt that we had been supernaturally helped out of a frightening situation and we were greatly relieved and thankful.

Now the angel of the Lord came... Judges 6:11a (NKJV)

Dear Father, I'm so thankful that you are a God who seeks those who are lost, sometimes physically, sometimes spiritually. That night we were lost and you sent help in the form of an angelic dog. Thank you! Amen.

January 31

The Dizzy Duck

It was in San Mateo, California by an inlet near the Bay. We watched spellbound as a colorful Mallard spun around and around in the water. Was he wounded? We couldn't tell. He would drift toward us and then away, always within a spin, but never stopped — sometimes twirling faster, sometimes more slowly. At one point he violently bumped into the edge of a dock across from us; it didn't even slow him down. An apparently concerned Mallard, no doubt a long-time buddy, swam near him, watching, but not able to do anything to help. He continued to whirl.

Fifteen minutes went by. We didn't know what to do. He obviously needed help but we could not reach him. The sun was setting. The night air brought a penetrating chill. We gave up and started to walk away, but turned back to check on him just one last time and, to our amazement, he suddenly, without a hint of disorientation, stopped turning. He swam straight to the shore with the other ducks and settled down for the night. Our mouths hung open. What nerve! All that show for nothing? Was he just turning in circles because he felt like it? We'll never know.

This dizzy duck reminded me so much of myself that it made me laugh. Maybe you can identify. Our Best Friend stands by and patiently watches until we're tired of the dizziness of the busyness, and then, like Martha in the Bible, we finally learn about the part that can't be taken away — time spent with Jesus, our best friend, our only Rest. More time spent with Him keeps us focused on what He has called us to do, no more, no less, and then we will find that He will even miraculously expand our time into being all that we need in order that we might accomplish all that we are required to do!

> *But the Lord said to her, 'My dear Martha, you are so upset over all these details! There is really only one thing worth being concerned about. Mary has discovered it—and I won't take it away from her.'* Luke 10:41, 42 (NLT)

Dear Lord Jesus, how often I need to hear you remind me of the same thing — that I am too caught up and anxious about things! Lord, help me to slow down and take the time to sit at your feet and listen to your word. Oh, what a fresh breeze to a harried soul is just a moment of acknowledging that you are available, waiting, wanting to give us just the word that we need today. Help us to take those special moments of receiving a touch of refreshing eternity into our clock-driven little dizzying lives here on earth. Amen.

FEBRUARY

February 1

Eternal Life — a New Perspective

It was one of those rare times when Don needed to go out of town. I had looked forward to being alone, and, after all, he was only going to be gone for three days and two nights. But I missed him far more than I thought I would. I lay down beside him the night he came home and listened to his slow breathing as he moved into sleep. I snuggled up against him, and placed my head on his chest. I sniffed him, drawing in his familiar scent and listened to the steady beat of his heart. He felt big and strong and alive — yes, *alive*. But I thought about the possibility of losing him — that someday the body his dear spirit resides in now, will not continue. But he will. His spirit will go on into a new life, a new existence, and one day, at the Resurrection, he will receive a new, transformed, glorified body, one that will never know death. He will continue to exist through an ageless eternity. He will rejoice and praise God forever.

As I lay there next to Don, my inner being quaked with a sense of wonder because I knew this was not only true of him, it was also true of me and all the saints who live side-by-side with me now, and all the men and women of faith, who have lived before: Abraham, Isaac, Jacob, Joseph, Job, Isaiah, Jeremiah, King David, St. Paul, St. John, Martin Luther, Teresa of Avila, Brother Lawrence, St. Augustine, C. S. Lewis, Emily Dickinson and Grandma and Mama and on and on. We will continue on in the Presence of our Creator, continue to grow throughout eternity in the knowledge of the mysterious, yet Self-revealing One, our Heavenly Father and Jesus Christ, who came to Earth as His expressed image. We, as human beings purchased by His blood, are indeed fearfully and wonderfully made, redeemed members of humankind, eternal beings, created in the image of God and are the ultimate of all of God's creations.

The "eternal" moment that I spent with my husband asleep at my side changed forever the way I related to him, others and myself. It was a supernatural glimpse of whom we are in Christ Jesus, beings not moving through time, but those through whom eternity moves as He, who is our Eternal life, lives within us.

> *And this is the promise that He has promised us — eternal life.* I John 2:25 (NKJV)

Dear Lord and Savior, when I think of the reality of what you have given us — eternal life in you — it fills me with wonder. There are no words to express my gratitude but I simply want to thank you for giving me a future to be spent in eternity with you. Amen.

February 2

The Face at the Window

It was in the middle of the night, dark and silent. I awoke with a start and realized I was not going to go back to sleep, so I quietly slipped out of bed. I went into the kitchen, thinking to myself, *perhaps a small cup of warm milk.* I poured cold milk into a delicate little cup made in Sweden that I had found at a thrift shop. I placed it in the microwave to heat for 45 seconds. When I took it out, I decided to sit down in the darkness of the living room and just enjoy it.

It was then that I heard it, a kind of snapping noise. Unclear of its direction, I realized with a start, that Don had left the back window open. Was someone outside on the patio? I moved ever so slowly toward the open window, trying to peer through the darkness. What was it? I saw someone slowly, slowly moving toward the window. My heart began to race. It was a rather large person with lots of hair sticking up all over. I felt a shot of adrenaline quickly drive itself through my entire system. The milk trembled in the little Swedish demitasse cup.

Then something happened to change my experience of this fearful sight. The person coming toward me was: myself! The window was partially closed on the side through which I was looking and I had seen the reflection of — me! I sighed with relief and I sat down and enjoyed my milk.

Well, wasn't it Pogo who said something like, "We have seen the enemy and they is us?" Are you your own worst enemy? I know that's true of me. Did you know that scripture tells us that anything that is a friend of the world within us is our enemy because that part of us is at enmity with God. Maybe it's time to find the enemy within and make sure that part gets "converted" — daily!

> *Do you not know that friendship with the world is enmity with God? Therefore whoever wishes to be a friend of the world becomes an enemy of God.* James 4:4 (NRSVA)

Lord, wake me up! Help me see where I am in love with the world's values and help me to, instead, fall more in love with you. Amen.

February 3

Famous Last Words

Think about it. What "famous (regretted) last words" have you spoken about yourself? You know — the things that you were sure were absolutely true at the time, until the reality of self-knowledge took over! How about the following? "Open marriage? Sure, I'm not the jealous type." Or how about: "I don't need to ask for directions; I know exactly how to get there," or "No, I'm not at all sensitive, I just want to know the truth."

The scripture verse that made me the most uncomfortable before I became a Christian is now one I have come to appreciate greatly and it is this: "The heart is deceitful above all things and desperately wicked; who can know it?" In spite of our deceitful hearts, in spite of our woeful lack of self-knowledge, there is One who knows and loves us anyway. He will reveal to us what we need to know about our inner selves in order that we might grow and repent and be humbled before our Lord, or be healed and restored. If we ask Him to do this inner work, He will, in His time. We don't have to dig and grope around in the dark past. I have found that, when I am ready, He will bring to me a truth about myself through a memory, or a revelation dream, a word of Scripture, or the wise comment of a friend. This is all so that I might grow in Him when I have been wounded by someone else's deceitful heart or have sinned by following my own devious heart. When we place Him in charge of such self-growth, He will deal with us in just the way we need — whether with firm voice, or a soft and comforting touch. He knows exactly what we require in order to get to where we are supposed to be going, and He will lead the way. It is up to us to follow and not turn away from the truth He reveals.

The heart is deceitful above all things, and desperately wicked; Who can know it? I the Lord, search the heart, I test the mind, Even to give every man according to his ways, And according to the fruit of his doings. Jeremiah 17:9, 10 (NKJV)

Lord, you are omniscient and therefore know all about me. Help me stay on the track of the spiritual growth you have ordained for me. Amen.

February 4

The Sound of the Magic Violin

I believe that every day we are touched with something beautiful, or meaningful or educational, and whenever that happens it is meant for us to receive it, not just from whomever or whatever brings it our way, but to receive it as a gift from the Lord, a token of His caring and love for us. It's up to us to recognize and catch these precious signs of God's love.

I remember clearly one such gift of beauty. It was a shopping day in Pasadena. I was walking along Raymond Avenue south of Old Town. I unexpectedly heard something — a beautiful sound coming from the historic Hotel Green across the street. I stopped on the sidewalk and looked around. What was the origin of this lovely, magical refrain? I thought perhaps there was a party with entertainment somewhere, but I could see no sign of that. I tried to trace the sound of the music with my eyes and found myself looking up to a third story window where stood a young man in a light brown suit. His hair and skin were dark. He had flung the window shutters open and was standing there alone, playing his violin for all the world to enjoy, for *me* to enjoy! The sweet, plaintive melody, the beauty of the old hotel, the garden rich with a myriad of flowers and the green lawns, all combined to transport me. For a moment I found myself in a Spanish Villa, in the nineteenth century, enraptured by the sights and sounds of a different world, serenaded by a handsome Spaniard.

But it all soon came to an end. I was brought back to reality quickly as I nearly fell off the sidewalk curb! However, the memory lingered, as all such lovely moments should, and my inner bliss continued on in my heart, for it is there, any time I choose to recall it.

Sometimes these beautiful touches from God last only a second or two, sometimes much longer. Sometimes they are so quiet and transient that we could easily miss them altogether. Sometimes they are as clear and ringing of the glories of God as this special moment on that ordinary day of shopping. My part is to catch these moments as they fly through my life and to then say, "Thank you, Lord, for your gift of love to me today." Won't you make a point of looking for these gifts too, so that you might let your Lord please you? It gives His generous heart great joy when we say, "Thank you, Lord, for this special gift, just for me!"

There I will give you my love. Song of Solomon 7:12b (NKJV)

Oh my dear Lord Jesus, how precious are these lovely gifts you give to us! They remind us that you love us so very much! Give us eyes and ears to discover each one, and help us to remember to thank you and then give us opportunities to share with others. Amen.

February 5

Food for Thought?

In May of 1997 Swiss brain scientists announced the discovery of a new disease. The word *disease* is probably a misnomer, however, unless one is poor. It is called *gourmand syndrome.* The symptoms are: one desires to eat only the best of foods, preferably in the best of restaurants. It is caused, apparently, by the destruction of a particular part of the right front of the brain.

This bit of curious news got me to thinking. Having suffered with compulsive eating most of my life, wouldn't it be nice if researchers could discover exactly where in the brain to give over eaters like me a zap of something — say, a laser beam — thereby changing our appetites completely and forever? We would thereafter only desire the healthiest of meals, significantly decreasing our appetites for fatty, salty and refined foods!

Then I thought about our spiritual appetites. It reminded me of something I heard from Raymond Jones, MFCC (expert on addictions). He believes that we have the old nature, hungry for "food" that will feed our appetites for self-indulgent compulsions, but from which we fail to admit we need deliverance. We also have our new, born again selves, hungry for those things like enjoying nature, reaching out to others in love, listening to uplifting music, Christian fellowship, reading the Bible, and prayer, and much more, all of which will feed our spirits. The part of us we feed the most will be the part that will grow to be the stronger of the two. We have a choice which inner self we feed. Which am I feeding today? Which are you feeding? When the spiritual life becomes the stronger of the two inner beings, then we will become vessels of honor, ready for doing good in the world for God's purposes and for His glory.

> *But in a great house there are not only vessels of gold and silver, but also of wood and clay, some for honor and some for dishonor. Therefore if anyone cleanses himself from the latter, he will be a vessel for honor, sanctified and useful for the Master, prepared for every good work. Flee also youthful lusts; but pursue righteousness, faith, love, peace with those who call on the Lord out of a pure heart.* 2 Timothy 2:20-22 (NKJV)

Dear Lord, help me to resist doing those things that would feed the old nature within me that needs to die, and help me to feed the life of the born-again self within me by doing those things that will help me to grow and mature spiritually. Oh yes, and help me to discern the difference. Amen.

February 6

Freedom from Religion?

As Don and I were on our way to Shasta Lake in California we noticed a sign announcing that a certain portion of the highway was being maintained by a group called, "Freedom from Religion." I wondered at that. What did it really mean? How did such a group come about? What kind of religious bondage had the founders experienced to have to start a foundation to help set people free from all religion? Was there any particular religion that they had in mind? Was the group founded by atheists who never believed anything in the first place? Or, perhaps they are a Christian group that believes that Christianity cannot be defined as a religion, because unlike all other religions, it is not brought into being by human beings, but by God himself, a relationship, not a religion.

A 1998 Gallop Poll tells us that 2% of immigrants entering the U.S. do so because they are seeking religious freedom. It's because they know something we native-born U.S. citizens sometimes forget: Here in this great country, we have it all — Freedom to believe in anything, freedom to believe in nothing. Freedom of choice. How blessed we are!

Deliver me from my persecutors, for they are stronger than I.
Psalm 142:6 (NKJV)

Dear Heavenly Father, I confess that I have taken for granted the freedom we have to worship in this country. I have not suffered persecution like those in Paul's day nor like those in many other countries suffer even now. I acknowledge that there are those believers around the world who are suffering for Jesus' sake even at this very moment. I ask today that you comfort them, give them supernatural courage to continue in their faith, send them helpers, human or angelic, and may they be blessed by your Holy Spirit, knowing that you are with them, never forsaking them, to the end. Amen.

February 7

Time with Daddy

When Garth Brooks' daughter, Allie, was born in 1996, I heard that he was truly enamored with her. Shortly after she was born, he set aside a period of two hours to have their first conversation. He found himself telling her two things, "Be happy," which he said many times. The rest of the two-hour "conversation" was spent in silence and he reported that it was wonderful.

This story helped me visualize this: I'm a child of about four, sitting on Father God's lap, gazing into His eyes. He's telling me to be happy. But wait! Does God really want me to be happy? What a surprise! I have to admit that I have often questioned that. But to continue the visualization, and the best part of all — I am just *there* in His presence, drinking in the motherhood and fatherhood of the One who cherishes and loves me. That is what our "quiet time" with God may be like for us. Oh, but how often I've made it a dutiful obligation — reading and praying and then sometimes even glad it's finally over, checking that off my list and getting up to do something "important."

But what if I should just bask in the light of His presence, just be with Him, not having to *do* anything, but just "being?" I want to try that; don't you?

> *"So you should not be like cowering, fearful slaves. You should behave instead like God's very own children, adopted into his family—calling him "Father, dear Father."* Romans 8:15 (NLT)

Dear Daddy, how strange in seems to call you that! But you have made it so by adopting me into your family. As I imagine that I'm a child sitting on your lap and leaning against your strong chest, teach me how to sit here with you and let us be still together so that I may soak into my Spirit your very essence. Amen.

February 8

Generosity — The Gift of Giving

I am fortunate enough to have one of the most generous friends in the world — I'm sure of it. Her name is Ruth. She has gone out of her way to help innumerable people and animals in a myriad of ways. It may involve giving of self, or money or material gifts. When she gives money it is more often than not to those who are in no way connected with a non-profit organization of any kind, so she can't deduct such donations on her income tax returns. She seems to know what a person needs the most, and finds a way to give just that perfect thing. For me, she has made sure I got to go to special events — the most memorable being the Three Tenors at Dodger Stadium in 1994! There they were: Carreras, Domingo, Pavarotti, right in front of us, in person! What an unforgettable treat!

When living in Arizona, she made sure that when I came to California and stayed with her, I would get trips to the beach so I could enjoy the ocean because she knew that's what I missed the most. She treats people to things like movies, plays, museums, beautiful places, wonderful restaurants and even took me once to her masseuse when I was extremely stressed, so I could enjoy a relaxing massage. She cannot be considered "rich"; this giving is a matter of sacrifice for her. But she must have learned the secret — it's more blessed to give than to receive, because it's such a habit with her that I don't even think she knows about how much more generous she is than other people. There is no way I could ever repay her, but I know she wouldn't even think of that, or want me to try. What a gift this gift of giving is. I want more of it in my life.

Give, and you will receive. Your gift will return to you in full—pressed down, shaken together to make room for more, running over, and poured into your lap. The amount you give will determine the amount you get back. Luke 6:38 (NLT)

Dear Father, you are the one who has given us everything and shared with us everything — the earth and all its fullness, the sun, the rain, the stars, the moon, and far beyond that — your very own beloved Son.

Please teach me how to let go of what I have for the sake of others, whether it is time or things, money or love. Amen.

February 9

The Earth — a Geodesic Dome

In the 1970s I had a dream in which the Lord showed me the whole Earth as seen from a distance with spokes of light that met in triangles, which He told me (within the dream) were the connections of Christians, and that this connecting would continue until it covered the whole earth. I watched, spellbound, as the Earth shone more and more brightly as the connections multiplied. And the dark areas in between the sectors of these light spokes became more and more light with more and more spokes.

If this was a "true" vision, then perhaps someday I will witness this in reality. The image reminded me of Buckminster Fuller's geodesic dome. Brendan Gill describes it succinctly in his book "Late Bloomers" like this, "...a system of interlocking triangles that encloses the maximum volume of space with the least amount of material...." Metaphorically, they express what Fuller hoped to establish as the guiding principle of mankind: "to do more with less in order that people everywhere should have enough of everything." This, then, is perhaps a spiritual picture of the coming reign of Jesus Christ on the Earth.

Years after this dream, I had another dream in which I was told to pray for all the nations of the world. I have begun to do this, one nation at a time. I have found a remarkable book that helps me know how to pray; it is called, "Operation World" and it is a prayer guide for every nation.

Do you have a burden for the world? If so, perhaps God is also calling you to pray for all the nations, that some out of every people group will come to know about God's love for them through the Gospel of our Lord Jesus Christ!

They shall not hurt nor destroy in all My holy mountain, For the earth shall be full of the knowledge of the Lord as the waters cover the sea. Isaiah 11:9 (NKJV)

Lord, give me a love for all nations and a burden to pray until I see this prophecy from Isaiah come to pass. Amen.

February 10

A Little Problem

In 1998 when a high official of our government found himself embroiled in a sex scandal, a little boy in Truth or Consequences, New Mexico, was asked about the meaning of his town's name. He said something like, "There might be a little problem and it might get bigger." Well, that's it in a nutshell, isn't it? Remember your Father or Mother warning you, "Oh, what a tangled web we weave when first we practice to deceive?" How true a statement about lies that is. What happens with liars is that they forget what they told to whom, and eventually, it comes back to haunt them, doesn't it? As a child, it was so ground into me not to lie that I seldom did, but I have been lied to. This has always come as a great shock — since I project onto others my own values, it's hard to believe that someone who smiles and looks you straight in the eye and tells you something, could actually be purposely deceiving you — and as Grandma used to call it, "telling an untruth."

We don't like to think about it, do we? But it happens, and there are con artists who do lie. This may be to the elderly, for instance, in order to get money from them in a myriad of schemes. There is the well-known "pigeon drop", investment scams, telemarketers who con the elderly, and fly-by-night so-called construction workers, as well as robbers who pretend to be from the gas or electric company and people who sue because they fell on your property ("accidentally on purpose"). Just recently we received an E-mail purportedly from the IRS informing us of a refund we were entitled to. All we had to do was give them personal information, including a credit card number and detailed bank information! We already knew that the IRS does not communicate in this way and never asks for personal information of this kind. All these scams are aimed at the most unsuspecting victims.

Psychologists tell us those of us who are most inclined to be fooled are those who always want to think the best of others and be kind, considerate and thoughtful. Well, that's me, so the keys, I've learned, for keeping one's self from being bilked or robbed are: Ask for IDs; know that if it sounds too good to be true, it is; don't open your door to strangers, and get references for workers. And that's just a beginning. But the Lord cares for us and as we listen to His Spirit, we will hear little warnings from Him. Let us remain truthful, but be cautious and responsible in our day-to-day business and dealings with others. (If you suspect you are a victim of fraud, you may call KNOW FRAUD by calling 1-877-987-3728 or 1-877-FTC-HELP. The calls are free.)

> *Beware of false prophets, who come to you in sheep's clothing, but inwardly they are ravenous wolves.* Matthew 7:15 (NKJV)

Dear Lord, first of all, I want to ask that you help me guard my lips, so that I won't be the one who tells a lie. Then, I ask you to help the elderly and others who are too trusting to sense your warning and to be wise. Amen.

February 11

Miraculous Moments

Have they happened to you? — Strange, inexplicable but wonderful moments in your life? I've had it happen just a few times. The first was when I was a teenage girl and I was walking alone, down our old dirt driveway in Pasadena. I looked up in the sky and there was a small, low, white cloud. Within the cloud was what I can only describe as a "piece of rainbow", softly glowing. There was no rain; in fact, the sun was shining. It might have been the sun shining through ice crystals, but it was a warm and balmy day. It was a wonder to me! Like a visitation, I felt that some holy being, perhaps an angel, was looking down at me from within that small rainbow-clothed cumulus cloud. It was not just an ordinary occurrence. It was special; no one could ever convince me otherwise.

> *I have set my rainbow in the clouds, and it will be the sign of the covenant between me and the earth. Whenever I bring clouds over the earth and the rainbow appears in the clouds, I will remember my covenant between me and you and all living creatures of every kind.* Genesis 9:13-15 (NIV)

Dear Maker of Heaven and Earth, I thank you for these special moments in my life that are like my own personal miracles, wonders to my soul. Help me to always see them and always receive them and always thank you for them. Amen.

February 12

Talents

As a young person I didn't understand what it meant to be "talented" or "gifted." I didn't understand discipline. But now I know that it is a matter of God's encouraging us, helping us believe that He believes in us, and helping us to find out what our talents and gifts are as well as what they are not. This is all for the purpose of bringing us to the place where we can do that thing that we are most uniquely qualified to do. He knows that when we find that purpose and follow it that we are deeply satisfied and happy, and that we can rejoice in our work. Let's not disappoint the Holy Spirit by refusing to acknowledge our gifts, or hiding behind false humility; we can't take praise for gifts that were given to us, but we can receive appreciation for what we do with them, as we take responsibility and learn, through discipline, to properly use those gifts.

> *...and he has filled him with the Spirit of God, with skill, ability and knowledge in all kinds of crafts—to make artistic designs for work in gold, silver and bronze, to cut and set*

stones, to work in wood and to engage in all kinds of artistic craftsmanship. Exodus 35:31-33 (NIV)

Lord God, you who have given to all some gift or gifts, help me to know what my gifts are, help me to discipline myself to hone them. Then help me to use them for your sake and the sake of others. Amen.

February 13

It's About the Rain

The lightning and thunder were incredible, continuing on and on for many minutes. Don and I stood outside and watched this natural fireworks display — so brilliant, so beautiful, so terrible in the night. Finally, the rain stopped and there was a stillness everywhere, yet the air was alive, full of charged negative ions, fresh and invigorating.

Sometimes my soul feels like a dry and thirsty land and I need a spiritual rain to come down upon me, to bring me life, to heal me, to bless me. But how can I receive such a blessing if I don't stop to ask, to wait, to wonder at His soothing touch, which he pours out faithfully, generously, when I take the time to draw near to Him?

He draws up the water vapor and then distills it into rain.
The rain pours down from the clouds, and everyone benefits.
Job 36:27, 28 (NLT)

Lord, thank you for these times of rain upon the earth that remind me that I can call upon you to pour out abundantly the water of life upon my thirsty soul. Amen.

February 14

St. Valentine's Day

This is the day set aside to remember those we love, especially in a romantic way. But it began as a day to celebrate the memory of St. Valentine. It is said that he lived near Rome in or about the year of A.D. 270. It was a time when Christians were being imprisoned, tortured and murdered for being followers of Jesus Christ. In the end he gave his life because of His faithfulness in witnessing for His Lord.

In today's world in the United States, we don't hear much of those who have suffered for their faith. One exception is those students at Columbine High School in Littleton, Colorado who spoke out about their beliefs. This may have lost their lives because of their confession of faith in Christ. In other countries, there are those who suffer daily because they have chosen to follow Jesus. There are those who are persecuted, tortured, martyred. Let's not forget these who suffer for Jesus' sake. Who knows, the time may come when we too will be privileged to suffer in the same manner, and then who will be praying for us?

Therefore...I was not disobedient to the heavenly vision...
Acts 26:19 (NKJV)

Lord God, thank you for those like St. Valentine who were and are faithful witnesses to the heavenly vision, even to death. Today we pray for those who suffer for your sake, Lord, wherever they may be in the world, and ask that you give them peace, patience, comfort and courage. Amen.

February 15

Answers to Unspoken Prayers

It was St. Valentine's Day and we had guests arriving by car from out of state about dinnertime. We had all planned to go out to eat together, but I decided to fix dinner myself and have it waiting for them when they arrived. The table was all set and I felt it would be special to have something to put by each place setting, but I didn't have time to go shopping. Then the doorbell rang. It was my next-door neighbor, Lucile, who brought us a Valentine card and along with it, five little picture cards with scripture verses printed on each. There, before I even asked, was the answer: I put one at everyone's place setting. As the guests sat down at the table, they were delighted to each find a little token of love. I told them the source, my sweet neighbor, and the other source, the Lord.

Isn't it wonderful that sometimes we get these little gifts from God, answers to our unspoken requests? How lovely that Lucile answered the little voice in her spirit that suggested she take the cards over along with her Valentine card to us! I want to be like that — the one who obeys such urgings so that I will be part of the Lord's answers to someone else's unspoken prayer.

Before they call I will answer, while they are yet speaking I will hear. Isaiah 65:24 (NRSV)

Lord, thank you for sometimes giving us the small things that we didn't even have time to ask for! We are in awe of such gentle, loving-kindness. Lord, make us more like you. Amen.

February 16

The Good Samaritan, South Pasadena Version
or
Knock, Knock, Who's There?

It was a sleepy Saturday afternoon in our quiet little town of South Pasadena, California. I was just about to doze off when I heard footsteps — someone running down the sidewalk by the house just outside our bedroom. I could tell this person was not just jogging; the sound was too fast and too loud. A few moments later the front door bell rang. I did not connect these two incidents. I did not want to get up. A few moments after this, the doorbell rang again. I heard my husband and son, Dan, in the TV room. They were watching a football game. *Why don't they go to the door?* Maybe they couldn't hear the doorbell. Even so, I was *not* going to get up; I wanted to rest. Then I heard someone run up the walk by the back gate. A young woman's voice called out, "Don...Pat...Don...Pat." I didn't recognize the voice but at this point, realizing something must be wrong, I jumped up and ran outside. It was our next-door neighbor. I called out after her, "Teri!"

"Oh, I'm so sorry I scared you, but it sounds like there is something or someone in the trunk of your car. Bob [her husband] and I were working outside when we began to hear it. He heard it too, didn't you, Bob?"

Bob smiled and nodded, looking down from his perch on the top of their roof where he was cleaning out their rain gutters with a broom, "Yeah, I did," he said without much enthusiasm. I had the feeling that he would have preferred not to have been asked.

"What? What do you mean?" I was incredulous.

"It's making a noise, a knocking sound."

I followed her to where my car was parked. Sure enough, there was a clear knocking noise coming from the trunk of my 20-year old Cadillac.

"Listen," she said, as she knocked on the top of the car trunk.

"Knock, knock," the car trunk repeated immediately.

Just to check it out, *I* knocked on the car trunk twice and, again, it obediently echoed back with two knocks. I rushed to the house to get the car key. When I got back to the car and tried to unlock the trunk, it was stuck! I couldn't open it. I went back to get Don. He came out and couldn't open it either. Finally, he sat on the trunk as I turned the key. The trunk opened up to reveal: the ugly computer table that I had found by a trash bin. Don hadn't wanted to keep it and it had stayed in the trunk, waiting to be discarded. Somehow, its presence had managed to keep the automatic trunk closure mechanism from working correctly. The strange knocking noise stopped once the trunk was closed properly, never to repeat its message for "help" again.

We all laughed heartily and Teri said she must have been reading too many mysteries lately. She was a good sport and a good neighbor. Certainly no one could accuse Teri of being one of those people who won't "get involved."

Then a Samaritan traveling down the road came to where the hurt man was. When he saw the man, he felt very sorry for him. Luke 10:33 (NCV)

Lord God, there are times when we are supposed to get involved and yet we are afraid. Help us to be courageous and do the right thing. Amen.

February 17

Lucy, Super Dog

Our dog, Lucy, has a toy called "Mad Dog." She was terribly afraid of it at first. It is oblong, white, yellow and red and gives out a yelping sound when squeezed. We forgot about it and it rested under an end table for weeks. Then one day I heard her going after something, growling, and scuffling. Sure enough! She had taken on "Mad Dog" again. She would bark at it and hit it with her paw and then back off, too fearful to proceed. But the next day and the next she would go back again and try once more to subdue the enemy. She discovered that it would "yelp" if she bit it in the middle, so she learned to grab it only at the ends. She would hold on to it longer and longer each day, until finally, she "overcame" her fear of it! She had figured it out. It was not really a threat. She overcame Mad Dog; Lucy won!

For me Lucy is a good example of bravado — courage to go after an enemy, to face that which is feared. Sometimes what we thought was an enemy might just be a big cowering bully who backs off at the least bit of assertiveness. Sometimes giants are really pussycats. So, today, what am I afraid of? Whatever it is, with God's help, I think I'll just follow Lucy's example and go after it!

David said to Saul, "Let no one lose heart on account of this Philistine; your servant will go and fight him. 1 Samuel 17:32 (NIV)

Dear Lord, give us courage to fight the Goliaths in our lives. Amen.

February 18

The Warmest of Memories

I believe I was about ten when my mother caused the fire. It was bedtime and she was trying to find the Mentholatum™. It had apparently rolled under the bed, where it was too dark to see it. So — she lit a match! She looked further and further under the bed until, just as she found it, the filmy cotton gauze that hung down from the box spring caught fire! It was like lightening!

My often inappropriately hysterical Mom said, and I'll never forget it, partly because it was so atypical, "Dad, the bed's on fire." She said it as though she was saying, "Dad, the cat wants out."

"What?!" he screamed and jumped out of bed like a jack-in-the-box.

In a flash he had the box spring and mattress up against the wall and was beating the fire out, sort of. To me, it didn't seem to be doing the job. I decided to help; I got a pan of water. Dad looked at it for a split second as though it couldn't possibly do anything, but then he grabbed it from my outstretched hand and poured it over the flames anyway. I don't believe it did help much, but I felt that I was part of the solution to this exciting crisis. I think, however, suffocation was the preferred method of quenching the thing, and finally, the flames ceased.

Someone called the fire department. They arrived after Dad had dragged the mattress outside. It had a black hole about the size of a cantaloupe on the upper right hand side. The firemen warned my parents to keep a watch on it, that it could appear to be out but at anytime could erupt into flame again. I had no idea such a thing could happen; I was learning something very important. We did know it was smoldering. The smell was most unpleasant — like old damp rags.

I think the thing I like most about this story is how, after it was all over, my parents, who were financially strapped, never acted as though something awful had happened, (though it was clear they would have to purchase a new mattress)! I don't know where they slept that night. They just had a great old laugh about it. Later, they told friends over and over how calmly my mother had announced, "Dad, the bed's on fire." I can hear her soft voice speaking those words to this day. Their sense of humor was one of the best qualities my parents possessed. So, this story brings back a (no pun intended) warm memory.

So I decided it was more important to enjoy life. The best that people can do here on earth is to eat, drink, and enjoy life, because these joys will help them do the hard work God gives them here on earth. Ecclesiastes 8:15 (NCV)

Heavenly Father, I thank you for the gift of humor and the experience of joy in our lives. Help us to laugh more and enjoy all the good things that you have lavished upon us and even when we are without, help us to be filled with the good memories of the days of our lives. Amen.

February 19

The Smell of It

Smells are so much a part of life, aren't they? Yet, how often do we take the time to actually try to smell what is around us? While walking home from work one day in South Pasadena, I decided to make a goal of discovering what I could smell along the way. At first there was fertilizer, then something that smelled like cinnamon, next something cooking (hominy grits?). Then there were roses and, later on, fresh cut grass. Certain trees seemed to have a scent I'd never noticed before as I walked beneath them. There was the smell of gasoline fumes from cars going by.

Everything seems to have a smell, but it takes a special kind of concentration to pick up the scents. They say people remember smells more than anything else. When we smell something we once smelled, even long ago, a whole scene from our past can spring into our minds, returning it all to us, as though it just happened yesterday. Such memories pack a great emotional punch.

But what's the spiritual application? There is also a spiritual sense of smell. Did you know that the Bible tells us that there is a sweet fragrance of the knowledge of God? I find that mysterious and strange, but I want to emit the aroma of one who knows God.

Now thanks be to God who always leads us in triumph in Christ, and through us diffuses the fragrance of His knowledge in every place. 2 Corinthians 2:13 (NKJV)

Lord, I long to be able to find the fragrance of knowledge of you in every place. And, for myself, let me offer up the sacrifice of praise that it might be a sweet smelling aroma to you this day. Amen.

February 20

The Sounds of the Earth

One morning I decided to listen to all the sounds in the gardens at Descanso in La Canada-Flintridge, California as I slowly meandered along paths lined with numerous shades of green and beneath groves of ancient California Oak trees. As I walked, these are some of things I heard:

- A single oak leaf falling to the forest floor
- A child crying in the distance
- A Chinese family of three, speaking Mandarin, enjoying the beauty of the gardens
- Birds that I can't see making high squeaking sounds
- My own feet crunching leaves on the path
- A soft wind high in the California Oaks
- The sound of fern leaves caressing each other
- Something small, unknown moving in the bushes
- A distant siren
- Squirrels rustling leaves as they forage for acorns
- The chirping of crickets hidden in the underbrush, and
- The different quacks of a variety of ducks.

What a joy is the sense of hearing! My grandmother on my dad's side of the family, Florence Harper, was deaf and for most of her life went without hearing aids until late in life when she did begin to hear with their help. Perhaps someday I will lose this precious sense, but may God help me store up memories of the wondrous sounds of the earth, and meanwhile may I have my spiritual ears open to what God is saying in the world around me.

...but blessed...are your ears for they hear. Matthew 13:16 (NKJV)

Dear Lord, thank you for the gift of physical hearing. Bless those who do not hear the sounds of earth, but may they be tuned in to that which is even more valuable — the sound of your inner voice calling them, teaching them and leading them. Amen.

February 21

Asking for What We Want

By the time I was about 10 and my brother, Preston, was 9, I realized that, for whatever reason, he tended to get what he wanted by simply asking, and, believe me, he asked for a lot, and often. I, however, was much quieter and did not ask for much at all — ever — but when I did, I did not very often get it. One day while Mom, Dad, my brother and I were taking our regular Sunday afternoon drive I had an overwhelming desire for an ice cream cone. I didn't want to ask, but, oh! How I wanted that cone. So I came up with the best solution I could at the time: I heard my own small voice saying before I thought the whole thing through: "Preston wants an ice cream cone." The minute the words got out of my mouth, I knew my ruse would not work. My parents and my brother all scoffed and laughed at me. And no, I didn't get an ice cream cone. This became one of our family's stories, told over and over, at my expense.

Once I became a Christian and realized that part of my regular prayer life was asking God for something, the asking did not come easily. But I did find that no matter what I asked, I always knew that He heard and honored my request, even if the answer was not *yes*, but *no* or *wait*. God is the Good Father who listens to the shyest of his children, even me, even you. He always hears. He always answers. He always respects and honors us. Is there something for which you have been too shy to ask? Ask now, and know that He will answer that request, in the way that is wisest and best. You can trust Him with the answer.

If you ask anything in my name, I will do it. John 14:14 (NKJV)

Dear Father, thank you for being such a good listener and a wise answerer! The thing that I've had a hard time asking you for is _____ . I ask now in the name of Jesus, that my request be granted if it is in accordance with your will. If not, then instead of my request, give me what I truly need rather than what I urgently want. Amen.

February 22

The Perfect Match

Sometimes I see colors in the world around me that give me a real kick. Yes! Like a jolt of pleasure. For instance, one spring several friends and I went out into the Southern California countryside to see the wild flowers. In one area of gently sloping hills there were a myriad of bright yellow mustard flowers blooming. Through these hills ran a narrow dirt road. On the road, slowly rambling along, there was an old truck with a wooden bed — all ordinary, except for one thing: The wooden slats on the bed of the truck were painted exactly the same color of yellow gold as the wild flowers. Eureka! It was a peak color experience!

Want to hear about another one? My friend, Birgitta, had made Don and me an exquisite patchwork pillow as a gift. It had many colors: lavender, orange, beige and green. I placed it on a green leather chair where it found a comfortable home. Later that day I threw across the back of the chair a lavender shirt! Eureka! There it was again, that surprise of perfectly, deeply satisfying color matches.

Another time: I see Lucy, our dog, bouncing toward me with her yellow-green tennis ball across a patch of greenish-yellow grass! Ah! Another perfect match!

But my favorite: My husband has large blue eyes. Sometimes when I look up at him on a clear summer day, the sky is just exactly the same color! It's as though I'm looking through him to the heavens! It's just that perfect a match that makes me, well, in this case sigh with affection and appreciation!

So what does all this have to do with life and meaning and stuff like that? Well, everyone has a place in his or her spirit that is looking for a perfect match — oh, not for a mate, but for a god! They try different gods such as money and the things it buys — power, fame, drugs, sex, or success, but none of these things ever fulfill the longing we have inside; our deepest need is not met. But when we seek for Jesus Christ with all of our heart, He is the One who can give us the living water that satisfies that inner thirst because He is the water of life. He will give us Himself, and that oneness, that communion is the one thing that will satisfy that deepest longing. In Him we find the "perfect match." It happens when we truly touch God and we are touched by Him. We may think we have found Him, but, in truth, He has found us.

Delight yourself in the Lord and He will give you the desires of your heart. Psalm 37:4 (NKJV)

Dear Lord and Savior, please bring to us those times when we experience a "perfect fit" in our relationship with you. Answer the longings of that empty place in our souls. And when those dry times come to us — and they will come — please bring us back into that relationship that once again will thrill our souls, as a first love returning, fresh and beautiful and full of wonder. Amen.

February 23

Lumgigi People

Mama lost her daddy, Jesse Nelson, when she was nine years old. After that Grandma had to raise four children on her own. They had very little in material goods on Grandma's small salary. She was a one-room schoolhouse teacher in Oklahoma and also had a night job as a pianist at the movie house before "talkies." As for toys, Mama had some marbles — just a few. One of them she named Lumgigi. She was playing with Lumgigi one day when it rolled away from her and through a crack in the floor. It disappeared from view and she cried and cried as though she had lost a best friend. She and her siblings didn't want to make the crack in the floor bigger, but they couldn't reach the spot from under the house. She never saw Lumgigi again.

The crack and the few marbles told me something about my mom that she didn't tell me — they must have been very poor. I also see the marble as a metaphor of those of us who will "fall through the cracks" of world systems. I have felt like one of those Lumgigi people. I have fallen through the cracks by being kind of weird and not like other people in some ways. But even this I can think of with joy because whenever I have fallen through the cracks, there was a hand to catch me. I was valuable to God and He made sure I didn't get lost from His view. God has caught me and held me in the palm of His hand. God loves Lumgigi people.

A man was there named Zacchaeus, who was a very important tax collector, and he was wealthy. He wanted to see who Jesus was, but he was not able because he was too short to see above the crowd. He ran ahead to a place where Jesus would come, and he climbed a sycamore tree so he could see him. When Jesus came to that place, he looked up and said to him, 'Zacchaeus, hurry and come down! I must stay at your house today.' Luke 19:2-5 (NCV)

Dear Lord Jesus, I understand how Zacchaeus felt and yet you looked up into that tree and saw him! And you wanted to go to his house! How delighted and surprised he must have been, but Jesus, you didn't judge him by his profession or by his appearance; you saw how open his heart was and how in wonder he was of you. I want to be that way toward you too. Please feel welcome in my home and in my heart this day. Amen.

February 24

The Tiny Ones

In the early 1900s Grandma gave birth to seven children. Four survived but three little ones were stillborn or died in babyhood. Mom remembered one of them. She was about six at the time. It was wrapped in a piece of sheeting and placed in a breadbox instead of a casket to be buried the next day. When no one was looking, she sneaked into the kitchen and opened the box and unwrapped it. It was a little boy. Mama knew it was probably not right that she did this, but she needed to know and no one was talking about it. In those days secrets abounded. A little brother died that day. I don't even know if he had been given a name. Certainly there was not much of a ritual burial or a funeral service. Now there is no one (besides me) in my family who remembers about the existence of this tiny child who was my uncle. I want to remember him.

I believe that the little ones who die in the womb need to be remembered. In 1963 I had a miscarriage. It broke my heart. I had felt so connected to that little life. However, I conceived again a few months later and was carrying our second son, Daniel, during the time I would have carried the other baby to term. A few months after Daniel was born, I had a dream in which Daniel and the other child, a little boy, were playing together, just a few months apart in age. The baby was so real to me, that I named him Jonathan. Maybe this was just a wish fulfillment dream but perhaps it was more than that. Maybe children lost in miscarriage or abortion are taken into Heaven where they will await our coming to meet them. Such a possibility comforts my heart.

When Elizabeth heard Mary's greeting, the unborn baby inside her jumped.... Luke 1:41 (NCV)

Dear Father in Heaven, if it is true that you do create spirits for all the unborn then they must leave this world guileless and you surely welcome them back into your presence and take care of them. I ask that you comfort all those who have lost a child from the womb and I ask forgiveness for all those who have taken a life from the womb, for surely they did not know what they were doing. Amen.

February 25

Fear on Hold

I've rarely felt courageous in my life, except for one occasion. I was alone with our two sons, Michael and Daniel, ages two and four. They had gone to sleep and I was sleeping in the living room of our tiny house by myself. Someone trying to open the front door awakened me. The only thing that mattered to me at that moment was that my children be protected. I found myself grabbing a sheet and putting it in front of myself and heading for the door. It opened! I screamed — well, no, it was more of a deep, horrendous-sounding low growl that came out of my mouth, and I continued to move forward, feeling like a menacing threat to anyone daring to enter our house. My next-door neighbor, a young man stood there for a split second, his mouth open. He then backed off, apologizing in extreme embarrassment all the way down the steps. "Sorry Mam, I got the wrong house."

Well, that's it — my appointment with courage. But I've heard that the Spanish word "macho" means not only manly and virile, but it has to do with bravery, but the kind of bravery that is concerned with one doing something *in spite* of the fear to do it. Now that, I can do, and often — not that anyone would notice. Who knows or notices that I am trembling when driving L.A. freeways at night? Who knows that I'm afraid to go into an unfamiliar store and shop? Who knows how hard it is for me to go up and speak to people at church, since, by nature, I am shy? Who knows that I fear answering phones? Well, there is someone who knows. God knows and He also is the one that empowers me to do these small, courageous acts that are so unimpressive to the world!

The Lord is my light and my salvation; Whom shall I fear? The Lord is the strength of my life; Of whom shall I be afraid? Psalm 27:1 (NKJV)

Lord, thank you for giving me courage to do the little things. When I remember that you are with me, I know I don't have to be afraid. Amen.

February 26

Memories from the Rock

Don and I were strolling through Pasadena's Old Town one summer evening. We happened on a small shop, *The Game Keeper*, in an alley where games and puzzles of all kinds are sold. I was drawn toward a fishbowl in which there were no fish; instead there were some unidentifiable little round objects. When I got closer I saw the sign adhered to the bowl that read, "Break your own geode - $1.00." I reached into the jar and picked up one of them and found myself traveling back in time.

My father's hobby was to find, cut and polish semi-precious stones. He had a workshop in an old converted shed several yards away from our house. He would wet the stones and show me what they were prone to look like after being polished. Sometimes I would wait to see for myself. It was a process that always brought out the rich colors and complex designs in what looked liked ordinary pebbles.

The most fascinating of the rocks he worked with were the geodes. Most were somewhat larger than a baseball and looked like dusty potatoes, newly harvested. There was nothing attractive about them. However, my father assured me there was a surprise waiting to be discovered within. To get to the treasure, he would saw them in half. I can still hear the shrill whir of the blade as it cut through the stone, and I waited in anticipation to see what would be inside. It always took so long — longer than I thought I had patience to endure as I sat on the shed step and wiggled my bare toes in the dust.

Then the moment would come! He would open up the geode to reveal a magical, miniature cavern of white and lavender crystals. It was worth the wait. Now 60 plus years later, I stood and looked at the little geode in the palm of my hand. The owner of the store said, "You can have that if you like." I was surprised and moved by the gift, tucked it into my pocket and when I got home I placed it on the coffee table beside a little box where I keep some of the rough and polished moss agate, moonstones and chrysolite that my father gave me years ago.

I don't want to break open the geode. I want it whole. I already know what's inside, how rough and ugly have been some of the past years since daddy's death — just like that ugly "potato" rock. There have been so many painful memories to relive and so many true offenses for which I needed to forgive my father. I have had to slice through them all before I was ready and able to remember the good things and the happy moments that he gave me — the times of sitting on the old workshop steps, waiting for him to polish a stone or open a geode. Now I can finally remember the good — the old treasures hidden inside passed the ugly shell of unforgiveness that needed to be broken through. That man at the game store in Old Town gave me so much more than a little geode. He gave me back a moment out of my past that I thought I had lost forever.

> *But when you are praying, first forgive anyone you are holding a grudge against, so that your Father in heaven will forgive your sins, too.* Mark 11:25 (NLT)

Dear Heavenly Father, thank you for helping us to forgive our parents for any hurtful offenses. If the readers need to forgive their parents, help them to take the first step by being willing to do what may be the beginning of a process of forgiving that will set them free from their past. Amen.

February 27

Rats!

When I was a child we lived in a very old home on the southern edge of Pasadena; it was next to the last home on South Euclid Avenue and for some reason was called the water house. Part of the frame of the house was made with logs, which we discovered when we did some remodeling. It was built right on top the dirt with no cement foundation underneath and no crawl space. This being the case, the house had rats.

We never got rid of them; they made noises at night, moving and scratching and squeaking inside of walls. Daddy set traps, but though we often caught one at a time, we never got all of them. One of their favorite places to visit was our upstairs bathroom. My grandma used Cutacura™ soap, which she wrapped up and kept as her own. I was not allowed to use it (I used Palmolive™).

Each evening one of the last things we were to do was to put the soap bars away. If we forgot, the rats would come dine on them during the night. If it were a new bar, they would leave large teeth marks on it — sometimes devouring a quarter of it. If it were smaller, they would carry it off and we would never see it again. If it were mid-sized, they would try to carry it off and drop it on the floor, making a clatter that would wake us up, and one of us would have to get up and go redeem it. Daddy often put rattraps in the bathroom near the toilet and under the sink, and sometimes they would be caught, but not die right away. They would slap and drag the trap around. It was Daddy's job to take the rat out of the trap. I never asked what he did with the corpses — ugly and huge with long hairless tails. It seemed just one of life's little normal nuisances at the time. Now it makes me shudder.

I sometimes wonder if God did not create certain kinds of creatures in the world as figurative symbols to teach us about evil, like snakes and deadly spiders and, yes, rats. These rats came in the night to steal, even as the enemy of our souls would seek to nibble away at our faith. All I have to say about this is: Beware of the "rats."

A thief comes to steal and kill and destroy, but I came to give life—life in all its fullness. John 10:10 (NCV)

Dear Lord Jesus, thank you for giving us warnings about the enemy of our souls. We praise you that you are the One who came to give us life. Help us to receive that life today and deliver us from evil. Amen.

February 28

Granny and the Future

Granny, Florence Crier Harper, my father's mother, put a red henna rinse on her white head of hair. It was thick and long and someone said that she had always been proud of it, that it had been a source of vanity. She had bright little brown eyes that were set in her face at an upward angle. I remember clearly her coming to see us in California in the 1950s. During her visit we drove her to Manhattan Beach so she could see the California coast. She had never seen the ocean before and it was a breath-taking wonder to her. As we were riding in the car, she was sitting very straight, looking ahead. She told me, "You must always look ahead so you know exactly what is going to happen and where you are going." That message ingrained itself into my heart. I truly believed her. You were, as a child, supposed to believe what your elders told you, weren't you? This put a great burden on me. I was supposed to see what was going to happen in advance and I must not let up on this responsibility. It filled me with fear. What if I should miss something? Not see what was coming? On the way home I was resting in the back seat and a great fear came upon me. I couldn't see where the car was going! What if we were to have an accident? I would need to see it coming. I jumped up in a panic, vowing to never look away — just in case — when I was riding in a car.

Poor little Granny had no idea what horror her guardianship theory of an unknown future put into me, and it has taken a long time for me to let the future rest in God's hands. Even now, I sometimes take it back, try to prophesy what's to come, or just get into a panic about what I don't know. Worrying, after all, supposedly prepares us for the worst! But God is faithful to teach me to leave it all up to him. I'm glad I don't know the future. How many of us would want to know, for instance, the number of our days, the way in which we will die, the losses we will encounter along life's road? Whatever befalls us during our earthly journey, we know, by faith, that we have a Companion along the way and that's all we really need to know.

For I know the thoughts that I think toward you, says the Lord, thoughts of peace and not of evil, to give you a future and a hope. Jeremiah 29:11 (NKJV)

Dear Father, I ask that you help me trust you with my future, whatever it may bring. I pray that you will teach me to allow each day to come — one at a time. I want to receive your guidance for all future days, knowing you will be there with me, for that is surely the most important thing of all — that I will not be alone in any of my tomorrows but may count on you to be there for me. Amen.

February 29

Old Sins that Hang Around

Aunt Flossie was one of Grandma Jessie's (my mother's mother) sisters. She was in her eighties when she came to live with us, and I was in my teens. The explanation of her extreme forgetfulness was that she was "senile," the catchall word of the day for any form of dementia. She was plump and rosy-cheeked with her pure white hair tied in a tiny knot on the top of her head. Though half Cherokee, her skin had little of that lovely golden brown hue. She had been somewhat wealthy and well known in her day. She had attended the New England Conservatory of Music, which she occasionally proclaimed in the best Bostonian accent. She had studied piano and voice, but by the time I met her, these talents had faded away into her lost past. However, her pride and her dignity were almost always intact. She thought she was living in a time perhaps 50 years earlier. She believed her sister was her maid. She ordered her around and Grandma, ever humble, did as she asked.

If she said something about their mother as though she were still alive, Grandma could not allow her to believe that lie for a moment. One such correction came as Aunt Flossie looked off into the distance. She said with great feeling and tears in her eyes, "Oh look. It's my mother; she's calling me." Grandma was adamant: "Floss, Mama has been dead for 30 years!" Aunt Flossie replied, "Dead, Mama dead?! Oh, no!" And then she would weep for just a moment or two before forgetting what had been said.

One of my best memories of her is the morning she sat in her favorite spot on our old shaky wooden balcony and looked down the three hundred foot dirt driveway. "See there!" she said, her keen eyes fixed on a nonexistent spot at the end of the drive, "That dead man's been left hanging there for a week; someone should cut him down." What scenes from her past must she have been digging up with such a picture as that!

It makes me wonder at the imaginary dead things that are hanging around in my own mind — past sins, forgiven by God, but neither forgotten nor forgiven by me. Why? Oh, partly it's because I'm too proud to admit, even now, that I did such things — so ashamed, that somehow I still imagine that if I make myself suffer for them by adding guilt and remorse, I will help myself look more pious! Well, time to let them go, cut those old dead bodies down!

I—yes, I alone—am the one who blots out your sins for my own sake and will never think of them again. Isaiah 43:25 (NLT)

Dear Lord, thank you for forgiving and forgetting my sins. I, here and now, forgive myself for my sins even as you have forgiven me. May I never remember them except in the context of having compassion for others who have sinned or in the context of receiving the natural consequences of these things of which I am guilty. I promise you Lord, that I will no longer punish myself. Amen.

MARCH

March 1

The Weapons of Warfare

You no doubt know about what the U. S. Forces call "smart bombs." They can penetrate the roof of a bunker. A smart fuse is programmed to count floors of a bunker and it detonates when it reaches the designated floor! Sounds awesome, doesn't it?

What do we have as spiritual weapons that can compare to that? We are told that our weapons are not in the realm of the physical. Why is that? Because our enemy is not in the "flesh" but in the sphere of spiritual realities and it is part of our responsibility to be aware of our enemy. So how do we pray? How do we do the spiritual warfare that is necessary? It is by faith, with the entire armor of God, which has been provided by God (See Ephesians 6:11-17). There is only one offensive weapon, the sword of the Spirit, which is the word of God. We are to be armed with a working knowledge of the Bible. That is what the Captain of the Lord's Host is calling us to!

Are you ready? Am I? We never know when the attacker will come; be we are to be prepared to do battle by feeding our spirits with the knowledge that is contained in Scripture, so that when the enemy comes with lies, we will respond with the truth. This is not only our right but also our responsibility and we are authorized to do so!

No weapon formed against you will prosper. Isaiah 54:17 (NKJV)

Lord, remind us to be armed with your word, that we may stand against the deceitfulness of the spiritual enemy. By your Spirit, help us to recall Scripture, so that we will be able to apply it to each situation in which we fight against spiritual enemies just as Jesus did when He was tempted by Satan. Amen.

March 2

The Joy of Words

As I shared once before, my mother's father, Jesse Nelson, died when she was nine. I missed meeting him, but the few things my mother told me about him say a world of who he was. I know that his favorite composer was Robert Shumann and that his favorite composition was Traumerei (Op. 15, No.7), a rather plaintive song without words. The most important thing I know about him is that his children were encouraged to read and that he taught them, when they were reading, to always have a dictionary nearby and always look up any word that was unfamiliar to them. My Mother passed this on to me and I still adhere to this rule. Yes, I have learned to love words — to read them and to write them!

And books, what wonderful, taken-for-granted pleasures they bring. What would my early life have been without books — without the classics that my mother read to us as children — "Black Beauty," "My Friend Flicka," "Little Women," "Little Men," "Rebecca of Sunny Brook Farm." Later, once I became a believer, it's been the wonderful works by Christian authors that have taught me so much — C. S. Lewis, Oswald Chambers, Richard J. Foster, Dallas Willard, Billy Graham, Madam Guyon, John Hyde, St. Augustine, Evelyn Underhill, Brother Lawrence, St. Francis of Assisi. The list goes on and on. What amazing resources we have! We can avail ourselves of so much knowledge from these great saints who have gone before us!

But above all, there is *the* Book – the Bible, with a life of its own, because it was written by dozens of God-inspired writers for a period of more than three thousand years. I read it every day and every day it speaks to me. The "old" words become fresh as God brings them to life within — food for my hungry soul and spirit!

How sweet are your words to my taste; Sweeter than honey to my mouth! Through your precepts I get understanding; Therefore I hate every false way. Your word is a lamp to my feet and a light to my path! (Psalm 119:103-105 NKJV)

Dear Lord, thank you for the blessed words that you have given us in your book — the Bible! Amen.

March 3

A Choice of Attitude

One of my daughters-in-law, Karen, tells a poignant story of living a desperately poor life in Arkansas. Her family lived in California until her father discovered that he had cancer. He wanted to go "home" to Arkansas for his final years, and so they all packed up and left. They stayed there for a period of three years, and when she was nine he passed away. During that time, they lived in the poorest of areas, with only the barest necessities provided.

However, as Karen tells the story, she displays not the slightest hint of self-pity in her voice. She tells it in the context of all that she learned, especially how unimportant the material things in this life really are. It was important to be where they were for their father's sake, but the winters were cold and she and her sister had only one pair of gloves. They would take turns wearing them, or one would use the left hand glove, the other the right. Instead of an attitude of "poor me" over having had such an experience of forced sharing, Karen laughs about the time her sister made her fall down in the snow, get all wet and dirty, so she would have to go into the house, and then her sister could have both gloves for a change!

Now that's called making the best of a bad situation! What an attitude. How wonderful that we all have a choice about how we experience what happens to us, no matter how "bad" the circumstances are! (I can't help adding that I'm proud of my daughter-in-law and I'm proud of my son, Mike, for choosing her as his wife.)

Now these are the ones sown among thorns; they are the ones who hear the word, and the cares of this world, the deceitfulness of riches, and the desires for other things entering in choke the word, and it becomes unfruitful. Mark 4:19 (NCV)

Lord, it's so easy to believe that if we just have something more or different, that we will be happy. Help us to see that the key is within ourselves as we choose an attitude of contentment, over a life of self-pity and complaint. Amen.

March 4

The Final Release

Today on my morning walk, I saw something small and white in the street. Curious, I checked it out. It was half of a tiny bird's egg. The little being who had inhabited it would now be in its nest, and will soon be eating and growing and learning to fly. I thought, as I cupped that fragile shell in my palm, that death is like that — leaving the confines of this body, and flying away. I think I got the idea from something that happened when a friend of ours died last year.

I was watching a television news report about the setting free of an owl that had recovered from injuries and was being released into the wild. I held my breath as a hand reached for the latch and opened the cage door. My heart felt lighter as I watched that exquisite bird lift off and reach for the sky, gliding into the heavens. Free, it soared until it was out of the camera's view.

That night we drove to the hospital to visit our friend, "Art," who was gravely ill. We had all prayed for his healing, but it hadn't happened. Don, as his pastor, was allowed to visit him, but I was not able to because he was in intensive care. As we left the hospital, I suddenly saw in my mind's eye, a replay of the stately owl I'd seen on TV a few hours earlier — freed from its cage. I turned to Don and I said, "I don't think Art is going to live much longer; he's going to fly away." I somehow just knew. And that's what happened about two hours later. It was time for him to be set free, free from the cage, free from the shell of the body, free to fly into the heavenly realm.

So this body that can be destroyed will clothe itself with that which can never be destroyed, and this body that dies will clothe itself with that which can never die. When this happens, this Scripture will be made true: "Death is destroyed forever in victory." Isaiah 25:8 - 1 Corinthians 15:54 (NCV)

Lord God, help us not to dread death, but to know that we will be freed from our bodies in order that we may enter into a Heavenly Realm. Amen.

March 5

Forgiving Preston

My brother, Preston, is hardest of all of my relatives to write about, but I must do it. I remember him both as a gentle soul and as an ambassador of evil. He was good looking and self-conscious. He was smart and terribly neat, could have been an engineer, was a welder. He was a natural artist, but had no training. He had turquoise blue eyes, long curly eyelashes, curly brown hair and strong Cherokee, as well as Negroid features, for which he was teased in high school, and called the "n" word (I suspect that our family from my mother's side has some black blood in our ancestry, but from whence this connection might have come, I will never know.).

When I accepted Christ at the age of 18, Preston was enraged and jumped on a stool in the kitchen and over and over yelled down at me, "You belong to me" until I was cowering on the floor. However, I did not give up on my faith. Up until that time my brother had had power over me, but no longer.

At some point he decided to become a Christian, but it was a difficult thing for him to follow Jesus. It became clear to us that he had a mental illness. When he found a medication that helped him we had moments of quiet sanity together, but it did not last. He grew worse and one horrible spring day in 1982, he took his own life and he took Daddy with him.

Afterwards I felt the Lord was asking me, "Will you forgive your brother?" I said immediately, "Yes, of course I will," knowing that it was out of a tortured, fickle brain chemistry that he had acted; no one can know what kind of hell he experienced in his soul, and life was a horror that he wanted to leave, but perhaps was not brave enough to leave it by himself.

So why do you condemn another believer? Why do you look down on another believer? Remember, we will all stand before the judgment seat of God. For the Scriptures say, 'As surely as I live,' says the LORD, every knee will bend to me, and every tongue will confess and give praise to God.' Yes, each of us will give a personal account to God. Romans 14:10-12 (NLT)

Dear Father, you know all about us and why we do the things we do. You know my brother and I believe he is Home with you where he could find the healing he never received here. Thank you that we can entirely entrust to you our loved ones, no matter how sadly or badly they have sinned. Amen.

March 6

My Sister and Alcoholism

My sister, Sylvia, was my idol when I was young. She was beautiful and funny and great at telling stories. But by the age of 16 she was already an alcoholic. She was sweet when sober and a terror when drunk. She had four children and all were victims too as she was not capable of raising them. She spent the better part of her life under the spell of alcohol. Her death at a relatively early age (60) was no doubt partially due to her alcoholism.

Even though her life exhibited little of the fruit of the Spirit of God, she had accepted Christ and had said on many occasions that she loved Him and knew that she would go to Heaven.

The tragedy was that her life was largely wasted because of alcoholism. I remember seeing it happening when I was a teenager. I, in a rare display of anger, picked up a glass of beer and doused her with it, saying, "Don't you see what this is doing to you?"

Some people can drink. Some can't. My sister could not.

Wine produces mockers; liquor leads to brawls. Whoever is led astray by drink cannot be wise. Proverbs 20:1 (NLT)

Lord, there are those in our lives who suffer from alcoholism. Help us to know how to help them, but not enable them. Amen.

March 7

In Times Like These

In the spring of the year 2000 there was a devastating fire in Los Alamos, New Mexico. My friends, Birgitta and Zhenya Kovalenko had to evacuate for a week, but when they returned they were greatly relieved to discover that their home had not been destroyed. However, friends from their church were not so fortunate. Once evacuees were allowed back into the town, their church arranged a special breakfast.

During public prayer time one of those whose house had burned down, expressed gratitude to God, first for his wife and then for having his attic and garage cleaned out. He said he felt his soul and attitude had been cleaned up too! Others recounted how fortunate they were for they had lost only material things. Then there was another couple that had been several miles away (in Santa Fe) when they heard the evacuation order over the emergency radio station. They interrupted their business and sped back to Los Alamos, only to discover that their street was already blocked off with a police barricade, but the husband was determined to return to rescue their animals, so the police finally let him through, giving him five minutes. He found their two dogs and one cat (which usually hid under the house) waiting quietly by their front yard fence. He put them in the car and sped off, just as fire was breaking out in their back yard, a fire that later burned their house to the ground, but they were grateful because their pets were saved.

I was deeply moved to hear of the lovely spirit these people who lost "everything" were able to radiate. What a beautiful expression of God's grace in and through them.

What is more, I consider everything a loss compared to the surpassing greatness of knowing Christ Jesus my Lord, for

whose sake I have lost all things. I consider them rubbish, that I may gain Christ and be found in him, not having a righteousness of my own that comes from the law, but that which is through faith in Christ—the righteousness that comes from God and is by faith. I want to know Christ and the power of his resurrection and the fellowship of sharing in his sufferings, becoming like him in his death, and so, somehow, to attain to the resurrection from the dead.
Philippians 3:8, 9 (NIV)

Lord God, thank you for the courage of those who continue on with gracious spirits, even when they have lost everything of material value, and may they find comfort in You, the treasure of their hearts. Amen.

March 8

Surprising Joy

Just thinking of my first son, Michael, makes me smile. He is a warm and gregarious person, full of fun and energy. What a treat to have such a person as my very own son. Meeting Michael is like meeting a human party! Even though he's capable of hard work, he also really knows how to play. He's a magician and can do magic tricks for the children in us all — sleight of hand with cards and coins and so clever that you just can't catch him at it! He loves to go to movies. He loves to laugh. He loves fun.

Now, I'm ashamed to say that I don't think of Jesus this way. I can't imagine Jesus having fun, laughing at jokes and playing games. But I know I'm wrong. Jesus loved a good meal at a friend's house, and weddings were a great celebration. After all, His first recorded miracle was to make sure the wine supply didn't dry up at a wedding reception. Now, don't you think he must have been having fun?

Once when Don and I were going through a difficult time, when rumors and lies were being spoken about us, the Lord woke me with this wonderful inner picture of himself: He was seated on a hillside teaching, his face was alight with a joyful radiance. He was waving his arms about with energy and enthusiasm and saying to the crowd that sat around Him [and it was as though I was truly there, an invisible onlooker] the most remarkable, unexpected things. How could He be so full of such authentic cheer when predicting for some of us what He knew would come — evil spoken against us? I want more of that kind of overcoming joy. I take Him and my life and my religion far too seriously sometimes, just so I'll be "appropriate." I think I'd rather just go for the joy!

> *Blessed are you when they revile and persecute you, and say*
> *all kinds of evil against you falsely for My sake. Rejoice and*
> *be exceedingly glad, for great is your reward in heaven...*
> Matthew 5:11, 12 (NKJV)

Dear Lord, thank you for giving us that wonderful, surprising lesson in the Sermon on the Mount. Let us believe you and give us that supernatural joy that only you can, in spite of all that is going on around us, even persecution. Amen.

March 9

Models of Courage

I think of our son, Daniel, as brave, wise and smart. I admire him as well as love him. I experience him as a quiet and private person. He has great integrity and good boundaries. He has a perpetual twinkle in his eye that seems to be saying *I know something you don't*. What has Dan taught me? When Daniel had a severe inner struggle in his twenties, I watched him face it head on. I was amazed at his courage. When I had run into similar kinds of problems earlier, I had run from them. But not Daniel. He became my hero and my guide, not just my son. He is way ahead of me in many ways. That's about the brave part. The "wise" has to do with his selection of a marvelous woman as a wife, Becki, whom I love dearly and the way that he has nurtured and protected and cherished their talented, beautiful daughter, Kaylee. The "smart" has to do with his skill as a computer programmer.

However, my most favorite example of heroism is in Jesus. When I see Him in my mind's eye, now that I am in my seventies, I see a young man, less than half my age, but full of courage, heading toward Jerusalem his entire life. I can take courage in His courage. I can overcome, not because I imitate Him, but because He has made His own courage available to me.

Is there any where in your life that you are you lacking courage? If so, remember that it is in *our* weakness that we experience *His* strength. As we reach out and ask the Great Overcomer for help, it will be there for us!

And He said to me, 'My grace is sufficient for you, for my strength is made perfect in weakness.' Therefore most gladly I will rather boast in my infirmities, that the power of Christ may rest upon me. 2 Corinthians 12:9 (NKJV)

Lord, please be my strength in weakness, and give me courage when I am in fear. Amen.

March 10

Glories in the Morning Sky

It was a dark morning in the desert. The earth all around us was overshadowed with deep, gray clouds. As I glanced up I saw where the sun must be beyond them — a bright, translucent spot of brilliance, but wait! No, there the sun was, just peaking through to the right! I looked back to the *other* "sun"; it was still there, in a gentler kind of glory, easier on the eye, and yet spreading its rays in its own mysterious way. Some call this a "sun dog." Others a "perihelion" which is Greek for "beside the sun."

I'll never know what caused that phenomenon, but it was so breathtakingly beautiful that it was just what I needed at that moment — a reminder of the Lord of Creation, who surprises us on dark days with the light of His presence. But — and this is important — we need to realize such surprises can come in different places than we would at first have looked. And it is there, in that unexpected place that He amazes us, comforts us, and cheers us with His glory. His power has been there all along, just awaiting a minuscule change of our focus to catch that moment of His reaching out toward us. When we do, we can embrace His love and light with open hearts.

That was the true Light which gives light to every man who comes into the world. John 1:9 (NKJV)

Lord Jesus, we know that you are *the* Light and the source of our light. Help us not to be afraid to welcome that light into our inner most beings, even the darkest of places. And then, may we be transformed by your brilliance into the person you want us to be — lights in the world. Amen.

March 11

The Grandest Place of All

The Grand Canyon in Arizona is the longest, deepest canyon on earth. It's been said that the sight of it causes people to gasp for breath and tears to run down faces, and that it is so far beyond what one can imagine, that it can never be expected. No picture, no movie, no descriptive words can prepare one for its breath-taking magnificence.

I believe that's a little bit of how it will be when we enter eternity's Heaven. There is nothing, not in the Bible, not in any of the great art works of the world, not in any vision, not in any dream, that can possibly prepare us for the wonder of it. It is far above and beyond human comprehension. Jesus said He would prepare a place for us! God is a God of preparation. He prepared a way for us to come to Him before the world was brought into being. He prepared the world for His coming, and in so doing He helped us to prepare a place for Him in our hearts. Now He is preparing the world for His next coming. And He is continuing on in the process of making all ready, by preparing a place for us in Paradise.

We know through faith that this indescribable place awaits us, one that exists in another dimension beyond time and place as we know it, created just for us, created by the same God who created the Grand Canyon, the planets, the galaxies, and the universe. Not only that, but He knows us, each one, intimately and therefore, He knows just what will make us serenely and supremely filled with joy, a place reserved for us.

I go to prepare a place for you...And where I go you know, and the way you know. John 14:2-4 (NKJV)

Lord Jesus, we, as we exist in time, cannot comprehend all that you have prepared and accomplished in Eternity. You exist in dimensions that we cannot know, but by faith, we thank you for what you have done, and are doing, and what you will do. Amen.

March 12

Grandma and the Doves

Grandma, on my mother's side, "Jessie" Nelson Edwards, lived with us from the time I was four until I left home to be married at the age of 21. I loved her dearly, and she influenced my life more than almost anyone. She took me to a beautiful park in Pasadena one day when I was about seven. We walked through a flower garden and she pointed out the beauty of each special blossom, the variety of colors, the slightly unique scent of each one. As we strolled together, we could hear doves calling out from somewhere in the branches of the Oak trees on the edge of the park. She told me that doves have messages that you can make out if you listen carefully. One is, "What *hour* is it?" and the other, "It's a *boy!*" or "it's a *girl.*" (It's been years since I've heard just this call from doves, but in the 40s it was most common.) I was at that age where I knew it couldn't really be true that doves talk, but I believed just a little for the joy of it.

There were not many times like this with grandma, but they were precious and unforgettable, lasting me for a lifetime, and this one walk alone, started me on a lifetime love affair with doves.

The time of singing has come, And the voice of the turtle dove is heard in our land. Song of Solomon 2:12b (NKJV)

Dear Father, thank you for the special gift of grandmothers and the special gift of the doves, and their unique place in our world. Help me to have eyes to see the wonder of such precious moments like simple walks in a park that you so freely give to all. Amen.

March 13

Hands

My childhood friend was watching me play the piano. He then said, "Ick. Your hands look like spiders!" There was a bit of truth in that I thought, as I looked down at my long fingers, but up until that cruel remark, I had thought my hands were my best feature!

I'm glad for these hands, these fingers. They have served me well. Though I've enjoyed the hobby of playing the piano, they've been my livelihood, as I was a secretary and typist for more than 40 years. Yes, they have served me well, and continue to do so even as I type this out at this moment, and see the words appearing before me on the computer screen.

I remember other hands: My mother's, freckled with age spots of which she was so ashamed that she often wore gloves. I can see my father's fingers at an old age, red and swollen with rheumatoid arthritis, ironically screaming pain about which he never, ever spoke. I can see Grandma's hands, her wrinkled fingers going through her little pine box of lace handkerchiefs.

I can see Jesus' hands too, in different poses: Working with wood, in prayer, open and giving, throwing the tables over in the temple, pointing the way, reaching out and touching someone who needs healing. And yet the most important view of His hands is the one in which I see that they are scarred where they have been pierced through with nails, wounded for my (our) iniquities. That was the cost of my salvation — nail-scarred hands that now hold mine as I walk on in this life of faith.

See, I have inscribed you on the palms of My hands... Isaiah 49:16 (NKJV)

Lord God, you hold out your hands to help and heal and deliver. Help me to remember that these are the hands that you allowed to be scarred for my sake. Amen.

March 14

The Heavy-handed God — Part 1

I used to be a student of drama. One of the worst things an actor can run across is what is known as a "heavy-handed" director! This is a director who gives you no freedom to make choices, one who interprets the character for you and does "line readings" [i.e., tells you how a line should be read]. However, it is strange to me that sometimes God becomes the one who is heavy-handed. It has happened to me, but only on a few occasions, throughout my Christian walk.

The first was shortly after I had become a Christian. I wanted to become a cosmetologist. Even though a new Christian, I knew God was telling me "no" when I felt a pressure on me, almost physical, pushing me down! I wanted God's will but I also wanted to do what I wanted to do, and so I tried to ignore it (this heavy hand) but it would not go away. I had to drop out of class in order to get some peace! I'll bet that was the first time the school counselor ever heard that excuse: "God wants me to stop taking this course." Once I did obey, however, the pressure was released immediately. I was free!

Whoever falls on that stone will be broken... Luke 20:18 (NKJV)

Lord, thank you that you are the stone on which we fall and are broken, as we are humbled before you in obedience. Amen.

March 15

The Heavy-handed God — Part 2

It happened again. In 1959, Don had asked me to marry him. I said "yes." We got the ring and set the date. Then, it returned — that old heavy-handed business. It is an awful feeling and one that you cannot get rid of, or ignore. I didn't want to tell Don, but finally realized that I had to. I shared this strange phenomenon with him and told him I could not marry him, at least not yet. So, the date was scratched off the calendar, and back went the ring to the jeweler. Almost a year later Don asked me again. Willing to wait. No pressure. This time the answer was "yes." The heavy-handedness didn't return, and we were married the following April.

Even now I have no idea why God wanted us to wait, but we obeyed. Don had no experience whatsoever that even came close to my experience with God's "heavy hand." But he respected me. He believed me.

Everyone has different, unique experiences. All are to be respected. Because I respect these differences I've been privy to some amazing stories about ways that God has spoken to His people.

For you are my lamp, O Lord; The Lord shall enlighten my darkness. 2 Samuel 22:29 (NKJV)

Lord, help me to recognize your voice in whatever ways you choose speak to me or lead me. Amen.

March 16

The Heavy-handed God — Part 3

And years later, it happened once more. One day when I planned to go fix dinner and take care of the child of a young mother who was pregnant and ill, I felt it again — that heavy hand! *Oh, no! Now, Lord, what could possibly be wrong with my doing this good deed?* So — I went. It was a nightmare experience, but only because the inner child-self in me could not cope with the child in that house. He was more than an imp. The experience so wounded that part of me that it took me several weeks to recover! The Lord tried to spare me pain and I rejected His warning.

Now if perchance, you ever feel a heaviness upon your spirit, it might be God giving you a warning. I can't help giving a little advice here: Take heed!

For day and night your hand was heavy upon me. Psalm 32:4 (NKJV)

Lord, help me not to run from your warning messages. And thank you, God, for that dreadful but caring heavy hand of warning you sometimes place on your followers. Keep it there when we need it and don't take it from us until we do your will! Amen.

March 17

St. Patrick's Day

This day is about more than just wearing the green. St. Patrick lived in the fifth century. It is said that he was taken captive and brought to Ireland as a boy of 16 where he worked as a slave, herding sheep for six years. He was a Christian in a pagan land. During that time, he went through a dramatic change of heart. He experienced an inner transformation as his faith grew deeper and stronger, after which he miraculously escaped from slavery and from Ireland. Later in his life, however, he obeyed the call of God to return to that country, and he is credited with bringing the gospel to Ireland in the year 431 A.D.

There are missionaries around the world today who have followed the call of God and gone to a foreign country where they tell of the love of Jesus Christ. These are those who sacrifice much, leaving their homelands and families and going to distant, foreign places where they must adapt to new cultures, climates and environments. I hope your church is actively supporting and praying for missionaries who have followed this God-inspired vision. I believe that to do so, to have an arm of your own congregation, reaching out somewhere else in the world, whether it is from the United States to Burkina Faso, or Ghana to the United States, is absolutely vital for your church's spiritual survival.

> *And a vision appeared to Paul in the night. A man of Macedonia stood and pleaded with him, saying, 'Come over into Macedonia and help us.'* Acts 16:9 (NKJV)

Lord, place on my heart at least one missionary that I may pray for daily. Amen.

March 18

My Buddy

Some years ago I took part in a mentor school program called Adult Buddy Who Cares (ABC) at an elementary school near Phoenix. The buddies were to spend an hour each week with a student. At first I was afraid and shy to do this. I asked for a boy because I had sons and thought maybe that would make it easier for me. I was worried about our first meeting with Marc. However, my husband, a former elementary school teacher, suggested that I begin by asking him to draw a picture of his family. This got us off to a great start.

Soon I learned that the best thing to do during this time was to let Marc do what he wanted — I was just there for him. Sometimes that would involve using flash cards to work on his reading or math, but mostly it meant playing games. Our favorite during the two years I spent with Marc was "Ants in the Pants." The object is to flip the colorful, plastic "ants" into a pair of rigid plastic pants. At first I felt silly playing games, but soon I found that I was having a great time myself. If I missed a week, Marc would chide me.

Over the time we were together we became closer and more relaxed. Finally, I found that he would, without even knowing it, kind of lean up against me on occasion. I just loved it! Then my time with

Marc was over; the buddy program is not for those beyond the second grade.

When the school put on a great celebration for all the buddies and children at the end of the year, Marc brought me a card. It said, "Dear Buddy, I had a good time with you. I like you. Love, Marc." I told him I would save it forever. And I will.

I tell this story because it just may be that God wants you to become a mentor to a child or a young person. There's such a great need. Please pray about it.

And Jesus called a little child to Him, set him in the midst of them... Matthew 18:3 (NKJV)

Father, show me if you want me to help a child in some way. Amen.

March 19

A Little Hard of Hearing?

Stopping in Santa Fe, New Mexico, on our way to visit friends in Los Alamos, we had a scrumptious meal in a lovely Mexican restaurant overlooking the town square. They served, along with the cheese enchiladas, some delicious, but spicy re-fried beans. After leaving there, we passed a guided tour group of people looking through the oldest adobe building in Santa Fe. I heard what the docent was saying and repeated it to my husband, "The beams are carbon-dated," I said. What he heard was something else and maybe partially due to the state of his digestion, for his reply was, "Yes, those beans were carbonated."

The older I am the more I mishear what is happening around me. For instance, one day I thought Don must be having a hard time with clearing his throat until I discovered it was the coffee maker just beginning to percolate!

But, you know, I have faith that my "inner ears" are getting better at hearing. All my adult life I've wanted to truly hear what Jesus is saying to me. Sometimes I've heard a soft voice speaking words inside my head; but mostly it's a gentle sense in my heart that I just know what He is saying to me — a word of love, of encouragement, of correction, or sense of direction. I believe God speaks, in one way or another, to everyone. He may speak to us through a sermon, when we read Scripture, or through something beautiful in His creation. Listening carefully and searchingly takes time and practice. If you and I make a point to add this discipline to our lives, it will change us forever.

> *For God may speak in one way, or another....* Job 33:14 (NKJV)

Lord, I want to have inner ears that know how to hear you. Help me to keep a date with you every day and to, for at least a few moments, just listen. Amen.

March 20

Ideals, Lost and Found

When I first went into psycho-therapy many years ago, I told my counselor about a man I had been in love with when I was in my teens, my piano teacher. My therapist assured me, so to speak, that that was not really love — that instead I had been idealizing him. Whatever that bit of so-called wisdom was supposed to create in me, what it managed to do was make me feel that I did not know how to love, even my own husband. I began to feel like some kind of mutant — something deeply wrong with me, this woman who did not know how to love. It took me a long time to discover what genuine love is, but when I did, I was able to realize that I was indeed capable of it after all.

Many years later, I went back into therapy with another counselor and, for some reason, I told him about the music teacher I had loved, never having been fully convinced that I had not loved him. (By the way, I've discovered that sometimes this need to return to past experiences occurs so that we can learn what we missed; we keep going back to something because we know somewhere deep inside that we have not yet found out the truth.) My new therapist was gifted with keen discernment and somehow saw in his mind's eye the man himself! It was as though God was showing him my teacher's character and he began to praise him. He could see how I could have loved him. He was noble. He was strong. He was a good man! So you see, sometimes, we can reclaim what we've given up. In this case this experience of going back restored in me the memory of a love that had, after all, been real, even if from the heart of a very young girl!

> *And they shall rebuild the old ruins, They shall raise up the former desolations, and they shall repair the ruined cities...*
> Isaiah 61:4 (NKJV)

Dear Father, thank you for your willingness to give back to me the inner things that I have lost on the way to growing up, and restore the things in me that have been torn down. Amen.

March 21

The Invisible

I laughed when I saw that a 15-year old girl who wrote Ann Landers had signed her name "No Name or City or State or Country." Now that's a real need for anonymity. But I understand. There is something within me that wants to be invisible, but only some times. On those days I try to find something gray to wear. Most of the time I want to be seen; I'll even wear cranberry red. In fact, there is something in me that fears invisibility. There is a little "Patty" in me who wants to be heard and is afraid that she will not be. When I read Lynn Redgrave's book "This is Living," I felt I understood deeply how she felt shortly after her father's death when she found his diaries. In them was recorded all in his life that truly mattered to him. She looked up the date of her birth, March 8, 1943, and found a long, detailed entry, but no mention of her own birth, not one word. As she put it, "No Lynn."

My own eyes filled with tears as I read. But there is hope for us who fear we don't "count." We can combat that fear with the knowledge that He, the one with all knowledge, knows all there is to know about us. He keeps His eye on us. He cares. He loves. We are written in his "diary." What comfort, what joy to have such a wonderful Father God!

And in Your book they all were written, The days fashioned for me when as yet there were none of them. Psalm 139:16 (NKJV)

Lord, on the days I feel invisible, help me to remember that I am never invisible to You. Thank you for caring for us "little" persons, each of us, even me. Amen.

March 22

God's Will Vs Mine

When my husband and I were in Taiwan for a year in 1963, we traveled everywhere by public transportation. One time, after getting lost and going around and around in circles on the same crowded bus, I was fed up. I finally found a different bus, the right one. Once safely home, I said, "OK, Lord, we really need a car. Please make it possible." Immediately I was filled with a deep sense of incredible joy. I knew without a doubt that we would get a car. The Lord had heard my prayer and was going to answer according to my wishes.

The car, however, never materialized. Yes, the Lord had heard our prayer and He did answer, and the answer was "no" to this particular prayer, but it was "yes" to other prayers. We continued to use the public transportation system and, therefore, Don had many opportunities to tell others about the love of Christ during his travels. He even led two people to the Lord on a train trip from Taipei to Taichung.

Now, whenever I pray and get that wonderful feeling of joy welling up within me, I no longer believe it's telling me that I'm necessarily going to get *my* way. What it means is that God is going to have *His* way — God's will done on Earth as it is in Heaven, whether it's exactly what I think I want or not!

Your will be done on earth as it is in Heaven. Matthew 6:10 (NKJV)

Father, I don't always know what to pray, and when I do pray, I, of course, want my way. So Lord, may your will be done in my life and may I be willing to do my part to get it done. Amen.

March 23

A Belated Answer

In 1963 I prayed for a healing for my little niece, Laura. So lovely she was, with huge blue green eyes and soft blond hair and yet she had one foot significantly larger than the other. I believed then that God would heal her. But He did not, and somewhere inside of me I resented that "no" answer for years. Then in 1997 Laura, then a woman in her thirties, found a doctor who X-rayed her foot and found that the difference in size had to do with additional muscle tissue, not from skeletal size! Underneath this tissue, both feet were almost exactly the same. In October of 1997 she had surgery and it was successful. Laura is now able to wear the same size shoe for both feet, is able to wear sandals for the first time in her life, and I know that God's answer was not "no" after all, but "wait." He heard that prayer and He determined how and when it would be answered.

For a thousand years in your sight are like yesterday when it is past and like a watch in the night. Psalm 90:4 (NKJV)

Lord God, forgive me for my anger at you over unanswered prayer. I thank you for your perfect timing for all things and ask that you give me patience to endure the waiting periods that you have ordained. Amen.

March 24

Witchcraft in the Church

In November of 1997 the Associated Press reported that a blind physicist who wanted to advance a Braille system for computers had his grant request rejected by the Education Department because his typewritten application wasn't double-spaced! This is an example of extreme legalism in society.

But as bad as that may seem, when in the Church, legalism is even worse. Paul likens it to witchcraft. *"O foolish Galatians! Who,"* he asks, *"has bewitched you?"* (Gal. 3:1) This kind of witchcraft almost took over one of the churches where my husband was a pastor. We felt the presence of a controlling spirit. The rigidity of leadership in requiring obedience to all rules *they* had set up became overwhelming. Nothing that my husband could do was right. It was as though trying harder only made it worse for a group of people who were focused on finding error in his ways. And they did, of course.

Whenever we look for error in humans, we will find it. It's not possible to win in a war with legalists. However, in the end, grace won and as the legalists left, those in search of grace came and the church grew. But, I offer a word of warning: Beware! Such people come in all kinds of costumes. They always look pious, but they want control and will plant seeds of discontent and undermine spiritual freedom. Pray that your Church will remain free of these enemies of the message of God's liberty and grace.

Now the Lord is the Spirit; and where the Spirit of the Lord is, there is liberty. 2 Corinthians 3:17 (NKJV)

Heavenly Father, may the Spirit of grace rule in my place of worship so that the Spirit of the Lord will bring liberty to all. Amen.

March 25

The Letter

My grandmother (Jessie) once told me a humorous story about one of her sisters who tried the patience of all those around her whenever she received a letter. She would hold it up to the light and peer through it. She would turn it over and over in her hands and examine it. She would look at the handwriting and inspect the quality of the stationary. She would check out the postmark. All the while she would be mumbling repeatedly, "I wonder who sent this." Finally those watching would blurt out, "Well, for heaven's sake, Ola, just open it!"

Maybe Ola was a bit eccentric, but I think I understand her. I'll bet she loved suspense and she savored every moment of the ritual leading up to the actual opening of the letter. She must have possessed the virtue of patience, and she certainly could not have been accused of having a problem with impulse control, but rather knew all about delayed gratification before such terms were in use. Maybe she daydreamed — *Could it be from a secret admirer? A would-be suitor? An acceptance of a manuscript? A check from an anonymous benefactor?* What patience she had. What joy in anticipation! When she finally opened it, I wonder if the discovery of the contents ever lived up to her expectations!

When we open the Bible in the morning as part of our daily spiritual discipline, do we look forward to that with anticipation? What will God's love letter say to me today? If we do have such a relationship with Him, we will, by faith, believe that He will speak to us that special personal word that will give us manna (bread) for the day and enlighten our spirits.

> *...man shall not live by bread alone; but man lives by every word that proceeds from the mouth of the LORD.* Deuteronomy 8:3 (NKJV)

Lord God, I long to know that you care about me so much that, if I take the time to listen, you will speak a personal word to me today. Help me to hear you. Amen.

March 26

Lost Things

How many things have you lost, or were destroyed or stolen in your life? What kind of things were they? How did you respond? I was fortunate to hear Gladys Alyward, missionary to China, (the one about whom the movie *The Inn of the Sixth Happiness* was made), speak shortly after I became a Christian. She joined our Baptist mission team and came to speak to the men on skid row at the Los Angeles Mission in the late 1950s. She told of having one of her mission homes in China burn down. When it happened, she said that she began to cry but suddenly she heard the Lord speak to her saying, "Don't ever cry over things, only over people."

That word has stayed with me through the years. I try to make sure my heart is deeply set in heaven, where my true treasure is, though sometimes it is difficult. Where are your true treasures? Where are mine? On Earth or in Heaven?

Don't store up treasures here on earth, where they can be eaten by moths and get rusty, and where thieves break in and steal. Store your treasures in heaven, where they will never become moth-eaten or rusty and where they will be safe from thieves. Wherever your treasure is, there your heart and thoughts will also be. Matthew 6:19-21 (NLT)

Heavenly Father, Jesus taught us to be careful about what we deem to be most precious in our lives. Sometimes I think I am not attached, until I lose something, and then I find I was more attached than I ever imagined. Thank you for teaching me through such losses, where my true treasure should be. Amen.

March 27

Lost Things of the World

In November 1997 it was reported by the Associated Press that the Naval Research Laboratory records that chronicle some of the most significant technical achievements in the 20th century were inadvertently destroyed by the National Archives. This meant that the historical record of our nation's scientific and technological heritage had suffered a serious and irreparable loss. Rear Adm. Paul G. Gaffney II, Chief of Naval Research, wrote National Archivist John Carlin, protesting the destruction of the records. Records such as those about American pioneers in high-frequency radio, work of the inventors of radar, and war records of the applied technology in campaigns against Nazi Germany and Japan were all lost.

There have been other even greater losses in history. For instance, the library at Antioch where thousands of books were destroyed. And another, Herod's temple in Jerusalem, where all Jewish records of heritage were destroyed.

What do you cherish most? What do you most hope will never be destroyed among your personal effects? Most people will answer: Pictures, treasured mementos and correspondence, the family Bible, and the like. I believe that the essence of these things, though lost in the physical world, is not lost to God. I know that He remembers it all and those things of spiritual value will be restored if it is within His great plan. So entrust it all to him — that anniversary ring that was lost, that record of personal histories, even those cherished memories destroyed by Alzheimer's disease. All are in His care.

He gathers the waters of the sea together as a heap; He lays up the deep in storehouses. Psalm 33:7 (NKJV)

Lord, I trust you to keep for me all the things of the heart that I have lost. Every memory that was a treasure, I believe you will restore to me, either now or in eternity, and the rest I give to you as a sacrifice, for it is you that I love more than all other treasures. Amen.

March 28

Precious Things Lost, Then Found

I was in the shower when I glanced down and saw that my ring was missing its sapphire stone. I was tempted to cry, but then I let go of it in my mind, realizing it was only a thing. However, as soon as I made the decision to let it go, I saw in my mind's eye exactly where it was — under my bed two feet from the foot of the bed and ten inches under it. I never doubted for a moment that it was there and so, even without looking, I just reached under the bed and grasped it. I had received back what I had lost.

Isn't it wonderful that God cares for even these little things that have sentimental value to us? He understands about looking for lost things. It's been rare that I've found something this way — by God showing me something, but it has happened three times in my life.

Do you remember the parable of the woman who lost a coin? She refused to give up. She looked and looked until she found it, which would not have been easy on the dirt floors of those days. But this looking for, without ceasing, is what we are to do when it comes to the Kingdom of Heaven. We are to look and look until we find it and then our hearts will rejoice along with the angels of Heaven!

Or what woman, having ten silver coins, if she loses one coin, does not light a lamp, sweep the house and, seek diligently until she finds it? Luke 15:8 (NKJV)

Lord, since I found you, I have felt I found the Kingdom of Heaven, but I want to know what it means to search daily for that kingdom. I want to see your presence wherever I look. Teach my spirit to not only look, but also how to find. Amen.

March 29

The City of Love and Lights

How I had dreamed about Paris, France! It would be wonderful, magical, a city filled with romance, music, strolling lovers, the art of the masters. But when we arrived in Paris in the summer of 1981, it was the eve of Bastille Day and we couldn't find anywhere to exchange money. I had to wait in an underground railroad station, hungry with my blood sugar dropping lower by the minute, while Don searched for a place to exchange dollars for francs. I couldn't have been more disappointed or miserable. I watched disgusted, as teen age boys enjoyed a spitting contest, trying to see who could spit the highest and the farthest on the wall across from me.

Don finally returned with the proper currency and as we walked along a Paris street, I just sat down on a tree stump and cried, "I want to go home. I hate Paris." I didn't really mean it, of course, and the days that followed changed my first despairing perception as we spent time seeing the wonders I had dreamed about. But, you know, somehow our day dreams never include sore feet, jet lag, rude beggars and getting lost, do they!?

Oh, but there is a place I dream about, a place I'll go some day and there will not be any disappointment, because it will be far more beautiful than any place I can possibly imagine. Isn't it wonderful to know that, when the time comes, we'll get to go there and it won't just be for a vacation — we'll go to stay — forever in the true and eternal City of Love and Lights?

He replied, "Truly I tell you, today you will be with me in Paradise." Luke 23:43 (NRSV)

Dear Lord, on the bad days in Earth's time, help me to remember the future I'll enjoy in the Paradise of Eternity. Amen.

March 30

To Trust More

There are those in my life who have profoundly influenced my faith by their words. One such person was Henrietta Mears who said when asked at a conference I attended, "Ms. Mears, what would you do differently if you had your life to live over?" Her answer was simple, but all encompassing. She said, "I would trust God more." I decided that I would do that in my life — just starting out as I was on my Christian journey.

And so, that little sentence set me on my way. Had she not said it, I would not have believed God as much as I have through my Christian journey, and yet, I can say the same thing when asked, "What would you do differently?" I would have to answer, "Trust God more." I have so often failed to trust enough. Yet God is gracious and has given me repeated opportunities to trust again in similar situations, until I "get it right." There is always room for more trust on our part. God is worthy of absolute trust with no trace of wavering.

> *Blessed is the man who trusts in the Lord, and whose hope is the Lord, For he shall be like a tree planted by the water...*
> Jeremiah 17:7, 8 (NKJV)

Lord, I want to learn how to trust in you more. Show me where I need to let go. Show me when I wrongly take things into my own hands instead of giving them to you. Please give me a new measure of faith today and every day, so that my trust may be in you alone and in no other. Amen.

March 31

More Than One Way to Get Lost

In October 1997, Scott Adams, cartoon strip writer of *Dilbert* set up a hoax with the help of Pierluigi Zappacosta, vice chairman of Logitech

New Ventures Group in San Jose, California. He was to head up a meeting in which he was to crisply define the company's goals. Instead, using doublespeak he proposed a totally impossible mission statement that was both long and incomprehensible. All the while the chairman is nodding in agreement, as though he fully understood, followed by most executives in the meeting nodding right along with him!

Now, isn't this some kind of statement about leaders and followers? What were they thinking? Maybe "This guy isn't making any sense, but I'd better pretend to go along with it."

Well, as far as hoaxes go, it is Satan who, with the help of countless so-called "leaders" is trying to win over to his way of thinking all those who don't know for sure what or whom to follow. He would like for us to believe that all roads lead to Heaven. When you are tempted to believe this, think about it! In all the religions of the world, the only God who comes down from Heaven is Jesus Christ. The only one who died for the sins of the world is Jesus. The only one who is both servant and King is Jesus Christ. And He comes to find us; we don't have to go find Him. What a unique and wonderful Savior!

> *...I am the way, the truth and the life. No one comes to the Father except through me.* John 14:6 (NKJV)

Lord, how can we thank you for not only leading the way, but also *being* the way. Let us lose ourselves in this Way that you have provided, because then we will be finding ourselves in you. Amen.

APRIL

April 1

Fools

Well, here it is April Fool's Day — again! Rarely have I ever been able to fool anyone on this day. Even when I try, I start laughing and give it away. Once only I almost succeeded. I went outside to go to work and rushed back in, telling my husband in an alarmed voice, "Honey, my car's gone! It's been stolen." He jumped up and started to run outside, but then I started giggling and he knew!

My dear friend, Birgitta Kovalenko's son, David, played a great joke on her one year. He lives in Sweden and she lives in the States, but she was planning a visit him and his family. He wrote her an E-mail that said: "Dear Mother, Annette [his wife] and I have a great opportunity to travel to do a film in Kenya [He owns a production company]. We'll be leaving just as you arrive and we will only be gone for two weeks. We're so glad you're coming because you can take care of the girls [their three young daughters] while you're here."

Birgitta was shocked. What! She wouldn't even get to spend time with her son and his wife, one of the main reasons she was going, and now she was expected to spend most of her time in Sweden baby-sitting! She was in a quandary about how to answer. It was hard to turn them down, but the truth was, she didn't want to do it. After all, she had also planned to spend time there with her daughter and her children! How relieved she was when her husband, Eugene, gave her a second E-mail that David had sent to him. It said, "April Fool! Give this to mother when she has suffered enough!" She burst out laughing! Her son knew how to pull off the best of April Fool's Day jokes.

The fool has said in his heart, 'There is no God.' Psalm 14:1 (NKJV)

Lord, if I'm one of those people who gets fooled a lot on this April day, help me to take heart. According to you, I am not a fool because I truly believe in you. Amen.

April 2

Hidden Messages of Love

Before the foundation of the world, God knew He would bring us into existence. He knew, as He formed the universe and our little earth and all of its wonders that someday, you or I would not only look at, but truly see, something special in the natural world that He created by His own Word. So yesterday when my friend, Ruth, and I walked to the end of the pier at Seal Beach and looked down into the dark green water, He also knew that we would be totally delighted to see a seal popping its head up directly beneath us. He knew that she and I, both loving the sea and all its teeming life, would believe in our hearts that the seal came to say "hello" to us as a messenger from Him. Our knowing these things, I believe, truly touches the heart of our Lord, who in just such gentle ways reaches out to us with messengers from His wondrous world every single day, if we will only open our inner eyes to discover them.

> *But now ask the beasts, and they will teach you; And the birds of the air, and they will tell you; Or speak to the earth, and it will teach you; and the fish of the sea will explain to you.* Job 12:7, 8 (NKJV)

Thank you, Lord for special touches that you give to us every day in your wonderful world, and forgive us for the many times we've been too distracted to notice. Help us see by your appointed messengers, such as that exuberant seal that day, the little gifts you reach out and offer to us along today's path. Amen.

April 3

Pretty Is...

I have in my memory some interesting advice that Mom gave me other than the usual "Haste-makes-waste" and "A-stitch-in-time..." and "Rise to the occasion," kinds of tips. But among her out-of-the-ordinary bits of advice were: "Never buy a red coat. People will say 'Oh, there comes Patty in her red coat.'" Here's another: "Never tell a dirty joke. You will be remembered for it." But the one I heard the most often was "Pretty is as pretty does." This one, though well known, made the deepest impression on me. It gave me a goal to strive for and that, of course, was to behave in an attractive way and not be "shallow." (Mom talked a lot about how important it was not to be shallow.)

I have to ask myself once in a while if I am too concerned with my appearance. Is jewelry more important than it should be to me? Am I "label" conscious? Does a "bad hair day" make my whole day bad? Do I judge myself by my appearance or do I judge others by theirs? Am I, in other words, "shallow"? I believe that, in varying degrees, we all are, but we can work on focusing on our inner life. That is what God is interested in — our character and our heart.

> *Don't be concerned about the outward beauty that depends on fancy hairstyles, expensive jewelry, or beautiful clothes. You should be known for the beauty that comes from within, the unfading beauty of a gentle and quiet spirit, which is so precious to God.* 1 Peter 3:3, 4 (NLT)

Lord, help me not to be overly concerned about my outward appearance. Instead, help me to focus on transforming my inner life. Amen.

April 4

The Tomato, the Dude and Appearances

I was in a hurry, of course. I needed only the ingredients for a salad that I was to take to a dinner party that night. I had carefully selected one huge, hothouse tomato. I had weighed it. The cost would be $1.17! The checker was new and nervous. And slow. As the tomato was weighed, I watched the price come up on the display units in front of me, "23 cents" it glowed. I glanced at the "dude" in line behind me. His boots, jeans, shades and cowboy hat gave me a pretty good idea about his response to what I was about to do. Racing through my mind was my time limit, and the money, not much for either party (the market or me) in this picture! But, I couldn't do it. I could not steal the pennies, no matter how little the number. I told the cashier, "I'm sorry, but that tomato — it's a green house tomato." She was surprised and sweet and pleased at my honesty, and — again — slow. I was cringing as I thought about the man behind me and avoided looking at him. *Sometimes a sensitive conscience surely causes more trouble than it's worth, Lord — for everyone!*

Then the man behind me spoke, "Well, an honest person. That's something we don't see too often these days," he said as he gleamed a bright smile at me. After the checker found out the correct price, she punched it in. By that time, even I was smiling when he spoke once again, "Yep, when the Holy Spirit speaks to ya', you just have to do what He says." The young man who was bagging my groceries was also smiling as he witnessed this little scenario.

As I left, I realized I learned more than just a lesson about honesty. I had learned something about not judging by appearances. If we can learn that, we will be more like our Lord, who looks not on the outward appearance, but on the heart.

Do not judge according to appearance, but judge with righteous judgment. John 7:24 (NKJV)

Give me, Lord, spiritual eyes to see beyond what my physical eyes behold. Amen.

April 5

Old Songs and the Healing of Memories

There is almost nothing that brings back memories for me more abruptly than hearing an old song. I was sitting at the computer and about to begin a writer's market survey report when Mike, my son, came in and turned on the radio and the song, "I'll Walk Alone" came on. And — snap! — just like that, the emotions of that era came back to me. It would have been sometime in 1944. That song had been on the Nov. 4, 1944 broadcast of "Your Hit Parade."

Well, what was I feeling at that age (I would have been nine years old)? It wasn't comfortable for me to do it but I decided to sit still and just let the feelings come as I drifted back in time. I found that I felt: lonely, sad, tearful, bereft, hopeful, gentle, guilty and scared. *What do I do with these old feelings?* I continued to sit quietly and wait as I invited Jesus to show me how He was there for me in 1944. I waited until I experienced His presence in that long-ago moment. It is not that He wasn't there at the time, of course. It was that I didn't know that He was, but when I waited, I was able to receive His presence there. This was a moment of healing for that sad child of nine.

When we ask God to come, He will come in order to be a comforter in that distant moment by showing us how He was always there for us, even then. But He is here with me, with you, right now. He is present even in those times when it seems least likely. He is there because He is God, because He is omnipresent and because He has promised, and He doesn't break His promises.

I am with you always, even to the end of the age. Matthew 28:20 (NKJV)

Dear Lord, thank you for being with me yesterday and today and tomorrow. Thank you for being an omnipresent God and for being our companion, day by day, throughout our lives. Amen.

April 6

On Being Used and Using

God provides us with things to use but he provides us with human beings to love. Have you ever been treated as a thing, something to be used, instead of as a person? The first time I had this experience happened as I was just beginning my secretarial career. I was given a typing test at an employment agency. My typing speed was about 85 words per minute. There was a great display of pleasure by my agent. She looked at the wpm speed and said to her fellow agents, "Hey, look what we have here." The word "what" stuck in my mind. I was not a person to her; I was a moneymaking machine! I was a thing — an 85-wpm typing asset. I hated that feeling.

I recently saw a movie where the husband treated his wife as a business asset because she helped him in his long successful career. When she decided to leave him, he was disappointed because he would lose her business help and support; he showed no heartbreak over the loss of her as a wife or a lover or as a person, only as a thing!

When we feel we are being used, there are times we need to confront the person who is using us, but with nothing less than our own humanity! If, however, we watch our own behavior and find that we are using others rather than honoring them, we need to remember *their* humanity, that they have feelings, a heart, and a soul. We need to look past what they can do *for* us and see through to their spirit beings. We can learn to do this with discipline and the Spirit of the Lord as our teacher.

> *When Simon saw that the Holy Spirit was given when the apostles placed their hands upon people's heads, he offered money to buy this power. 'Let me have this power, too,' he exclaimed, 'so that when I lay my hands on people, they will receive the Holy Spirit!' But Peter replied, 'May your money perish with you for thinking God's gift can be bought!'* Acts 8:18-20 (NLT)

Dear Holy Spirit, help us to be used only by You and may we do it gladly in any situation to which you call us. Also, Lord, help us to know if we are using others. If we have attempted to "buy" your favor or bargain with you, forgive us and help us to treat you, not as a means to get our way, but as One with whom we have a loving, honoring relationship. Amen.

April 7

Slow, Sweet Spiritual Growth

How beautiful are the stalagmites and stalactites that rise and hang from the depths of Crystal Caves in Pennsylvania. How steady and unrelenting, the drip, drip, drip of liquid limestone that has continued for hundreds of thousands of years to make these beautiful formations.

We too, are built up slowly in our spiritual lives. Each day we need to enjoy our time with the Lord and in His word and in prayer. Nothing happens over night. There is no "instant" spirituality that glows from our face when we leave our room, like Moses face glowed when he came down from Mount Sinai. No, we learn day-by-day, bit-by-bit, and we are built up into something beautiful in the eyes of God and into someone who, eventually, will be appealing to those around us. Not everyone will notice, but whenever someone asks about your joy or your peace, you will have an answer for him or her and be a witness of the Good News — that the Kingdom of Heaven is at hand! And then they may want to spend time in the Master's presence too.

Whom will he teach knowledge? And whom will he make to understand the message? Those just weaned from milk? Those just drawn from the breasts? For precept must be upon precept, precept upon precept, Line upon line, line upon line, Here a little, there a little. Isaiah 28:9, 10 (NKJV)

Dear Teacher and Friend, every time we spend even a few moments praising you and speaking to you and listening to you and being silent with you, we grow spiritually if we do so in spirit and in truth. Help us then, to remember to take the time to do these things, for there is nothing on earth or in heaven that is more important. Amen.

April 8

A Carefully Considered Gift

As a child we lived next to Mr. Smales who had a large garden, a grove of plum trees and an assortment of chickens including little bantams. I can see his firm face clearly in my mind's eye — the sharp, keen eyes, the square-set jaw. He and Daddy would lean on and talk over the old run-down barbed wire fence between our properties, often about "the good old days" and laugh and joke with one another. On my eighth birthday Mr. Smales reached into his shirt pocket and pulled out a crisp dollar bill and started to hand it to me. I looked at it in surprise; it was a lot of money. I wanted it, oh, how I wanted it! But I felt it was not right to take it, so I looked down at the ground, and said, "No thank you."

Mr. Smales crouched down, no doubt with difficulty, and proceeded to explain things to me. In essence what he said was something like this: "Now, Patty, I want you to know something so listen to what I'm going to tell you. Money is very, very important to people. Before giving money away, people will think very carefully about that decision. People don't just give money away without cautiously considering the consequences. They thoroughly think through whether they really want to give it away or not. So, when someone offers you money, you can be sure they know for certain that they want to give it to you. So now, Patty, take this dollar. I thought it through before I offered it, and I really want you to have it as a gift." I looked over to Daddy who was watching from a short distance and he nodded in approval. I thought to myself that Mr. Smales must have told him what he was going to do and that he had Daddy's permission already. I confidently reached out my little hand and received the dollar bill and politely thanked Mr. Smales. It's a lesson I've never forgotten!

The Bible teaches us about counting the cost. It is something that Jesus Christ did before He came to Earth. So, when with such forethought, He offered so much, we know He planned it in advance and fulfilled all that He came to do. He is Love and to Him, we, the creatures He made, were worth it all. Most of my readers already know the Lord, but if there is one out there who does not, don't refuse the greatest of all gifts. Reach out your child-like hand and take it and say "Thank you." Jesus already counted the cost.

For God so loved the world that He gave His only begotten Son, that whoever believes in Him should not perish but have everlasting life. John 3:16 (NKJV)

Dear Jesus, Thank you for making the choice to give up your glory and come down here to Earth. Thank you for taking on yourself my sin so that I could take on your righteousness. Amen.

April 9

Snipe Hunting

One of the first dates I had with Don (my husband) was to go "snipe hunting." He told me about his plans for the evening with such a twinkle in his eye that I suspected there was some joke going on. He got a couple of brown paper bags to catch them in and a stick with which to "stun" them. He wasn't very clear about what they were, so I went with him, suspicious, but curious. I don't want to give away any secrets, but let's just say that we didn't find a single one, and that was the last I heard of the snipes.[2]

Do you ever go on snipe hunts or on wild goose chases? You move. You change jobs. You think you are going for such and such a purpose but when you arrive, you find that the circumstances are quite different than you expected.

It happens to me a lot. God seldom gives us the whole picture. We go in obedience and find out on the way what the circumstances are. This is the walk of faith that God wants for each of His children. Where does God want you to go today?

Show me your ways, O Lord; Teach me Your paths. Lead me in Your truth and teach me.... Psalm 25:4, 5 (NKJV)

Dear Lord, give me courage to take steps of faith, knowing that when I take the first step you will show me the way to the next and the next. Amen.

---

[2] Snipes are small brownish birds with extremely long beaks that they use to pull worms out of the ground!

April 10

A Song of Welcome

My friend, "Annie," had studied voice and majored in music but I had never heard her sing. One day when she came over for a visit, I sat down at the piano and started to go through some old songs. Among them was "All the Things you Are," by Jerome Kern. We sang it together. She then told me that it was the song her mother sang to her while she was still in the womb. What a love gift for an unborn child!

Annie is full of life, vibrant and hopeful, a delight to be around. I can't help but believe that hearing a melody of joy sung to her day after day before her birth, not only made her feel welcomed into the world, but has colored her whole existence. Knowing she was wanted and loved must be one of the reasons she is such a joyful, loving person today.

I believe that even those of us who were not so beautifully welcomed into the world by our parents, can, by faith, receive and believe that Jesus knew us from our mother's womb and cradled us there. He called each of us into being and was the One who blessed us as we were born, rejoicing at our births. When we entered the world, even if no one else cared, He smiled and said to us, "Welcome my child. I love you." So we too, can have a joyful life, knowing that we are each a unique treasure, yes, even a "promised kiss of springtime."

> *Your have covered me in my mother's womb...My frame was not hidden from you when I was made in secret...Your eyes saw my substance, being yet unformed. And in Your book they all were written, The days fashioned for me, When as yet there were none of them.* Psalm 139:13-16 (NKJV)

Dear Father in Heaven, even those of us who were not desired by human parents, were desired by You. You brought us into being. Help us to receive with joy the wonderful gift of life on Earth that you have given to us. Amen.

April 11

Pecking Order

There is a pecking order on earth. It has to do with power over others when it comes to territory. I've watched it when I've seen birds feeding. I've seen it while duck watching at a near-by park. I saw it as a child when we raised chickens. Of course, it is present in human relationships too. I've seen it with people who have power over others because of their position; they guard their position jealousy.

I was once employed by an insurance company where there was no team work. Everyone sought his or her own good only. It was frightening. Every day I dreaded going to work. I had been fortunate to have never experienced this kind of workplace atmosphere until I was in my fifties. It was a lesson I needed to learn — that people do behave this way, but I was shocked. I was the newest employee and in an entry-level position as a receptionist and mail girl. Therefore, I was at the bottom of the heap.

Or was I? One morning the cleaning lady came in and I kept running into her in different offices as I delivered mail. I had been repeatedly put down by several co-workers that day and when I saw her I had a large envelope in my hand and I whacked her on the behind with it and made a joke about her following me around. I was trying to make it look like I was teasing, and she smiled, but I had spontaneously wanted to put her down. I found myself passing it on, like the old joke about the employee that goes home and kicks the dog. I was ashamed and shocked and was too guilty to ask her to forgive me. However, I did ask the Lord to forgive me. Every time I saw her after that, I went out of my way to acknowledge her in honor and respect, instead of treating her as someone "below" me.

Then Peter opened his mouth and said, 'In truth I perceive that God shows no partiality.' Acts 10:34 (NKJV)

Lord, help us to remember that you are no respecter of persons and neither should we be. Thank you that in your kingdom there is no pecking order. Amen.

April 12

Petals of Blessings

It was a warm day. There was a lovely breeze. I was just returning from shopping when I saw a young woman in a wheel chair being pushed across the walk in front of my car. Unexpectedly, I felt a great rush of compassion toward her. I prayed fervently, "Oh Father God, please help her. She needs you in her life." Later I got to wondering what happens when we pray such brief spur-of-the-moment prayers.

That night the answer came to me in a dream. The Lord spoke to me and showed me something about these kinds of prayers! He said that we could live our lives as though we are walking through life carrying hands filled with beautiful soft, pink petals, and as we go, we sprinkle them about for those whom we pass in order that they may be blessed. We do not see the results, but that should make no difference; we are to bless in this way anyway. So, now and again (not nearly often enough), I remember this, and I spend a day just blessing those around me with silent, little prayers: *Lord, help the new cashier as she learns her job. Father, bless that mother who is having to care for those three energetic children. Jesus, remind that young man who is driving too fast, to slow down. Lord, bless that pilot up there in that airliner.* And so I go about my day, blessing with these little prayers, and, at the end of that time, guess who feels the most blessed?

> *Prove Me now in this,' says the Lord of hosts, 'If I will not open for you the windows of heaven and pour out for you such blessing that there will not be room enough to receive it.'* Malachi 3:10 (NKJV)

Lord, help us to remember that within us is your Spirit at all times, ever longing for opportunities to bless all those around us. Remind us today that your loving power is loosed when we whisper prayers of blessings for others (pass out rose petals?) as we go about our day. Amen.

April 13

Consolation in Suffering

Sometimes I feel like God seems cruel — when life is so heartless and painful, when things have not only gone wrong, but horribly awry and we're weeping, our hearts torn apart in grief, and we wonder, *How could a good God allow this to happen?* One of my favorite movies is, "Return to Me." In it the character of Grace, played by Minnie Driver, says (after she has fallen in love, and then discovers to her horror that he was the widower of the woman whose heart she received as a transplant), "What was God *thinking*?" Oh, I can't tell you how many times I've asked the same question!

It's so easy to believe — when everything is fine, when days have gone smoothly by and everything has fallen into place and we are well and our loved ones are thriving — that God is good. Then all at once everything around us falls apart. Our world is shattered. Nine-Eleven changes everything. We discover a friend has betrayed us. Haiti is once again flooded and thousands are left homeless. We lose a job. A spouse files for divorce. A child dies. A volcano in Indonesia erupts and wipes out an entire village. Six are killed in a shooting in Tucson. And suddenly God does not seem so good anymore.

But God has not changed. He is ever the same. He is still here. He has not left. He is with us all in every sorrow, experiencing it, sharing it and helping us to carry every burden. When we feel pain, so does He. When there is devastation in any part of the world He cares. He weeps with those who weep. He is not some little piece of spirit tucked safely away in an isolation booth in our souls or in a far-away Heavenly hiding place. He lives in our entire body, including the parts that are in pain. He lives in our entire world including those areas that suffer beyond description, and He sees it all — the pain, the heartbreak, the hunger, the disease, the injustice. He feels it all; He does not exclude himself from our earthly suffering, physical or mental, emotional or spiritual. He sees and He cares and I believe that He longs to return to Earth as King of kings and Lord of lords as much as we who are the sheep of His pasture long for His second appearing.

God is our refuge and strength, A very present help in trouble. Therefore do not fear. Psalm 46:1, 2 (NKJV)

May your ways be known throughout the earth, your saving power among people everywhere. May the nations praise you, O God. Yes, may all the nations praise you. Let the whole world sing for joy, because you govern the nations with justice and guide the people of the whole world. Psalm 67:2-4 (NLT)

Lord, help us to be comforted by the knowledge that you care about all the suffering that goes on in our world including our own pain. We look to the time, our Heavenly King, when you will be recognized as Sovereign of the Nations, the one who will rule with justice and guide all the peoples of the Earth. But meanwhile, help me to care enough to **do** something about the wrongs and suffering that I see. Amen.

April 14

Rest — Part 1

OK. I'll admit it. I don't understand how to really rest — any kind of rest. There seems to be in me such a spirit of the work ethic that I even have busy dreams. I recently read a religious essay that said wool was not allowed in the Holy of Holies in Old Testament times. It suggested that this is because it causes one to sweat, and that sweat suggests the curse in Genesis 3. This would therefore, make sweat a reminder of sin, and no reminder of sin should enter the holiest of places, into the very Presence of God. I don't know if this speculation is accurate, but it's an interesting suggestion.

There are, of course, all kinds of sweat (More accurately known as perspiration if you were to ask my high school English teacher; "Sweat," she said, "refers only to animals."). There is the sweat of a good workout at the gym, the sweat of fear, the sweat of childbirth. There is the sweat of hard and satisfying physical labor. There is even sweat in a difficult time of intercessory prayer. So, I don't believe that sweat or perspiration is something to be avoided.

The "rest" that God calls us to is something that is, of course, on the inside, an inward place, where we may go into the Holy of Holies where the Lord himself dwells in the temple of our hearts, and find that as we make that precious connection with Him, we automatically go into a state of restfulness. That's what I want to learn to do more of, more often — to start my day that way with that kind of prayer. On the days that I begin, not by asking for anything, but by praising Him and telling Him how much I love Him, I'm sure I get closer and closer to that ideal rest — the rest that refreshes like a cool breeze on a clear spring day.

Then Jesus said, 'Come to me, all of you who are weary and carry heavy burdens, and I will give you rest.' Matthew 11:28 (NLT)

Lord, I want to be able to come to that inner place of rest with you and give you my burdens, but often my anxiety about them and the busyness of life seem to pull me away. Help me to overcome the temptation to go "do" and help me to learn to just "be" with you for a few moments each day so that I might truly be restored and refreshed by your strength and love. Amen.

April 15

Rest — Part 2

In an article by Natalie Angier entitled: *Busy as a Bee? Then Who's Doing the Work?* she reports that laziness is perfectly natural, perfectly sensible and shared by nearly every other species on the planet. She gets this information from biologists who engage in what is called "time budget analysis." Much to the surprise of almost everyone, these field scientists have discovered that the great majority of creatures spend most of their time doing nothing much at all, unless you include such activities as sitting, sprawling, dozing, rocking back and forth, and ambling around in circles.

I still puzzle over resting myself. Since retiring, I take a nap almost every day and, as good as it feels, I still have a sense of guilt about it. However, I've no doubt that there's a gene in me that believes in siestas. I once worked for a Frenchman who gave all his employees a two-hour lunch break so we could all go home and have a snooze. He thought of it as absolutely necessary and even part of a cultured life style and it seemed that, because of that respite, the afternoon workflow went much more easily for all of us.

But what about "resting in the Lord." How can we do that? How can we discipline ourselves to experience this apparent lack of activity and know that it is not only OK, but essential to our spiritual welfare to take time doing nothing in the presence of God? I think the answer is to just carve out the time to rest in His presence; and, like the result of those afternoon siestas, when we do, we will find that things will flow more smoothly.

'Take my yoke upon you. Let me teach you, because I am humble and gentle, and you will find rest for your souls.'
Matthew 11:28 (NLT)

For all who have entered into God's rest have rested from their labors, just as God did after creating the world.
Hebrews 4:10 (NLT)

Lord, help me to give myself permission to rest both physically and mentally. Help me to let go of work that you have not required that I take on, and help me to learn how to share with you the things you are requiring of me, and help me to know the difference. Amen.

April 16

A Robe for Ruben

Ruben was one of my mother's friends. They met in Kansas City some time in her early life, probably in her twenties. He had left school at the age of eight. He would write her occasionally, but always printed and used a small "i" instead of "I" when sharing something about himself. He explained that he did it this way because capitals should be used only for the Lord. He kept in contact with Mama and when he moved to California in the 1940s he came to visit us. Mama told me, "Now, make Ruben feel welcome. Go kiss him." I felt embarrassed but I did as she said and ran down our long dirt drive and welcomed him. (I don't recall kissing him, but I pretty much did what Mama had requested.) Ruben stayed in California and found work as a swing shift guard at a military installation. He came to dinner once a week for years and we did his laundry and ironing for him to earn a little bit of extra money.

One day over a simple dinner Ruben told us how he had become a Christian. He had a dream in which he tried to attend a wedding but was stopped and told that he could not enter because he was not wearing the proper wedding attire. He immediately woke up in great fear and distress. He realized he was a sinner and needed a Savior and so he found himself asking Jesus to forgive him for all of his sins. After this he felt a great peace in his heart and he knew that when he died he would be welcomed into the Kingdom of God.

That story impressed me greatly as a child. He moved further away and though he quit visiting, we kept in touch with Ruben for many years. He would send a little note along with a plain Christmas card, always saying pretty much the same thing, still using that lower case "i" when speaking about himself. Then one year the cards quit coming and our card was returned. We knew that Ruben must have died. Though saddened, we also rejoiced because we knew where he had gone and that there was no doubt that he was a welcome guest, because he had been given just the right garment to wear.

But when the king came in to see the guests, he saw a man there who did not have on a wedding garment, so he said to him, 'Friend, how did you come in here without a wedding garment?' And he was speechless. Matthew 22:11, 12 (NKJV)

Dear Lord, because of your mercy and grace, one day I will be given a beautiful white robe of righteousness to wear. I will wear it with gratitude and delight at the Wedding Feast for all believers! Amen.

April 17

In Need of Our Own Oil

I have learned that self-pity and bitterness are such poisons that they can spill out and around on those who are in the same room. I have one acquaintance that I will call "Justine." She can be so polluting that all her negativity is turned outward and all her energy is turned inward. It seems to me that she is a walking black hole. And yet it is just this kind of person who wants something from you or me. I don't and can't give them much and they do, eventually, go elsewhere to find their victims.

We need to be aware of this kind of person. They can be a type of soul vampire, looking to suck the spiritual life out of those who are spiritually alive so that they too can be spiritually alive. I believe what Justine really wanted is what I have found in my relationship with my Lord in the person of the Holy Spirit. This is something we cannot pass on because each individual needs to have his or her own abiding relationship with the Spirit of God. Jesus warns us about this kind of "thief" in the 25th chapter of Matthew. So, even though I cannot help Justine in the way she desires, I have encouraged her to find her own Source of spiritual life, and have not allowed her to "steal" mine. This may sound selfish, but the Bible calls this wisdom!

> *But the foolish ones [virgins] said to the wise, 'Give us some of your oil, because our lamps are going out.' The wise bridesmaids answered, 'No, the oil we have might not be enough for all of us. Go to the people who sell oil and buy some for yourselves.'* Matthew 25:8, 9 (NCV)

> *The leech has two daughters, Crying, 'Give! Give!'* Proverbs 30:15 (NKJV)

Lord God, help me to point the way to you and to neither a leech host nor a leech be! Amen.

April 18

Sacrifices of Praise

When my friend, Suzanne, came down with breast cancer, I was absolutely certain that God would heal her. In faith, I praised God for that healing. But the healing didn't come and she died after two years of constant prayer. The day she died I sat down at the piano and I played "In Moments Like These" by David Graham and I offered up a sacrifice of praise. No matter what happens, no matter how we feel, God is always worthy of our praises! So it was not easy, but as I offered up this sacrifice of adoration to Him, it was the beginning of the healing of my pain over her loss. So, even in the darkest moments, I've found, that as we praise and give thanks to Him, He enters into each situation in a living way.

> *Let them sacrifice the sacrifices of thanksgiving, And declare His works with rejoicing.* Psalm 107:22 (NKJV)

Lord God, even in the depths of despair, may my heart praise you who are always worthy of praise. Amen.

April 19

The Greatest Drama of All

When I took a summer course at the American Academy of Dramatic Arts in Pasadena, California, my instructor, Don Richardson, though he was Jewish, acknowledged the most dramatic occurrence in history to be the crucifixion of Jesus Christ. He said that it had all of the elements that make for a great drama: conflict, suffering, sacrifice, loyalty, betrayal, death, and grief. There was the horror of death by crucifixion. There was the betrayal by Judas who, in remorse, went and hanged himself. There were the Roman soldiers casting lots to see who would get Christ's robe. There were the weeping women, including Mary, the mother of Jesus. There was John, his closest friend, standing by and promising that he would become as a son to Mary.

My drama instructor didn't think of this scene as anything more than a pure and vital example of true drama! But those of us who know and love Jesus Christ know that it was, indeed, the greatest non-fiction drama in all of Earth's history — a moment of electrifying reality that pierced into earthly time from Heaven's eternity — that caused the grieving depths of nature to respond with a cloud cover so thick that it was the darkest day ever known on the Earth, that caused the ground to quake and give up some of its dead, and that caused the very veil that hung between the Holy place and Holy of Holies of the temple to be torn from top to bottom! In some way, as we come to that moment in the Eternal Now, we too can stand there at the foot of the cross of the God-man, the Lord Jesus Christ, and experience personally, the greatest human drama ever known upon the face of the earth.

Truly this man was the Son of God. Mark 15:39b (NKJV)

Dear Lord Jesus, we are in awe of that great and terrible sacrifice that you made for each one of us. The scene that we see as your Word describes it, is a wonder to us — God in the flesh, suffering, taking the burden of our sins upon yourself. We thank you for this indescribable gift, and we acknowledge with the words spoken by that centurion so long ago, "Truly this was the Son of God!" Amen.

April 20

The Battle in the Garden

Where was the greatest spiritual battle of all time really fought? My dear friend, Katie, suggested at a Bible study she was teaching, that Jesus fought His greatest battle in prayer, not on the Cross, but in the Garden of Gethsemane, the night *before* the day of the Crucifixion; that is where the victory was first won.

It was...

- . . .there where He, three times, asked His Heavenly Father that the cup He saw before Him be taken away;

- . . .there where He received the answer;
- . . .there where He answered back, "Not my will, but yours be done."
- . . .there where He sweat great drops of blood;
- . . .there where His soul was filled with sorrow unto death;
- . . .there where an angel came to minister to Him;
- . . .there where His disciples failed to pray with Him, and from
- . . .there that He got up and went out, knowing that the answer was "no," and knowing that He, having made the choice on His own and in prayer, would now be able to face the horrors of the day ahead.

An angel appeared to Him from heaven, strengthening Him, And being in agony, He prayed more earnestly. And His sweat became like great drops of blood falling down to the ground. When He rose up from prayer, and had come to His disciples...He said to them, 'Why do you sleep! Rise and pray, lest you enter into temptation.' Luke 22:43 - 46 (NKJV)

Lord, help us to remember that night in the garden, where and when you prayed until you were able to say: "Nevertheless not my will, but yours, be done." Amen.

April 21

Triumph in Time of Suffering

When He left the Garden of Gethsemane, Scripture tells us that Jesus knew what lay before Him, but perhaps it was there in that garden that the Father revealed to Jesus the glory that was to come; Perhaps it was there that Jesus foresaw himself as the Son of Man sitting at the right hand of the Mighty One and coming on the clouds of heaven. Remember, these are the very words that a short time later He spoke to Caiaphas. If he did see this vision of the future, then perhaps it was being in that state of hope and holding that vision in His heart that enabled Him to have the strength and determination to pick up that

Cross and go to that horrible physical death. And not only that, but the unimaginable spiritual crisis of separation from His Father for the first time in all eternity also faced Him. We don't have to imagine a pathetic, bowed-in-defeat Jesus after He left the garden, but rather a victorious Jesus, going forth in strength, empowered to do the perfect will of God the Father.

Yes we know, of course, that even by the time He left the garden, He would have been in a state of emotional and physical exhaustion, having had no sleep, and having experienced this great spiritual battle on His knees. And yes, it is true that as the night went on and as the day began, He became weakened physically from unspeakable beatings and floggings, but we don't ever need to see Him as spiritually weakened. Never. The amazing and wonderful thing is, that once He knew clearly what He was to do, there was no turning back. He knew precisely what lay before Him, and He went anyway.

Behold, I am the Lord, the God of all flesh. Is there anything too Hard for Me? Jeremiah 32:27 (NKJV)

Lord, by these words of yours to Jeremiah, and by your actions on the day of your death, we are not told it wouldn't be hard, just that it wouldn't be *too* hard. Enable us too, to do the hard things. Amen.

April 22

The Dividing Place of History

The Cross stands as the great dividing place of all time and the great meeting place of all time, and even space. It stands at a time and place when and where all nature moaned as it witnessed the suffering and death of the embodied Word of God, the very one who had spoken the world into existence. It was a time when the cloud cover above the earth was so thick that it became as night, when the Earth itself shook in response, and where the sin-caused separation between God and humankind was erased. When I meditate on the Cross, these are things I consider:

The Cross is:

- The meeting place of all that is natural and all that is supernatural,
- The place where Jesus stretched out His arms and embraced the world, and in so doing, embraced the sins of the world,
- A place where, even if I had been the only one who had ever sinned, Christ would have died for me alone,
- The place where His arms stretched backwards through time past and forwards through time future,
- The place between law and grace, between Heaven and Earth, between life and death,
- The place where mercy and truth met together,
- The place where righteousness and peace kissed each other,
- The great event in history that embraces the Ages,
- And it is that Cross that stands suspended in the Eternal Now, so that we, the children of humankind, have a place where, we, as sinners, may go with our burden of guilt and be washed clean and be set free of all that would separate us from God. And then we will be set on a new road, a new and living way, a road that begins with the gift of Eternal life right now, a life in relationship with The Heavenly Father and Jesus Christ, His only begotten Son, who loved us and gave himself for us.

Now it was the third hour and they crucified him. Mark 15:24 (NKJV)

Lord, this is such a short sentence in the Gospel of Mark. Yet it describes the single most defining moment in history. As I meditate on the High Holy Day of Good Friday, by your Holy Spirit, make that day real in my heart. Amen.

April 23

Easter

My favorite holiday (Holy Day) is Easter — the day of the miracle that changed history forever, the day that death was transformed into life. It is the day that took the fear out of death; because death, as we know, only involves the physical body and that death is but temporary because there will be a glorious day of resurrection for us all! Jesus went before us, the first of this great harvest to come (See 1 Corinthians 15:20)! Because He lives, we too shall live. Hallelujah! Christ is risen! He is risen indeed!

What a glorious time of year. What a wondrous miracle. The greatest miracle ever known to mankind on earth is what happened in that tomb when Jesus awoke, got up and walked out.

Death is swallowed up in victory. 1 Corinthians 15:54 (NKJV)

Jesus, you changed history; you changed the world, you change death into life. Though death may be all around us, it cannot capture us. We are alive forevermore in you. Amen.

April 24

The Perfect Touch

I've worked as a secretary/bookkeeper for many years. One job was in a place where there was much backbiting, cruelty, and competition. There was no teamwork. I repeatedly overheard one employee talking spitefully about another, and then would watch as she became sweet and friendly to the same employee, as though there was no animosity whatsoever between them. On one occasion a man who had identified himself as being a Christian became angry with me. His name was Fred. I walked into the office of one of our co-workers and overheard him talking about me in a derogatory, belittling fashion. He didn't see me at first because of a screen between us. I was devastated. The one person, whom I thought I might trust to be kind, was just like the others. The week that this happened, though not because of it, I quit my job.

The following Sunday morning I felt so disappointed and hurt about having to quit a job that I went forward for prayer after the church service. I was kneeling at the altar and an elder came and placed his hand on my shoulder and knelt beside me and prayed with me. He must have listened to the Holy Spirit for he did not say one word or ask one question. He behaved in the perfect manner for me to receive healing. He silently kept his hand on my shoulder and waited until I was through crying. And then, out of the darkness of pain, I began to sense the touch of God's light. When I turned to see who it was that had touched me and prayed for me, I was surprised to discover it was another Fred — this one a faithful brother in the Lord. I knew God had appointed him to take away the pain that the other Fred had caused! I marveled at this gift of healing for my aching heart that brought light into my place of darkness.

> *For it is the God who commanded light to shine out of darkness who has shone in our hearts to give the light of the knowledge of the glory of God in the face of Jesus Christ.* 2 Corinthians 4:6 (NKJV)

Dear Lord, you have sent the Holy Spirit to minister the light of your presence through others to me. Allow me to also be a minister of light, to bring healing to others when they are experiencing their own times of darkness. Amen.

April 25

The Wounds of a Friend

I've told you before about Suzanne, my friend who had breast cancer metastasized to bone. I was sure she would be healed, but she was not. I had prayed and prayed, somehow believing that the answer would come in spite of all evidence to the contrary. I believed healing had to do with the number of prayers released up to Heaven, that God would gather them up, save them for the miraculous moment, and then in one marvelous down pouring, empty them on Suzanne and the healing would be one that would bring her entire family to Christ in wonder and thanksgiving.

This, I realized later, was a magical-formula notion of prayer. I do still believe that sometimes God heals miraculously, but I also believe that whenever and however healing comes it is always of God. It may be an obvious miracle healing or through the medical establishment, or any mixture of both, but however it comes, it is still God's gift to us. However, we have all experienced the times that God has said, "no," and when He does, we need to accept that as an answer to prayer also. When He said "no" to our requests for the healing of Suzanne, I experienced it as a personal wound and I had to tell God, first of all, that I was angry with him, and later, that He had hurt me deeply by not healing her.

Have you ever been hurt in this way by God? It is an exquisite wounding that brings with it a sense of the depths of the intimate relationship we have with Him. He has entrusted us with a heart-rending disappointment, and has trusted us to continue to love Him unconditionally, even as He has loved us. Job is an example for us. He was sorely tried and Satan hoped that he would, as Job's wife put it, "curse God and die." He did not. Instead he said, "Though He slay me, yet will I trust him (Job 13:15).

Faithful are the wounds of a friend... Proverbs 27:6 (NKJV)

Dear Heavenly Friend, you sometimes wound those you love, and you have wounded me. Help me to trust that love kind of love, even when my heart is breaking. Amen.

April 26

The Universal Jesus

Sometimes dreams are more than just dreams. My dear friend, Connie Brooks, shared the following dream with me. She had awakened in the morning when her husband got up, but had then gone back to sleep for a moment. She says that she thought it was a dream, but that her husband, Brian, thought it was more like a vision. Whatever it was, during those few minutes Connie saw the following:

She looked out of their bedroom window. Across from their condo balcony and above the College of San Mateo and the surrounding trees was a column of clouds, the color of smoke. As she watched the cloud, she was astounded to see that out of it came a man whom she recognized as Jesus. There was a multitude of people surrounding Him in the clouds. After He appeared, He began to descend toward her, and as He did so, His face kept changing, or as she put it, "morphing." It became "everyman's" face. A series of many ethnic likenesses unfolded before her, but always it was clear that it was the same Jesus — Persian, Asian, Black African, Hispanic, and many more, all the major people groups of Earth.

Jesus came closer and closer to her until He was standing in front of her in their bedroom. She felt that all that time He was focusing on her as an individual, but at the same time realized that all others saw Him in the same manner, as though He were focusing on them as individuals too. As Jesus came closer, His presence was so awesome and overwhelming that she could no longer look at him, and weeping with joy, buried her face in a soft chair nearby. She shared her vision with her husband and later with me.

There is such a ring of truth about it, that I feel it was a vision from the Lord to her, yes, but one that was meant to be shared with others; that's why I include it in this book. I believe this genuine vision reveals the nature of the Lord Jesus, His identity with *all* humankind, all ethnic groups, and also that He appears to each of us as though He is focusing on us alone, our relationship with Him can be so intimate. That is the kind of universal, yet personal God He is, coming to the world, yes, but also coming to each of us individually.

For God so loved the world that He gave His only begotten son, that whosoever believes in Him should not parish but have everlasting life. John 3:16 (KJV)

Father God, thank you for sending your son to the whole world — all people groups, so that all may see Him, believe and have everlasting life. Amen.

April 27

Progress?

In 1998, my husband and I were living in Goodyear, Arizona. A few yards away from us "progress" was going on. More new homes were soon to be built, more farm land would be converted from AG (agricultural) to P.A.D. (Planned Area Development). The economy was booming. There was work to be had by all.

In the first two years we lived there I enjoyed seeing the red-winged black birds come and nest in the trees along the irrigation ditch that ran through the edge of the farmland property across from our housing development. But one day, bulldozers came through and tore out the trees in which they nested; they pulled them up by the roots and the reeds by the water were gone as well. Huge pipelines were laid in that waterway's place. Soon there were walls, walls and more walls, and lots of cement, more heat, and dust, more pounding and more building going on.

When I would drive by, I could see a few torn-out trees lying strewn across the land. And on their dried limbs, a few red-winged black birds, sat, as though waiting. Were they wondering what had happened to their nests, the eggs yet to be hatched or their little ones? Of course, they too were soon gone. After all, it was "progress," or at least it was change.

As we all know, in the world, for good or evil, there is constant change. But, it is a great comfort to remember that there is One in whom there is no change whatsoever forthcoming, nor needed — ever!

For I am the Lord, I do not change... Malachi 3:13 (NKJV)

Dear Lord, sometimes I am saddened when I see changes in my little world. Help me to be comforted in knowing that you at least, do not change, but remain forever the same. Amen.

April 28

Time Out of Mind

From tales my grandmother told me, the Cherokee nation had a history of suffering. One of the most well known of the Native American tragedies is now called "The Trail of Tears." It was the emigration, by force, of an entire nation that had lived on land that they had believed was given to them by the Great Spirit. It had been their land from "time out of mind."

My great aunt, Florence Evans, wrote in her memoirs, that when it was clear that his people had no choice but to go, John Ross, who had been their Chief for more than 40 years, spoke to them, giving a lesson out of the book of Job. I quote from her writings his message to the Cherokee nation on that day in 1832:

"There was once a very rich and respectable man called Job, who believed that God would forgive those that put trust in him. This good man was unfortunate enough to lose all his property — in one day — taken from him by his enemies. This man, Job, said he came naked into the world and he must return naked; what he had, had been given to him by the Lord and it was taken away, and blessed be the name of the Lord. His misfortune did not bring him to make use of any violent language, nor did he blame the Great Spirit; for he was never known during his existence to sin against the Great Spirit. The Great Spirit, in consequence of his cheerfulness, caused him to gather again double the amount of property he had lost...If the President of the white people should cease to protect us and our rights and should rob us of our rights, then I say to you, as Job said, 'My mother brought me naked into the world, and I must quit it naked.' Such is the bidding of the great Creator. 'The Lord giveth and the Lord taketh away; blessed be the name of the Lord.' This is what Job said when he was robbed. Bear like Job. Like Job may you be rewarded."

Have you been robbed of something? A happy secure childhood? Your dreams? Your health? It will be restored or you will receive something even better. And that, if not now, in your earthly future or in your heavenly Future. The curtain of the Third Act hasn't even gone up yet. And there will! Yes! There *will* be a happy outcome. Yes! Everything will work out! We will get a better-than-the-fairy-tale ending, that of the great and perfect mixture of love and justice that our hearts and spirits long for. Yes! We will live happily ever after — "Time out of mind."

> *For the Lamb who is in the midst of the throne will shepherd them and lead them to living fountains of waters. And God will wipe away every tear from their eyes.* Rev. 7:17 (NKJV)

Lord, we are in awe when we think of what you have in store for us in eternity. Thank you that you will make all things right in that Day that is to come. Amen.

April 29

Time Healing

My old home, the place where I lived from the age of 4 to 18 still stands, hidden among the trees and bushes on South Euclid Avenue in Pasadena, California. A few years ago I returned. It was time. The old dirt road that went back 300 feet was now paved beautifully with red brick. The date palm was twice as high as I remembered it. The Cyprus tree was gone, as was the arbor that my Dad had built for grape vines, his pride!

I had feared this trek back in time, but I need not have. I thought I would feel like a child again — fearful, haunted, ashamed. But I walked as a woman, no sense of fear, no sense of blame, just a feeling of freedom, knowing that all the old wounds had been healed. How had the healing happened? Through all good and simple things that God had brought into my life, such things as: special friends, prayers, flowers, songs, kittens, sunsets, butterflies and stars, I had reached out my heart to God for the last years, asking for healing, and all along, bit-by-bit, He had answered. Now on this day I stood tall, adult, proud and thankful, knowing my father would have loved this land now — even more. He would have rejoiced that it is in the hands of a landscape architect and nursery owner, who grows throughout its length and breadth, an incredible variety of beautiful, flourishing green shrubbery, trees, and flowers! Thank you, Lord God, for making this little piece of earth more joyful than ever and thank you, Lord God, for healing us along the way, even when we don't know you are doing it.

Create in me a clean heart, O God, and renew a steadfast spirit within me. Psalm 51:10 (NKJV)

Lord, I know that you want us to be healed in all the old, shameful places; help us to admit to you our need, so that we may allow you into those places to clean wounds and heal them, making us whole, making us new. Amen.

April 30

Into the Light

Gold and softly glowing was His light
Secretly touching me in the night
Almost forgot in the place where dreams die
At last recalled in a place children cry
There was a darkness that I once had known
But He drew me to the light of His throne
Marvelous, sparkling, clear and fine
I'm called out of the shadows that once were mine.

There have been many times of darkness in my life. But *always*, God has delivered me from the darkness and brought me back into His light.

If you have times of darkness, don't despair. It is temporary. It can be a test of your faith, a time to — more than ever — cast yourself on Him. Trust Him even in the midst of the darkest night. He will not let go of you and He will bring you into His daybreak.

If I say, 'Surely the darkness shall fall on me,' Even the night shall be light about me; Indeed, the darkness shall not hide from You, But the night shines as the day; The darkness and the light are both alike to You. Psalm 139:11, 12 (NKJV)

Lord, you are the God of Light and I trust that even though I may feel engulfed in darkness, you see all things clearly and will bring me into your place of perpetual light. Amen.

MAY

May 1

A Different Kind of Ending

At my first and only piano recital I played a piece called "May Night," by Selim Palmgren. I had so wanted to play Clair de Lune by Claude Debussy, but another student would be playing that, so I agreed to play the alternate selection. The day of the recital arrived and I walked out on stage, sat down and began to play. It was a requirement that the composition be memorized so I had no music in front of me. I got to the third and final section and hit a chord that I realized with dismay, was the wrong chord! It was the chord at the beginning of the piece, which was very similar, but not quite the same as the chord introducing the final section of the piece! I continued on, repeating the whole thing again, acting unruffled, but as I came to the end again, I felt at the mercy of my hands! *What notes would they play? Would I hit the right ones this time?* My hands struck the chord, and, oh no! I was back to beginning once more. *What should I do, just go on and on like a broken record?* The only solution I could come up with was to play a series of arpeggios (rolling chords) until I heard myself approaching the proper key, at which point I slowed down with a gentle pianissimo and struck the final chord. I got up, bowed, the audience applauded, and I walked off the stage.

To me, it was a total disaster; I could feel my whole body blushing! As a teenager might, I thought of just walking off and never coming back. However, there was another take on this whole scene that I didn't appreciate at the time. After all, I had managed to keep my composure. I had improvised an entirely new ending to a piece that was largely unknown, so no one would have noticed, and I had smiled and bowed, doing everything that was expected of me from the audience's point of view. How easy it is to look back now and see that that teenage girl was really pretty brave and creative!

But what about now, as adults on the stage of life? What do we do when things seem to go completely wrong? The same thing! With God's help (And I do believe God was there to help me at the recital even though I didn't know it at the time.), we can keep our composure. We can do the best we know how with what we've got. And we can trust God that there is another view of the whole thing that we may never know, until Eternity!

You will keep in perfect peace all who trust in you, whose thoughts are fixed on you! Isaiah 26:3 (NLT)

Father, there are times when I feel as though everything is going wrong. When such times come, and I know they will, help me to keep my mind on you, that my heart may be quieted and then help me to follow through on whatever I need to do. The rest I will leave in your hands. Amen.

May 2

Tuna Salad Surprise

I had been invited to a women's luncheon. All the guests were to bring a salad, and I chose to make my favorite, curried tuna. When I arrived at the home where we were gathering for the luncheon, I left my dish on the counter where several women were arranging the array of salads. A few seconds later I heard a loud "clink!" I said to a friend, "I hope that wasn't my crystal bowl breaking." But then I dismissed this as a possibility.

However, some minutes later when we all began to eat, my teeth crunched down on something hard in my own salad. *What could it be? Nothing that crunchy was in the recipe.* I surreptitiously slipped it out of my mouth. It was a small piece of glass. I couldn't believe it. Had the "clink" I heard been my bowl breaking and not one person noticed or bothered to do anything about it? I took another bite. Another piece of glass. There was no doubt that the salad I had brought had glass in it! *Lord, what should I do?* The answer was clear. The next thing I knew I heard myself warning everyone not to eat the tuna salad, that it had pieces of glass in it. And as strange as it seems, no one else had glass for lunch that day but me! I went over to check my bowl out and, yes, it had a large crack in it!

I thank the Lord for taking care of my friends and me by letting me be the first and only one to get the glass, and for helping me be bold enough to warn everyone else.

In my trouble I called to the LORD. I cried out to my God for help. From his temple he heard my voice; my call for help reached his ears. Psalm 18:6 (NCV)

Dear Lord, thank you for helping us in the midst of life's crises, even the little ones. Amen.

May 3

Passage to a Holy Place

I have read that the Ministry of Religious Affairs in Jerusalem has discovered and excavated a stairway and a secret passageway. It leads to a tiny chamber that is believed to be the Holy of Holies on the original site of King Solomon's Temple. It must be fascinating to take this tour, like going into ages past, moving down through the darkness of the cold, damp staircase, each step taking one further back in time, and then through the 400-yard tunnel leading to an ancient world of glory and riches. Think of it — into the very place that God himself dwelled among His people, where the priests could enter only once a year. Very few are allowed to take this tour, however. It can only be done by making special arrangements with the Ministry of Religious Affairs.

But there is a spiritual "tour" that is even more wondrous, that we are allowed to take, and it costs us nothing. It is a journey inward, where there is a spiritual throne room. We can enter the court of the King and reach out and touch the golden scepter without fear. As we go more deeply into this wondrous place, we discover that it is not small, but it expands to greater and greater dimensions of love because that is where the God who is the King of love dwells; and it is not dark because that is where the Father of Lights dwells. There is no law that says we may enter this place only once a year. We are invited to come, not just daily, but to enter and stay — forever. We are invited to make it the center of our being and to live our lives out of that place of holiness and beauty and rest.

But Oh! How difficult it is to stay. How easy it is to be pulled back and off center into the so-called realities of the world of hunger and labor, war and woundedness. If there's a secret to staying, I don't yet know what it is but I suspect it lies somewhere between God's gracious enabling and my steadfast self-discipline! Meanwhile I'm going to keep looking for concrete ways to keep my wandering heart there.

> *...Esther put on her royal robes and stood in the inner court of the king's palace...So it was when the king saw Queen Esther standing in the court, that she found favor in his sight, and the king held out to Esther the golden scepter that was in his hand. Then Esther went near and touched the top of the scepter.* Esther 5:1-3 (NKJV)

Dear Father of Love and Light, King of my heart, you who dwell in that secret, holy throne room within me, help me learn to keep my heart there with you and yet able, from that place of glory and opulence, to reach out and touch the world around me. Amen.

May 4

Honoring Others

One of the best lessons my mother ever taught me was not in words but through the way in which she related to people. How blessed I was and didn't know it, until I got out in the world and found the great numbers of people who are prejudiced against others! Mom just always treated everyone the same — no one, no matter how rich, how poor, how educated or uneducated, how white or how brown, deserved more or less honor than any other! All were interesting, whether she met them at work or on the bus, in church or at the Cherub Bin, her favorite thrift shop! She respected, loved and enjoyed people. Now, I'm deeply thankful for this wonderful lesson that was so ingrained in me. One reason is that it tells me she carried with her the spirit of Christ — the one who looks on the heart — not on the outward appearance! Thank you, Mama. I love you.

Do not judge according to appearance, but judge with righteous judgment. John 7:24 (NKJV)

Lord, help us to have the discernment and openness that you exhibited when you walked on the face of the Earth. Amen.

May 5

The Eye of the Storm

When my husband, our son, Michael, and I lived in Taiwan in 1963, we stayed on Yang Ming Shun Mountain, a few miles above the city of Taipei. We had been warned that a typhoon (a China Sea hurricane) was on its way. We prepared by moving all the furniture to one side of the house (away from the direction of the wind) and covering the windows and doors. Typhoon Gloria came with a horrible roar, and as we looked out of the one small window we had left unprotected, we saw walls of rain fly by, not falling downward, but rushing past horizontally. This was the largest typhoon to ever hit Taiwan at that time (sixth largest since). It dropped 49.13 inches of rain on the island. Large areas were completely flooded and many lost their lives.

It lasted for hours (and in some places days) and then, suddenly, it was quiet. We went outdoors and looked up. The sky was blue and the air eerily still. We were in the eye of the storm. It was passing directly above our mountain; the typhoon was not over, just taking an intermission, and it soon returned. It had lost velocity and the winds now blew in the opposite direction, and then after a few hours, it was gone and there was silence once more.

I will never forget that feeling of being in the quiet center of a whirling mass of wind and rain, and how utterly safe I knew I was at that moment. I felt that it was a picture, a view of life teaching me that the only way we can survive spiritually is to stay in the center of the place of rest, the heart of God. Oh, I've often moved, but I always go back. It's the only place where I know, without doubt, that my Father covers me with His feathers.

He shall cover you with His feathers, and under His wings you shall take refuge. Psalm 91:4 (NKJV)

Father in Haven, sometimes I fail to realize that there is no place on Earth that is truly safe. However, as your child, I know that I am in your care, that you are a sovereign God, and that nothing can happen to me without your permission. Amen.

May 6

The Upside Down Trees

Don and I were blessed to visit Glacier Gardens Rainforest Adventure. It is a botanical garden located in Juneau, Alaska. The most memorable part of our time there was the explanation of why there were some upside down trees at the entrance road. The tour guide told us that when he first started to prepare this land he had to clear some areas and used a bulldozer to do so. However, one day, while he was backing up, he accidentally ran into one of the great evergreen trees and toppled it over. He was horrified! After meditating on what he could do to atone for this tragedy, he decided that he could make this (and any other trees that fell or had to be removed) to be giant flower planters. Over the years he has planted each of the huge trees with trunks down into the earth and with roots reaching many feet into the air and in each are a myriad of flowers of all different colors, some gracefully hanging down.

So what lesson do I see in this? It reminds me that God can take the negatives of our lives and turn them into something amazingly beautiful. How? Because He is a God who transforms. Because He is a God who can make good come out of evil. He is a God who teaches that love is more powerful than hatred and that blessing is more powerful than cursing. And He is the One who can take a ruined life and turn it upside down and make it into something beautiful!

*And we know that God causes everything to work together for
the good of those who love God and are called according to
his purpose for them.* Romans 8:28 (NLT)

Father, do whatever you need to do to make good come out of all those
things that I experience as negative in my life. I know that you can do
this. Amen.

May 7

Lies vs. Truth — Part 1
When We Believe Lies

When we are hurt, what we really want to know, almost more than
anything else about God, is that all the things we fear about Him are
not true. In my own life, I've discovered the things I fear about God are
often the things that I feared or experienced in regard to my parents,
especially my Father. The things that make us afraid of our parents may
be due to real and terrible abuse, or they may be due to misperceptions.
For instance, as I shared earlier this year, if a parent grabs a child out of
the forbidden traffic-ridden streets and gives her a swat on the bottom,
this is considered by some to be an appropriate method (Or perhaps
spanking is not considered acceptable any longer?) of correction
because it should create within the child an equation of "If you do this,
it equals this [i.e., pain]." If the child thinks instead, "My mother
hurting me equals my mother hating me," then, for this child, this
correction has not created the desired results.

In my life, I have three specific things I have feared about God:
When I suffer, 1. God is punishing me because He does not truly love
me; 2. God caused this to happen; 3. God doesn't care what happens to
me.

Let's look at each of these, one at a time for the next three days:
The first may be corrected with the following statement: 1. God *allows*
things to occur in my life that He knows will ultimately teach me and
help me mature because He loves me.

When one of my friends was terminally ill, her greatest fear was
that she had done something to deserve it and that God was punishing

her. Her *inner* healing came when she reached a place of knowing in her spirit that God was not punishing her. Because of her illness we often prayed together and had marvelous visitations by the Holy Spirit. So even this illness, as we affirmed our love for the Lord in the midst of it, became the transforming trial that God used to glorify Himself and comfort and teach us.

> *And we know that all things work together for good to those who love God, to those who are the called according to His purpose.* Romans 8:28 (NKJV)

Lord, help us not to read lies about you into life's suffering, but rather help us to affirm our love for you in the midst of the suffering, that you may make even the darkest of times work toward good and bring into each of life's distresses your healing light. Amen.

May 8

Lies vs. Truth — Part 2
Fiery Trials

The second lie some of us are tempted to believe is, "God caused this trial to happen to me." Whereas, God is in charge of the universe, we must remember that the world is in a fallen state. The consequence of sin is a fallen world in which we find evil, suffering and sorrow. As human beings we will automatically partake of the results, for we are still in human bodies living in a world of sin. Ultimately the fact that there is suffering can be blamed on God only in the sense that He allowed freedom of choice in the world. The wills of human beings have made and continue to make sinful choices. However, the trials that come to us are within God's "permissive" will for us. The sufferings that come to us then, should be expected and are temporary experiences that will result in character building and, then, finally, in glory!

> *Beloved, do not think it strange concerning the fiery trial which is to try you, as though some strange thing happened to you; but rejoice to the extent that you partake of Christ's*

sufferings, that when His glory is revealed, you may also be glad with exceeding joy. I Peter 4:12 (NKJV)

But we also glory in tribulations, knowing that tribulation produces perseverance; and perseverance, character; and character, hope. Now hope does not disappoint, because the love of God has been poured out in our hearts by the Holy Spirit who was given to us. Romans 5:3-5 (NKJV)

Lord, help me to endure the difficult things that you allow in my life. I know they are the natural consequences of sin that are to be expected in this fallen world, but help me to receive them as from your hand, knowing, by faith, that I am sharing in your suffering and that I will share in your glory. Amen.

May 9

Lies vs. Truth — Part 3
The Weeping Jesus

The third lie that we are tempted to believe is, "God doesn't care." God not only cares deeply about us, but is aware of everything that we experience. When we suffer, He suffers, for if we invite Him to do so, He will enter into our suffering with us, sharing the burden of it. His sharing our suffering in this way is not only a comfort, but includes God's helping us find meaning in what's happening to us and what it is that He is teaching us. Or, we may discover how it is that He can be glorified through this experience we are enduring for His name's sake such as later being given an opportunity to help someone who has experienced the same kind of distress.

I've had a struggle with depression much of my life, but I have found that Jesus endures with me through these times of darkness. At one time when I would enter into states of depression, I would dream that I was in the hospital. In my last such dream, I got out of my hospital bed and knelt beside it, praying for the Lord to help me. Then I looked up and saw Jesus in the bed where I had been. He had tears streaming down His cheeks and on His face was a look of total understanding and compassion toward me. He spoke to me saying, "Do not think in terms of *'sick'*, but think in terms of *'we.'*" That was the answer for me; I have never needed to dream the hospital dream again, for I know that when I am in that dark state of skewed brain chemistry, "we" are together in it, Jesus and I. Some time later He added, "Your life is a series of deaths and resurrections!" And so it is! This gave me a new way of framing this challenge with which God has entrusted me!

> *But You, O Lord, are a God full of compassion, and gracious, Long-suffering and abundant in mercy and truth.* Psalm 86:15 (NKJV)

Dear Lord, thank you that you come to me in times of my human distress and share my suffering with me, giving me the grace I need to bear it, reminding me that I am not alone. Amen.

May 10

The True Diagnosis

In February of 1998 the Associated Press reported that there was a woman who had been misdiagnosed as having a type of blood cancer. What she really had was a case of malaria, the longest case on record! For seventy years this woman had suffered from something that needed five doses of the medication, chloroquine, in order for her to be completely cured. Now that's a long time to wait for a simple answer!

I have a friend who is working and working on getting her life together. She has tried everything that she can, all the while suffering a condition that she has not been willing to identify; it's called "original sin." But this is unacceptable news to her, as she believes in the pure goodness of human nature, in the reliability of the human heart, and in her all-sufficiency to discover her own path, her own answers, and all to the end of what? — Keeping in control of her own life!

However, only the Holy Spirit can diagnose her true malady for her. All she needs to do is ask: "Reveal to me that I have erred, cannot fix myself, and that I need a Helper." I believe that this prayer is always answered. She has a great fear of having to humble herself. However, we pray for her and we trust that one day she will humble herself before God. When she acknowledges her need for a deliverer (a Savior) she will find that "authentic self" she's been so desperately seeking. The only authentic self is the born-again self, the only heart to be trusted, the new one that the Lord promises to transform, the only path, not a self-guided tour up any and all alluring "mountains," but it is the simplicity of the gospel's message: Follow Jesus. He is the Way.

> *...always learning and never able to come to the knowledge of the truth.* 2 Timothy 3:7 (NKJV)

> *If you confess with your mouth that Jesus is Lord and believe in your heart that God raised him from the dead, you will be saved. For it is by believing in your heart that you are made right with God, and it is by confessing your mouth that you are saved. As the Scriptures tell us, "Anyone who trust in him will never be disgraced.". . . For everyone who calls upon the name of the Lord will be saved.* Romans 10:9-11; 13 (NLT)

Dear Holy Spirit, help us to come to the knowledge of the truth — our need for you to come to us and lift the load of our errors, mistakes and transgressions off of us and to give us your righteousness. Amen.

May 11

Memories of Mama

Following are some of the things that I recall about my mother, pictures that I hold dear to my heart.

- Mama, angry at the teacher who didn't notice I couldn't read in first grade;
- Mama, sitting with me day-after-day showing me how to do it — the phonics way.
- Mama, proudly showing me the childhood scar on her arm where she had been shot while balancing herself along the railroad tracks in Checotah, OK, assailant forever unknown.

- Mama, telling me about her favorite toy, a marble named Lumgigi, that had fallen through the floor boards of her childhood home, never to be retrieved.
- Mama, flaunting before my Dad, that chic black & white check wool jacket that she bought by matching, coin-for-coin, his beer money.
- Mama, secretly sitting at the old pedal Singer, sewing miniature dresses for my doll, Violet, yelling at me for catching her in the act.
- Mama, courageously storming that strange upstairs closet that had windows opening onto the easily-accessible roof, when I reported hearing "someone inside there."
- Mama, magical, choosing produce, showing me that you can tell exactly how much something weighs by simply holding it in your hand, and then proving to me how accurate she was, by using the scales!
- Mama, telling me to go choose my own switch from the Pepper tree in the back yard.
- Mama, making me take back to our 90-year-old neighbor, Mr. Post, the red pyracantha berries that I had stolen.
- Mama, lighting the underside of the bed on fire with a match while looking for a jar of Mentholatum™, and then saying in the calmest voice in which I ever heard her speak, "Dad, the bed's on fire."
- Mama, withering away, learning to lose her memory with a sad mixture of fear and acceptance, proclaiming to Don with indignity, "Yes, of course I know who that is. It's Pat."
- And sweet, shy Mama, in her eighties, learning for the first time how to speak the words, repeating after me, "I love you too."
- Mama, after fading away forever in 1984, in what perhaps was only a strange dream out of the Eternal Now, coming back to me to tell me what she had always wanted to say on her own without my prompting: "I want you to know that I always loved you." She spoke the words with depth and clarity as we embraced on a light-filled staircase suspended between Heaven and Earth.

Yes, Mama, I know that now. I know you loved me. I know.

...Forsake not the law of thy mother. Proverbs 1:8 (NKJV)

Dear Lord, I thank you for my mother. Thank you for giving her to me. Though she was not perfect, she was the perfect mother for me. Help those who have missed having a mother with a true mother's heart. Amen.

May 12

Getting Acquainted with Betrayal

It happened in an insurance office. I was delivering inter-office mail when I overheard the young woman who had trained me for my new job talking to our supervisor. She was telling him something about me that I had confided in her. I was absolutely shocked! I was being betrayed, a new experience for me! *What should I do, Lord?* I found myself walking right into the office, looking at him and then at her and saying, "You should be more careful about how loudly you are speaking if you don't want to be overheard." Both of them looked stunned. I walked away.

Where did I get such nerve? And it didn't stop there, this new found bravado; I almost ran after her when she came out of his office. Again, how did I get so brave? I confronted her, "We need to talk," I said, "I feel you betrayed a confidence." "Oh, no, I didn't tell him what you said," she lied to my face, smiling and looking me straight in the eye.

Well, what lesson did I learn? I learned that there are such people in the world, people who can lie, people without a conscience, people who manipulate and distort the truth to their own ends and who don't care who they hurt. Of course, I didn't want to know about such people, at least not first hand, but it was an important thing to learn. In his book, *Clergy Killers*, G. Lloyd Rediger, tells us that we have to face the facts with "street smarts" in the ministry. On the streets, he says, "Believe someone wants to kill you." For the clergy person, the needed knowledge is: "Believe that it is possible for someone to want to destroy you." Not a happy thought, is it? But when I had this experience in this office, I wondered why God had put me in that place, and I felt an answer in my heart: It was because when Don entered the ministry, we were going to meet some people like this and we needed to know that in order to be prepared. And that was the way it happened.

Even my best friend, the one I trusted completely, the one who shared my food, has turned against me. Psalm 41:9 (NLT)

Lord God, we ask that you keep us from being the friend that betrays another, and we ask that you help us, when we are betrayed, not to return this heart-breaking experience by getting even. We need you to give us the strength and will and power to forgive our enemies and go on with what you have called us to do. Amen.

May 13

More About Aunt Flossie

Dear Aunt Flossie! She was totally enamored with the pianist, Liberace, who had a TV program in the 50s. When he opened his show with *Liebestraum* by Listz, one of her favorite compositions, she would exclaim, "Just listen to that!" She would enjoy each week's show as though it were the first she'd ever seen. When he would smile and wink, it was for her and her alone, in this special private audience with this cheerful, delightful pianist. "Did you see that?" she would exclaim, "He's winking at me!" There was something so child-like, so filled with wonder as she watched enthralled.

Well, with Aunt Flossie, yes, it was a fantasy, but you and I have our own private audience with Someone more than special. It is with the Creator of the universe, with a God who has chosen to make us His friends! Yes, any time, He is there, waiting, longing for our attention to turn to Him, with joy, with thanksgiving, in need of help, or simply in want of His company. There is no blame when we are slow at coming, or late in turning to Him. There is no sarcastic, "Well-it's-about-time" expression on His face. Because He wants a relationship with us, to be one with us, we can be sure that whenever we come, he welcomes us. Isn't that a lovely and comforting thing to know?

> *I in them, and You in Me; that they may be made perfect in one, and that the world may know that You have sent Me, and have loved them as You have loved Me.* John 17:23 (NKJV)

Dear Father, we get so busy we do forget to turn to you, but we want to think of you often. Please help us to remember you many times throughout the day. Amen.

May 14

More About Grandma

My grandmother, Jessie Edwards, was strong and moral in character, having known the Lord for many, many years before I came along. Her life was difficult and filled with losses but she never complained. There was never an ounce of self-pity. She simply told of her experiences of hardship as "just the way life is" in her practical, down-to-earth manner. She came into my life when I was still a baby. I now know that the Lord gave her to me because she was able to give me the love that others around me could not. After she died, I found a little photo of myself as a baby and underneath in her handwriting was written, "Precious Patty." That was me. To her I was precious.

To God, even more, each of us is uniquely precious; we are His creation, His very own. I find comfort in that. I hope you do too.

> *But let my life now be precious in your sight.* 2 Kings 1:14 b (NKJV)

Lord, Help me to know that I am of great value to you. Amen.

May 15

Seeking for God

I felt lonely and sad that evening. Then I heard a bird, so close that I had to investigate. It was a tiny house swallow sitting on the ledge of the bathroom window. Our screens block the sun as well as the view through the window into the house, so I could get to within an inch of that little visitor without her even noticing me. I found God's message of consolation in the song of that bird that morning.

Do you imagine, dear reader, that God doesn't bother with such minutiae? Is He too busy? Is He too great? Or is it possible that He really is omniscient? — That He really does care about you and me individually and that the hairs on our head really are numbered? It is true!

Oh, I want to live my life looking for good in every day, looking for God in every day, believing that He wants to touch me in some way! In this book, I've often pointed out how God speaks to me in such simple ways, how He gets through in one way or another. One of the things I want for you, dear reader, is for you to find Him every day. He is everywhere. He is everywhen. And I promise that if you look for Him from your heart, you will find Him.

Then when you call upon me and come and pray to me, I will hear you. When you search for me, you will find me; if you seek me with all your heart. Jeremiah 29:12, 13 (NRSVA)

Gracious God, you speak to us, come to us, and touch us in many ways every day. Open our spiritual eyes so that we will see you this day and every day. Amen.

May 16

The Changing Speed of Time

It was my dear friend, Connie, who clued me in. There is a conspiracy going on in the cosmos. The earth is spinning faster and faster on its axis with all the clocks on earth joining in. We are left with the appearance of a 24-hour day, but what we actually have is a 20-hour day, or perhaps even less. Time is becoming compressed. This explains to us why we don't have the time we used to in order to accomplish what we once had been able to. Of course, some skeptics have suggested that we are moving slower as we get older! Absurd! After all, we have our own subjective experience that says it all, and in fewer words than ever before: Time is fickle!

Well, even so, we each of us have only so many days. When I went through a period of experiencing panic attacks, I kept feeling that the next moment I was going to die. The path out of this illusion was not easy and the spiritual part of the solution was two-fold. One was a dream that God gave me. In it I dreamed that I died, but what I found was that death is really just a birth from the womb of the earth, into a free and beautiful new heavenly life where loving beings will welcome me. The second thing that helped me was to remind myself that all my days are numbered. The Lord already knows how many; He has chosen not to burden us with the date of our death. He has that knowledge in His mind and hands and so I reminded myself that even if I were to die the next moment, as I feared I was going to, it could only happen if God chose it to happen. Even if the doctors say I'm "terminal" — what else is new? So are we all. No, it's up to God. He will, no matter who says what, keep us, body and soul, together, until it's time for us to leave, and when we do, it's OK because it's His timing, not ours.

My times are in Your hand. Psalm 31:15 (NKJV)

Dear Lord, I acknowledge that you are the keeper of my time clock. Every day is known to you. I give myself totally into your care, knowing that you will take my spirit from my body when it is according to your perfect will, and not one second sooner. Amen.

May 17

The Broken Branch

It was time for the trees in our yard to be trimmed. The workers had misunderstood; they thought they were to cut down the Lemon tree. I yelled at them, catching them just in time, but they had already cut one of the branches half way off. I told them to just leave it. In the 18 years that followed until the time we moved from that home in South Pasadena, the branch that hung there limply was still giving fruit just as plump and beautiful as the rest of the tree! I liked to look out a window and see that branch, because it never failed to remind me of myself. I've often felt like a broken branch, suffering things that I experienced as challenges but true difficulties none the less. Yet if that old broken branch could bear lemons, then I too could bear fruit for the Lord! And I've believed it, and my friends tell me it's true. So, if you feel "broken" in some way, please don't give up and allow yourself to feel "useless." If the Lord could use me, He can use you too!

The branch of my planting, the work of My hands, That I may be glorified. Isaiah 60:21b (NKJV)

Heavenly Father, thank you that you can use even those of us who are broken in some way, allowing us to bless others and glorify you. Amen.

May 18

Emotions Expressed

In writing workshops we are told: "Show! Don't tell." In other words instead of saying, "Janine was frightened" the writer should say, "Janine's pulse raced. She watched as her trembling hand slowly reached out to turn the knob on the door..." You get the picture? That's the point. How are emotions expressed in the Bible? Let's take some examples.

- Nehemiah when he heard that the wall of Jerusalem was broken down and its gates burned: "...when I heard these words...I sat down and wept, and mourned for many days." Nehemiah 1:3, 4
- When God did not respect Cain's offering: "...Cain was angry and his countenance fell." Genesis 1:5
- When Jacob took the blessing that Isaac meant for Esau, "And Esau lifted up his voice and wept." Genesis 27:39
- Job in the midst of his great suffering, calls out, "I have sewn sackcloth over my skin, And laid my head in the dust. My face is flushed from weeping. And on my eyelids is the shadow of death..." Job 16:15, 16.

But of all those who express emotion in the Scripture, almost no one can compare to David, who poured out his heart time and time again, all of his emotions spilling out toward the God he loved, "O My God, I cry in the daytime, but you do not hear; and in the night season, and am not silent..." (Psalm 22:2, NKJV) is but one example. It's good for us to see how David trusted God with everything in his heart; he was utterly authentic. Often when we are unable to express what we are feeling, we can find a Psalm that will give us the words we need in order to express the depths of our soul.

Out of the depths, I have cried to You, O Lord; Lord, hear my voice! Psalm 130:1, 2a (NKJV)

Lord God, thank you for providing us with the wonderful words of David, your servant, to help us to express what we feel whether praise or fear, pleas or thanksgiving. Amen.

May 19

The Mystery Gift

It came from an exclusive Beverly Hills shop, one I was familiar with only by name. It was a small package, wrapped in black and red tissue paper. There was no card. Inside was a small bag made of a colorful fabric, mostly red and white in a delicate paisley design. I used it and treasured it for years. I asked friends who I suspected might have sent it but all denied, quite convincingly, that they had not been the secret giver of this special little gift. So, sometimes even now, I wonder about who could have sent it to me. A secret admirer? Of course! Someone had to have gone to the trouble, someone who knew that I love the color red and the classic paisley pattern — the perfect little gift, with no thanks expected, just a generous gesture, and one I will never forget.

But when you do a charitable deed, do not let your left hand know what your right hand is doing, that your charitable deed may be in secret; and your Father who sees in secret will Himself reward you openly. Matthew 6:3, 4 (NKJV)

Lord, help me to be like you this gift giver, offering a little present here and there, without looking for praise or thanks. Amen.

May 20

Realistic Goals

The Competition

He won! He didn't think he could!
Not so for another, so sure he would.
Though days were the climb, only seconds the summit.
Yet after the goals' gained, the spirits can plummet.
But — if the climb's the better part of the test
Then, in just persevering, we aim for the best!
From hill top to hill top or valley between,
May in both I learn to be bright and serene.

I wrote this poem after watching a competitive race on TV. As you might have guessed, the runner favored to win, lost, and one not expected to, won! As I was rewriting this devotional, believe it or not, the same thing happened in a horserace on TV. On November 6, 2010, a horse named Zenyatta was racing the last race of her life in the Breeders' Cup Classic. She had raced 19 races and never lost, but this one was on dirt and not synthetic turf, and she was not used to having the dirt fly up at her. She was dead last for most of the race, but got all the way up to the front just in the last few seconds. However, though she was favored to win, she came in second. I felt sad for her and for the jockey. Did she know she lost? Did she compare herself to the winner? I think she did the best she could, stretched herself to the limit. So, in a way, she won!

In my own life, sometimes I feel like a winner; sometimes I feel like a loser. I aim too high and disappoint myself. Or I don't give it my best, and feel I've failed in my own eyes and failed the Lord. Or I "win" and I feel too proud. But what does the Lord want me to win? Success? Money? Prestige? For me, the answer has been "no!" However, my new goal is to aim at what the Lord has shown me to do for each day, one day at a time for the days that I have left, however few or many they may be! He will lead the way. I will follow. After all, He's already won the race.

> *...let us run with endurance the race that is set before us, looking unto Jesus, the author and finisher of our faith, who for the joy that was set before Him endured the cross, despising the shame, and has sat down at the right hand of the throne of God.* Hebrews 12:2 (NKJV)

Lord, help me to run only the race that you have set before me to run. And help me press on and to not to give up, knowing that you have gone before me. Amen.

May 21

God's Help in the Little Things

Has God ever helped you find something? I shared before (March 28) how the Lord showed me where to find the sapphire stone I had lost. I'm certain He wants to help us in little ways like this. Such help can come in many ways — knowledge that is from a divine source.

Another time (the first time) I experienced this was when I was taking care of Grandma when she was in her eighties and, as we said in those days, "senile." Basically what that meant was that her short-term memory was gone. Every day I would get her up and do her hair for her, brushing out the thinning silver strands and then placing it in a tiny bun on the top of her head with hairpins. One morning as I prepared to fix her hair, I looked around and could not find the hairpins anywhere! I was terribly annoyed and asked Grandma, "All right, you hid the hairpins, didn't you? Where did you put them?" She didn't know what I was talking about of course. "Oh Lord" I sighed, not even a prayer, just a lament toward Heaven. But at this point, something astonishing happened: I "saw" where the hairpins were. They appeared as a little picture in my mind's eye. I could have passed this up as just my imagination, but something told me to check it out. I reached in between the mattress and the bed springs of her bed in a particular spot, and there they were — every one of them! I fixed her hair in no time, but it was only later that I stopped to be amazed at this, the omniscience of God, and His willingness to share what He knew with a frustrated granddaughter!

Next time you lose something, pause for a moment and sigh a prayer toward God. He won't always help in this way but sometimes He just might! And one more thing — even if you never find the lost thing, know that God is the seeker and finder of lost souls, which are far most precious in His sight.

I will search for the lost, bring back those that strayed away, put bandages on those that were hurt, and make the weak strong. Ezekiel 34:16 (NCV)

Kind Shepherd, you are the one from whom nothing and from whom *no one* is hidden. Thank you for sometimes helping us find the things that are lost; but thank you far more for seeking out, finding, binding up wounds and healing lost souls. Amen.

May 22

Great Aunt Flossie's Baby Doll

One day Daddy brought my (great) Aunt Flossie a doll from his antique store. It was wearing an old, faded pink dress, and trimmed with what had once been white lace. The left side of her head was smashed in from some near fatal blow but it was partially covered with a tangled brown wig. Aunt Flossie loved that doll. It kept her company. She could talk to it or would comment, "Look at that poor, dear child. She has no family, you know," or she might whisper, "Poor little thing; she's an orphan you see."

However, when her daughter, Florence, traveled from New York to California to visit her mother, she got one look at that doll and was thoroughly disgusted. She immediately went out and bought her mother an elegant doll, dressed in pink taffeta, her head covered in blond curls, a perfect baby girl. Florence whisked away the pathetic child doll and, and with a self-righteous flourish, replaced her. "There, Mother! Here's a lovely new doll for you." But did Aunt Flossie appreciate this new and pristine version? Not one bit! She turned up her nose and commented icily, "Look at her! She's so spoiled. She really thinks she's something," and she refused to pay any attention to her after that first encounter.

Have you ever met people like Aunt Flossie's daughter, well meaning but arrogant fix-you-upper types? They rush into our lives, sure that they know exactly what we need to do to be healed, to be comforted or to be just, well, different! They are full of simplistic answers and maybe even scripture verses used like ammunition! Yet they fail in some fundamental way, because they fail to sit down and see who we really are, and what we really need! How much more welcome are friends who sit alongside and love us by their caring touch and loving silence! That's the kind of friend I want and that's the kind of friend I want to be.

Like one who takes away a garment in cold weather, And like vinegar on soda, Is one who sings songs to a heavy heart.
Proverbs 25:20 (NKJV)

Lord, help me forgive those who haven't yet learned to listen to your Spirit before offering help, and teach me to learn how to be a sensitive helper to those in need. Amen.

May 23

Adoring Eyes

Lucy (our dog) looks up at Don with a completely adoring expression in her soft brown eyes. He thinks, *Oh, she just loves me so much; how sweet.* Then he notices that her eyes are on the plate in his lap. She smells his chicken dinner and is waiting for a little tidbit. He is deflated, but then laughs at himself and at her!

Now isn't that the way we sometimes are with God? We look at Him adoringly, all the while hoping for some tidbit. We're not really adoring Him, but waiting to see what we can get. We don't fool God any more than Lucy fools Don!

I usually come to God wanting something, but there are a few occasions when I just want to be with Him, and when that's my goal, everything else seems to fall into place. I feel renewed and refreshed and ready for whatever the day brings.

Those who wait upon the Lord shall renew their strength; They shall mount up with wings like eagles, They shall run and not be weary, They shall walk and not faint. Isaiah 40:31 (NKJV)

Dear Father, we look to you in this quiet moment. We wait upon you with our inner eyes turned toward you. Right now we want nothing more, nothing less, than to be in your presence and to know you more deeply. Amen.

May 24

The Best Sermon

The father and son were neither one listening to the minister as he elegantly preached away from the high pulpit in the beautiful historic church. No, they were doing something far more important. The boy, less than a year old, was sitting on his father's lap and facing him. He smiled and looked into his father's eyes. The father returned that look with an adoring gaze of his own. This is what some would call "bonding." I believe it is a picture of what Jesus was speaking about when He said, "I and my Father are one." This silent metaphor of the Father's love was the sermon I took home with me that day, not the one preached from the pulpit. I will never forget the look of love and trust in the eyes of both father and child. That is what I long to experience more of with my Heavenly Father; don't you?

> *Holy Father keep through Your name those whom You have given Me, that they may be one as We are.* [Jesus' words] John 17:11 (NKJV)

Heavenly Father, I want to understand more about how I can reach out and touch you like that little boy touched the face of his father. I want to know in my heart that we are one. Amen.

May 25

The Attentive Father

Don and I walked along the Hermosa Beach pier. It was a cool day. The sky was filled with a magical mixture of luminescent white and deep gray clouds. The ocean waves roared and came crashing onto the shore, higher than we'd ever seen them before; they were breathtaking. Not one surfer dared to take them on. We could even glimpse an undertow eddy as we looked down into the sea.

Then along came a father and his son. The boy, about two years old, jogged in front of his father. He kept up the exact same pace for yards and yards toward the end of the pier. When we met up with them there, the father was showing the son a small stingray that a fisherman had left on the pier. It was still alive. The father gently lifted the creature up and tossed it back into the water. We all watched as the sea creature found its way into the depths where it was safe in its own realm once more. The boy and dad then made their way back to shore and the boy took up that same steady gate, again ahead of his Dad.

It was a picture of us in so many ways, going ahead some time, but had the father stopped, the boy would have too! He was on an invisible "leash." The tie between the father and son was almost palpable. The way the dad gave his son a lesson in kindness toward another living creature was rich with lessons of the preciousness of life. All this was a priceless gift to us as we watched a little bit of an ordinary day's drama in the life of a good father and a treasured son.

As for me, you uphold me in my integrity, and set me before your face forever. Psalm 41:12 (NKJV)

Lord, I believe that you keep me, and each of us, before your face forever, just like that little boy was constantly in the sight of his father. We have great need of a loving parent, watching over us at all times, for even though we are "grown-ups" there is still within each of us, a child who needs you every moment of every day. Amen.

May 26

A Child's Whisper

The little girl with curly dark hair and deep brown eyes looked adoringly at her Mother. "Mom, I need a hug," she said and her chubby little arms reached up toward her mommy. Her mom reached down and they embraced each other. I heard the child whisper into her mother's ear, "You are my very best friend."

What a wonderful picture that is of our Mother-God, El-Shaddai, who nourishes and blesses with abundance, the one who nurtures, the "many-breasted" one. I believe that if we are able to reach up to this Mother-God in our souls, El-Shaddai will reach down and embrace us in a spiritual hug. We of the Protestant profession often miss the good mother image that the Catholic Church offers, so we need to make an effort to find an image of God as one who holds all the finest feminine qualities, as well as the finest masculine qualities. After all, He made us all in His image.

> *By the God of your father who will help you, And by the Almighty who will bless you With blessings of heaven above, Blessings of the deep that lies beneath, Blessings of the breasts and of the womb.* Genesis 49:28 (NKJV)

Dear El-Shaddai, you hold within you all that we need in a parent, all of the qualities of both Mother-God and Father-God. Help us to receive you as both in our lives today and every day. Amen.

May 27

A Visitation

When I was a child my mother, in hushed tones, told me this story. I have attempted to recall her words as nearly as I can.

> *I want to tell you something that happened to me before you were born. I had to have an operation; an ovary needed to be removed. After my surgery, I did not do well. The doctors called my mother and other family members and told them that they should come and say good-bye to me because I was dying. I was in a Catholic hospital and I knew the nuns who came by to visit me were praying for me. After that phone call was made, I lay in my bed, all alone in my room, when all of a sudden I looked up and I saw Jesus standing at the foot of my bed. His arms were outstretched toward me, like this.* [She held her arms out in front of her to show me, and as she did, her expression changed; there was a look of love and joy and peace on

her face, as she was reflecting to me what Jesus looked like to her at that precious meeting.] *From that moment on I rallied. By the time my family members arrived I was sitting up in bed. Everyone, including the doctors, was shocked, so I told them about my Visitor, that Jesus had come to heal me.*

I was quiet after she told me this story. I thought about Jesus and how wonderful a thing it was that He had come to my mother. I knew that if He had not come, I would not have been born, for she would not have lived. Jesus came and reached out His arms to her and saved her life. My mother spoke of this only once. On one occasion I did ask her about it, but she was reticent to repeat it. It was a sacred memory, but I share it because I know my mother would not mind my telling her most wonderful secret with you, my dear readers.

Jesus immediately reached out his hand and caught him... Matthew 14:31a (NRSVA)

Lord, how often you reach out to us in compassion and love to catch us in so many different ways. Help us to see you in our hearts, even if we cannot see you as real and solidly as my mother did in that hospital on that day long ago. Amen.

May 28

Daddy's Beer, Mama's Coat and Sweet Revenge

Mom was utterly disgusted with Dad's love for beer. She finally hit upon a scheme to make a point. She told him, "Go ahead and drink your beer, but whatever you spend on beer, I'm going to put an equal amount of money into a jar." She continued to do this until she had enough money to go to one of the best department stores in town in that day (the 50s), The Broadway Pasadena, and buy a stylish black and white check mid-length pure wool coat. She looked smashing in it and wow! — Did she ever flaunt that! I don't think it made much difference to Daddy; he kept drinking that beer. But to her it was sweet revenge and she proved her point, and it made his beer drinking easier for her to bear.

I love this story about Mama because it displays her spunkiness of spirit. We usually can't change the behavior of those around us, but we can change our attitude and this coat spelled "attitude" in capital letters.

Is there something you can't change, but about which you can change your attitude? I've often misunderstood this guideline about attitude change. I thought I had to change myself, my instincts, my likes, my innate qualities. But now I don't believe that is what this means. When we lived the desert it was not my favorite place to be, but I learned to change my attitude. I accepted it! I, with God's help, came to a place of contentment. I now believe that when we start with a simple willingness to change, we will receive the supernatural help we need to make that inner transformation in our hearts.

...I have learned in whatever state I am, to be content....I can do all things through Christ who strengthens me. Philippians 4:11 & 13 (NKJV)

Dear Lord, I find that life is full of things that are difficult. Circumstances are not, in many ways, what I would desire, but I ask for your help to change my attitude from one of "put-upon" to one of gratitude and acceptance. Amen.

May 29

Stuck

There's a story I've heard about a little boy who was asked for instructions about how to get to "here from there." Perhaps it was to the Pasadena City Hall from his elementary school. He thought about it but all he could reply was, "You can't get there from here."

I've had that feeling. I'm referring to self-pity. We can't get out of that trap unless we give up the idea that someone else will come to help us. For this kind of self-induced hell, there is no one who can come into that place and rescue us, not until we ourselves reach out. Getting out is a choice that only we can make: I *will* reach out and give, not just take.

I will reach out and praise God, not pout. I will choose to be thankful, not resentful. I will choose to love and bless my enemies, not seek revenge. I will ask God to forgive me for the sin of self-pity and ask Him to help me have courage to go on. So, in the world of spiritual reality, you and I *can* get there from here!

> *Bring my soul out of prison, That I may praise Your name.*
> Psalm 142:7 (NKJV)

Holy Spirit, guard me against going inward into my own dark world and imprisoning myself. Remind me that I have a choice and that I can reach out to You and to others and receive the help I need. Amen.

May 30

Trapped

The little boy by the lakeside was being attacked by a Muscovy duck, and it was not much of a match! However, as we approached, we found out why: the boy had just happened to catch two of her new born chicks in his net while he was fishing (or so he said!). I sat down on the grass at the water's edge and together we worked to release them. We plopped them back in the water and they took off after the mother who waited off shore with the rest of her brood.

As I walked away, I felt good, like a kind of savior to the little ducklings. I thought about Jesus, the one who comes to pluck us out of traps we find ourselves in — sometimes of our own doing and other times because we are victims.

Some years ago, I found myself caught in a trap of fear and shame over having been sexually abused at a young age, but in His compassion, Jesus provided powerful intercessors who came to my aid. Jesus, through their prayers, lifted me up out of that web of self-hatred and the curse of a shattered personality. They prayed regularly for me over a period of many months.

Later I was privileged on several occasions to pray inner healing prayers for those who had suffered similarly. Once we are healed and made whole in a certain area where we have been wounded, we can then turn around and become instrumental in the healing of someone else. In whatever way we have been healed by God, we can have faith for the same healing of another.

> *He [Jesus] said, 'Go home to your family and tell them how much the Lord has done for you and how he has had mercy on you.'* (Mark 5:19 NCV)

Compassionate Lord God, I am so deeply and eternally grateful to you for reaching out and touching me in the places where I have been most wounded. I ask you now, in Jesus name, to reach out and touch those who are reading this book, who are hurting, having been victimized and wounded, and who need to know that you are a compassionate Savior. May they be open to your healing from whatever source you may send it. Amen.

May 31

Buildings of Earth, Buildings of Flesh

My favorite employer through a lifetime of office work is Whitney R. Smith, FAIA. He was a South Pasadena architect for many years, first with Smith and Williams, and then later on his own. I spent 17 years as his office manager. It was the best job I ever had — what a privilege it was working for a gifted architect. Being there taught me much, including learning to look at the world around me. Before that, I rarely paid attention to buildings. I was proud of his design of the Entrance Complex at the Huntington Library and Botanical Gardens in San Marino, the Tea House at Descanso Gardens in La Canada/Flintridge, the marvelous office building at 1414 Fair Oaks Avenue as well as many more, though lesser known, residences and other structures.

After starting this job, I found great pleasure at looking at my environment and appreciating the many beautiful structures that enhance my world! Buildings of great beauty are proudly and carefully cared for and national and local historical preservation societies guarantee that older buildings of beauty are preserved for future generations.

In the Old Testament, King David longed to build a house for God, but it was his son, Solomon, who finally built that marvelous structure. But we find in the New Testament, that the human body is called the "temple" of the Holy Spirit! These "temples" are, as the Psalmist says, "fearfully and wonderfully made." We are to take as much care of these physical forms entrusted to us, as historical preservation societies take care of extraordinary buildings. In other words: Preserve your body!

Don't you know that you yourselves are God's temple and that God's Spirit lives in you? 1 Corinthians 3:16 (NIV)

Lord, help us to take watchful care of the bodies that transport around our spirits as well as your Spirit in the world, so that our lives upon the Earth will be extended. Amen.

JUNE

June 1

The Outcasts of Ghana Witch Villages

In 1997 the Associated Press reported that for some women in Ghana (in Western Africa) the only safe refuge is in "witch villages." These are places where those who are accused of witchcraft might find asylum. Of course, this witchcraft cannot be proven, but when a baby dies, or there is illness or impotence, there has to be someone to blame and it is always a woman, usually an older woman, who is pointed out as the guilty party; she is blamed for the curse that caused the death or illness. These so-called witches may not even know what it is that they are supposed to have done. However, eventually, in the witch village they come to believe that they probably are witches and guilty of what they have been accused of.

When I read about this, my heart was breaking, but it is not just my heart, it is the heart of God that breaks over such injustice. How He would desire to see these women free — not just from these prison-like villages from which they cannot escape, but from the belief in lies and superstitions that send them there in the first place!

The Lord gives freedom to the prisoners. Psalm 146:7 (NKJV)

Lord, I pray for those everywhere who are imprisoned unjustly. May they be encouraged. May they find justice. May they find that there hope is in You. May they be comforted. Send angels, we ask, human or divine, to deliver them. Amen.

June 2

Supernatural Aromas

Have you ever smelled something that was not really there? It has happened to me three times. Once as I was praying for a lovely lady I know, I smelled cinnamon. I told her about it and reminded her of the verse, 2:13 Corinthians, about the fragrance of the knowledge of the Lord.

Another time, just after my sister died, I came home to find the entire house filled with the scent of fresh-cut flowers. But there were no flowers, no physical ones, that is. Did God allow my sister to leave me this gesture of love, an invisible bouquet, as a sweet good-bye?

But, the strangest experience of supernatural aromas was at a prayer meeting. I smelled three things, one after another. First, there was the sweet fragrance of fresh cut flowers, though there were none in the house (I know because I checked). This was followed by the odor of rich earth. Next, however, was the acrid odor of what could only be called the smell of death. I said "Lord, what does this mean?" I heard words from God that gave me a warning. Immediately following this, I was confronted with the spirit of legalism in a woman who had come to the meeting! These words that God spoke to me helped me cope with some comments she made to me that came almost in the form of a curse. I was able to "consider the source" because I was prepared with His warning:

> ...*the letter kills but the Spirit gives life.* 2 Corinthians 3:16 (NKJV)

Dear God, help us to overcome the spirit of legalism and receive the Spirit that gives life. Amen.

June 3

A Soft Word

My mother spent her last years in a convalescent hospital in Altadena, California. As I visited her one day, I was presented with an opportunity that I had not anticipated. When I arrived she was already in a wheel chair in her room. After our greeting I wheeled her outside and around the building, taking about 15 minutes to do so. On the way back to the front door, an imposing, angry woman confronted me. She came toward me yelling, "What do you mean by taking her away? She's my responsibility and I didn't know where she was!" I was about to answer in like manner, when I heard clearly in my spirit some words from scripture. Those words made me change my tack. I realized at this point that the angry woman must be my mother's new nurse, and I said, "Oh, of course. How thoughtless of me. I'm so sorry." She yelled once again, a little less vociferously, and I again answered with compliance. It worked. She realized I heard her and that I wouldn't do that again (and I didn't!) and she walked away with a satisfied huff.

Never did my mother have someone look after her more carefully than did Georgiana. She was there for Mama for the last two years of her life, and I was ever grateful for her. I treated her to lunch in appreciation once a year on her birthday for many years following my mother's death. But had I not listened to that little voice that reminded me of the scripture verse, things could have turned out very differently. And what were those words? Perhaps you've already guessed. They were simply:

A soft answer turns away wrath. Proverbs 15:1 (NKJV)

Lord, thank you for bringing to our minds just the right Scripture verse at just the right time. Amen.

June 4

Surprise Visits from Memories

Sometimes I have "visiting" memories that come unbidden to surprise and delight me. At this point in my life, these are almost always of something beautiful I've experienced in the past. It might be the memory of the way the sunlight glimmered on the ocean at Hermosa Beach, California on a certain fall day in October 1974. It might be the memory of the fireflies flitting across the damp lawn at St. John's College in Annapolis, Maryland in the summer of '95. It might be the recollection of the scent of the wild flowers as I opened the window of my little attic room one summer morning on the island of Gotland off the coast of Sweden. It might be the sound of my boys, ages three and five, giggling together over a silly secret.

Such times seem magical — as though one is being transported back to sweet and blessed moments, moments that were given to me, now mine, never lost. It is as though the Lord had stimulated a place in my brain where these sense memories are stored, springing them into my consciousness to give me encouragement, just when needed. As these lovely gifts come back to me, it's like sunshine through the trees, or moonlight on the water, or a gentle breeze at the seashore — refreshing, enchanting, and healing.

> *Like cold water to a weary soul, So is good news from a far country.* Proverbs 25:25 (NKJV)

Lord, thank you for causing the good memories I've stored away in the "far country" of my mind to spring forth at times like cool water when I need them most. Amen.

June 5

Prayer for the Little Things

I often go to thrift shops or re-sale shops to purchase my clothes. This is something my mother taught me years ago. What I've also learned is to ask the Lord to come along with me when I go shopping. Yes, I really mean this. I have often been in need of a particular item, prayed about it, felt led to go to a certain place, and there have found just what was needed, hanging on the rack, waiting for me to discover it.

My friend, Birgitta, recently called and left an intriguing message for me. "I had a wonderful answer to prayer and I want to share it with you." I called her as soon as I had a chance. This is what she shared, in her own words:

"I'm going to be singing in a production of the Messiah this coming weekend and just last weekend, the conductor told us that we are going to have to wear long black evening wear. I didn't have anything I could use. I knew all I could spend was $30, and I checked all the shops in Los Alamos but found nothing here. As the performance date approached, I felt increasingly nervous about it. Then yesterday, three days before the performance, I had an appointment in Santa Fe. On my way there I suddenly remembered that I could ask God to help me and I prayed in desperation for Him to 'lead me to the dress,' reminding Him I only had $30."

"After the appointment, I realized I was very close to a big shopping mall and I found myself headed for the most exclusive shop in Santa Fe. The thought came to me that I couldn't possibly find anything that inexpensive there, but still felt led to go there. I walked directly up to the sales lady in the dress section and, feeling a bit foolish, I told her what I needed and what I could spend. She measured me with her eyes and immediately walked over to a rack and picked out a long black two-piece, beaded silk gown. I was astonished! It was exquisite, but could I get into it? I tried it on and it was a perfect fit. "How," I asked, "can you afford to sell it for so little?" The sales lady said that it was too broad in the shoulders and too narrow in the hips for everyone else that had tried it on! It had been reduced several times. I was thrilled. It was just what I needed and more than I had expected. Now isn't that a wonderful answer to prayer?"

Well, there you are — a great example of the kind of help the Lord will give us if we ask Him. He wants us to have what we need and what we need to wear is part of that provision.

Her clothing is fine linen and purple. Proverbs 31:22b (NKJV)

Lord, next time I need to go shopping, come with me. Guide my steps. Give me a good sense of what is tasteful and appropriate and help me to spend my money wisely. Amen.

June 6

Joyful Rats

Did you hear about the giggling rats? In May of 1998, the Associated Press reported that Researchers at Bowling Green State University have been tickling rats and listening to them laugh by the use of a sophisticated instrument that registers high-pitched sounds humans can't hear. I laughed out loud when I read this. Even rats are playful!

I appreciate that God has put into rodents the ability to have such fun. Sometimes my "fun" capacity generator seems to be malfunctioning; I have a hard time having fun. Recently a friend asked me, "What do you do for fun?" I had this awful sinking feeling. I couldn't think of anything. *What's wrong with me? Have I had forgotten how? Or perhaps I have never learned?* Anyway, I decided to go about seriously pursuing this endeavor and didn't catch on for months that this *serious pursuit* is the opposite of what fun is all about.

Pursuing fun is not a pastime that can bring us happiness. So what should I do? Should! Yipes! I couldn't get away from trying. I've heard that happiness is that which we achieve because of what happens to us and that joy is what we can receive from God in spite of what happens to us. So, from here on out, I have decided not to *try* to have fun. If it happens to me, great! So I'll laugh when I laugh and cry when I cry and, and in the midst of life, I can have peace and know that God loves me in and through it all, even though the pursuit of happiness is not my priority.

Rejoice with those who rejoice, and weep with those who weep. Romans 12:15 (NKJV)

Lord, I know that you had a joyful life as well as a sorrowful life while you lived on the earth, and you accepted each experience that came to you. Help me to just be me and let others be themselves and let You be You. Amen.

June 7

When Wishes are Prayers

Many years ago I read a construction magazine that, believe it or not, had an article in it by Pat Boone. He wrote about deciding to go into show business and how some Christians had criticized him for this, but that he had felt called by God to do so. I felt such a strong sense in my soul that he was right about this that I heard myself saying, "I wish I could tell him that he did the right thing." I don't know why I thought he should care what I think, but anyway, a few weeks later my husband and I went to see an exclusive showing of *Close Encounters of a Third Kind* in Hollywood. We were among the first in line, though we noticed that someone had been shown in ahead of the rest of the crowd, *a celebrity, no doubt*, we thought.

When we arrived at our seats, we turned around and saw that just a few rows behind us sat Pat Boone. I walked over to him and told him I had seen the magazine feature and that I believed he had truly obeyed God in making the decision he made. He laughed and said, "I'm surprised that anyone even read the article." Anyway, I was satisfied. I had gotten my wish. I had delivered my message. Just a coincidence? Maybe, but I choose to believe that the Lord in some way appointed our steps so that we might have that little meeting that meant so much to me, and who knows? It may have been an encouragement to him as well.

The steps of the godly are directed by the LORD. He delights in every detail of their lives. Psalm 37:23 (NLT)

Lord, thank you that you hear our wishes as well as our prayers and answer even when we don't expect it! It is such a delight to have a God who sprinkles our lives with unexpected surprises. Help me not to miss a single one of them. Amen.

June 8

The "Lord, this is Jim" Story

Pat Boone reported on a TBN show some years ago that he had once heard Oral Roberts tell the following story that went something like this:

There was a farmer who did not know the Lord or go to church. He was getting up there in age and his family was concerned, but he had no spiritual inclinations, until, that is, one day when he was plowing a field. He knew that it was time. He looked up to Heaven and said, "Jesus, this is Jim." He didn't know how to pray, so he didn't say anything more, and he just kept on plowing. But the vital connection with eternal consequences had been made. He began to go to church and people were amazed at the change they observed in his life. A few weeks after this, however, he was struck by a car and was hospitalized in a coma. A minister visited him regularly and prayed for him but most people did not believe he would recover. However, one day as the minister was praying with his head down and one hand resting on the bed, he felt movement. He looked up and saw that Jim's eyes were open.

"Jim," he said, "we were all so worried about you."

"What happened? How long have I been here?" Jim asked.

"It's been several days; you were hit by a car. We didn't think you were going to make it."

"Oh," said Jim, "You didn't have to worry about that, I knew I was going to be all right, because some time between

when it happened and now, I don't know when exactly, I had a visitor. All He said was, "Jim, this is Jesus."

Oh! How I rejoiced when I heard this story. I knew that I could put my name in that sentence: "Pat, this is Jesus." You can put your name in that sentence too. Jesus knows you by name and He will "draw near" when you need Him!

...Jesus Himself drew near. Luke 24:15 (NKJV)

Lord Jesus, I want to have those precious moments where you break through from eternity into time and meet with me in special ways. Amen.

June 9

Prejudice

The word prejudice means to pre-judge something and is almost always considered a wrongful bias. I've been guilty of negative and positive pre-judging. In high school there were some Armenians and Asians who were so smart that I decided all Armenians and Asians must be extremely intelligent. I've prejudged some black friends as being great at sports, but upon getting to know them better, I discovered that they were not. Because of my loving black care giver, Adeline, as a child, I have an expectation that all black women will like me.

Have you been the object of someone's pre-judgment? I have. For instance I've experienced prejudice because: I'm a woman, I have big feet, I'm part Native American, and I'm a "senior." I've also occasionally experienced prejudice because I'm a Christian but that is the best kind, the one with reward promised.

The fact is: God makes no such judgments (looking on the externals), so neither should we as His followers. The book of Acts reports that in the early church the Jewish Christians were shocked to find that even Gentiles could become believers, but they recognized it as a work of God, realizing that He was without prejudice. We can make it one of our life's goals to look beyond, to see who and what is behind that which meets our eyes at first glance.

[Following are the words of the Apostle Peter] *Brothers, you know that in the early days God chose me from among you to preach the Good News to those who are not Jewish. They heard the Good News from me, and they believed. God, who knows the thoughts of everyone, accepted them. He showed this to us by giving them the Holy Spirit, just as he did to us. To God, those people are not different from us. When they believed, he made their hearts pure.* Acts 15:8 - 10 (NCV)

Our God, you who are without partiality, give us your vision of others that we might see the reality that rests behind changing and superficial appearances. Let us forgive those who have shown prejudice against us and we ask that you impart to them knowledge in place of their ignorance, and reconciliation in place of their fear. Amen.

June 10

A Teen's Wish Comes True

We were teenagers, my brother and I, that summer night when we went to see Harry Bellafonte at the Greek Theater in Southern California. We sat in one of the back rows. But no matter; it was a marvelous show! What stage presence he had! What energy! What charisma! Half way into his performance, he smiled at a girl in the front row and threw her a kiss. I don't know if I ever wished for anything harder than I did that night — wishing, oh wishing — that I had been that girl.

A few days later, something unexpected happened. My second cousin, rich, flamboyant Florence DuBosque, came for a visit. Upon hearing Bellafonte was in town, she exclaimed, "Oh! I absolutely adore him. Let's all go to see him." She immediately made reservations, and off we set for a night of glorious entertainment, all the way from Pasadena to the Greek Theater in a taxi cab! But where would we be sitting? I hadn't seen the tickets. I couldn't believe it; we were seated right smack dab in the middle of the front row. I waited expectantly through the performance. Could it be possible? Might my wish come true on this very night, what I had longed for just one week earlier? And then it happened. He sang that number (I've forgotten which song it was.) and at the end he looked at me, yes *me*, smiled and threw me a kiss! Oh, what joy! "Right at you, Baby," said Florence in my ear and everyone, *I mean everybody*, looked at me. I was special. I was "beautiful." I was alive. Life was good.

We don't need very many of those special moments, do we? Even one magical moment like that goes a long, long way. Through rare moments like these God cheers us on. We feel like He's smiling on us, like He's throwing us a kiss! We all need to watch for these moments as they fly by, and memorize them! Those recollections will come to us and bring us joy just when we need them most.

Happiness makes a person smile.... Proverbs 15:13a (NCV)

Lord Jesus, help me to recall joyful memories. Amen.

June 11

The Burden of Things

They were joyful and moderately poor. But the more they acquired, the less joyful they became, and finally they had happiness in things, but had lost the carefree spirit that comes with not being too weighted down by "things" — the responsibility that goes with those things, the guarding of them and the worries about losing them!

Oh, I know it's possible to have things and still have joy, but some of us might do better to sell at least some of what we have and give to the poor, just as Jesus told the rich young man to do (See Mark 10:21). That young man was asked by Jesus to sell everything he owned and to give the money to the poor and to come follow him. He couldn't do it! He sadly went away. Maybe he changed his mind and came and followed Jesus later on; we have no way of knowing. But to keep everything instead of finding and following the Lord — this is indeed a sad thing.

And then there were those in the area of the Gadarenes. Jesus cast the demons out of two men who lived in the nearby cemetery and sent the demons into a herd of pigs; they all plunged off of a cliff and were drowned. Did the people there want Him to stay in town? No! They had lost their source of livelihood! They came out in droves and begged him to leave! If I had been there I hope I would have wanted Jesus to stay.

Anyway, as I've looked around, I've seen this happen: a heaviness of spirit that comes with the weightiness of possessions. What a sad "price" to pay.

How hard it is for the rich to enter the Kingdom of God! Mark 10:23 (NLT)

. . . He gave them their request, But sent leanness into their soul. Psalm 106:15 (NKJV)

Wherever your treasure is, there your heart and thoughts will also be. Luke 12:34 (NLT)

Lord God, whatever I have, little or much, may I hold it ever so lightly, so that I might have a lightness of heart and help me to have a generous heart that gives joyfully and thereby stores up treasures in Heaven. Amen.

June 12

A Barrier of Protection

I had just become a Christian. My sister, Sylvia, had come for a visit, but started drinking. I previously explained that she had a problem with alcohol. When she drank she became another person, not the sweet, kind, funny sister I knew, but a cruel, sadistic, jealous and angry person. When she heard about my newfound faith, she made fun of me, then acted as though she was going to light a cigarette, striking a match. I sat frozen. She brought the match close to my face, my hair. Perhaps this went on for no more than a few seconds, but it seemed endless, as my heart pounded and tears welled up in my eyes.

Then something incredible happened. I sensed an invisible shield fall between the match's flame and me. I felt protected. I had a sense of unbelievable safety and peace in my heart. I wondered what it could be — *an angel perhaps?* I didn't know (still don't) but the fire didn't touch me. I believe I was supernaturally protected from harm. And my sister? Well, she suddenly blew out the match and the crisis was over, but I will always remember that marvelous feeling of a supernatural hedge that was placed around me.

I believe that God, anonymously and often, protects us in many ways during our lives and we are not even aware of such supernatural intervention most of the time. Let's thank Him for those times that we don't even know about.

> *When you pass through the waters, I will be with you; and through the rivers, they shall not overflow you. When you walk through the fire, you shall not be burned, nor shall the flame scorch you.* Isaiah 43:2 (NKJV)

Lord, thank you for protecting me. I know that my life is in your hands. I bless you for all the times that you sent an angel or appointed supernatural help for me even though I was not aware of it. Amen.

June 13

The Curse of the Shoulds

Sometimes I get into a mode of thinking of all the things I *should* be doing. I should write that letter, take the used clothes to the thrift shop, call that friend, take art lessons, always answer the phone no matter how busy I am, take a class in CPR, learn to swim, walk 45 minutes a day, pray more, take singing lessons again, complain less, learn Spanish, do the dishes immediately after eating, clean the toilet more often, sort the buttons in my sewing drawer, use some new recipes, plant an herb garden, brush our dog more often, blah, blah, blah! On and on the list goes. It is enough to make me stop and do nothing at all, just out of pure despair.

Once the Lord helped me through some of my neurotic guilt by saying something rather startling to me. It was, "Don't feel guilty about not using talents you were never given." Sounds kind of harsh, doesn't it? But not to me! It was a relief. I don't have either the natural gifts or the supernatural gifts to do it all.

But to encourage myself, I can tell you dear readers what I've learned to do. As I'm going to sleep at night, I talk to the Lord, the One who is interested in the details of my life, saying something like, "Lord, what was we did *together* today? Oh yes, I remember! I got up and had my quiet time, made breakfast, walked the dog, had lunch with a friend, wrote a little note to a friend, and made dinner. Thank you for helping me all along the way." Then I smile to myself and I feel at peace as I drift off to sleep.

I know that some people need a kick to get started, others need gentle words of encouragement, and some need to do less. I don't know where you are on that spectrum of workaholic to sloth, but God knows. So, we can ask His help in determining what He wants us to *do* each day. What is He telling us *not* to bother with? We can listen for a moment, and then do, or don't, as we're led by His Holy Spirit that dwells within.

The steps of the godly are directed by the LORD. He delights in every detail of their lives. Psalm 37:23 (NLT)

Lord, guide me each step of the way today, helping me to decide what needs to be done and what does not. Amen.

June 14

The Thing That Hurts the Most

In the book, "The Hiding Place," Corrie Ten Boom's father tells her (after her heart had been broken) something like this, "Corrie, it is taking love back that hurts." That has been a key bit of advice that I've believed and taken my entire adult life. Giving love and continuing to give love, even when it's not returned, hurts far less than withdrawing the love back inside of us. The temptation is to pull it back inside when it is not received or returned, but the godly thing to do is to release it toward a recipient, regardless of how unworthy that person may be. This has nothing to do with whether they deserve it or not. And note this: At this point, it's not about actions, only about the intents of the mind and soul. Love for someone, when taken back and turned inward, is a distortion of the essence of love. The nature of love is to go outward, to another, and that's why, when it's turned inward, it hurts so much! How wise Corrie's father was.

From whom are we prone to withdrawn love? A romantic attachment from the past — then we can send out good wishes to him or her; an adult child who has disobeyed and gone astray — we can ask God to bless and protect them; a long lost friend who betrayed us — send well wishes in the spiritual realm, in Jesus name, to that person just the same.

Take a moment. Is God reminding you of someone from whom you've withdrawn your love? If so, turn the love back outward toward that person and see how the hurt begins to go away. I know this works because I've done it — more than once.

> *But I say to you, love your enemies, bless those who curse you, do good to those who hate you, and pray for those who spitefully use you and persecute you....* Matthew 5:44 (NKJV)

Lord, teach me how to keep my love flowing, even toward those who are not my friends, even toward those who curse me or use me or persecute me. Then I will be like you. Amen.

June 15

The Homeless, The Hungry

The homeless man approached me, asking for money for food. From his appearance, I very much doubted that any money I would give him would go for that. I said, "There's a hamburger place right here. I'll go in with you and buy lunch for you." He smiled and followed me into the fast food restaurant. I told him about the homeless shelter nearby, and I stayed long enough to see him begin to wolf down that juicy hamburger. In this case, he really had been hungry. This is one way to help the needy without giving them the means to be tempted to use the money for whatever addictions they might have.

There are many people who are truly in need. There are those who are mentally ill and unable to work. There are entire families on the streets because of unemployment due to economic downturn. Yet there are also those who make a job of begging and don't ever try to do anything else; these are hardened users of those who work.

So what do we do? Perhaps it is arrogant of us to make judgments about these people, since there is no way we can have all the facts. So, if someone is hungry, perhaps the best thing to do is to simply give that person something to eat. We can carry around snacks such as fresh fruit or single servings of breakfast bars. Then we have done our part, and if they are taking advantage, that is between them and God. It's an alternative to doing nothing or doling out money that may be misused.

Those who shut their ears to the cries of the poor will be ignored in their own time of need. Proverbs 21:13 (NLT)

But if anyone has enough money to live well, and sees a brother or sister in need and refuses to help—how can God's love be in that person? 1 John 3:17 (NLT)

Lord, it breaks my heart to see so many homeless, hungry people. Help me to know what to do when I am approached, and teach me how to be prepared. Amen.

June 16

Lessons in Betrayal

I was furious with the Lord. Things had gotten out of hand. Everything had gone wrong. Why hadn't He warned me? How could He have let this happen? Why? Why? Why? Well, as you no doubt have reasoned out by now, bad things do happen to good people, and I figured I was a pretty good person. The old message we had in our souls, even as small children, is a cry for justice. Just think how often you've heard a child whine, "But it's not fair." Even though as adults we know that life isn't fair, we still have those times, at least I do, when I am shocked that it is not.

In this case I had experienced the betrayal of confidants. I had experienced betrayal before, but nothing like this, not from those I had believed to be my true friends. However, this unpleasant, painful experience changed my relationship to the Lord. Once I calmed my spirit down, I remembered that Jesus himself had experienced betrayal. I felt a new and sweet kinship with Him. I'd never understood before how heart breaking it must have been for Him to have Judas pretend to be a loyal follower and then betray Him with a kiss.

So though I suffered betrayal, I had found myself closer to my best Friend, the one who will never betray me, Jesus himself.

It is better to trust the LORD than to trust people. Psalm 118:8 (NCV)

Lord, I thank you that you are my true and faithful friend, the One in whom I will trust forever. Amen.

June 17

Lucy — From Mad Dog to the Sky

Late one night when my husband and I lived in the Phoenix area, I opened the bedroom window, propped my feet up on the windowsill, watched the lightening, and listened to the thunder and the rain. I didn't mind the monsoon season in Arizona. To me humidity has a softness to it compared to the harsh dry heat that we got during much of the year. Lucy (our dog), on the other hand, always hated the monsoon season, not because of the heat, but because of the sounds of the wind and thunder and the flashing of the lightning. But she moved on from her fear of Mad Dog (her stuffed toy) to taking on the sky. At a certain point she no longer cowered in the corner of the closet, hiding behind our clothes. No, Lucy came out of the closet! She began to take on that "big angry dog" in the sky with its deep, harsh barks and growls; she would go to the window and bark right back! Yes, she was a brave girl, and we encouraged that bravado! She found a way to deal with her fear and it worked! Good for her — what a creative dog!

I have lots of fears. I fear war. I fear violence. I fear change. I fear people that are controlling. I fear what others will think of me. I fear failure. I fear becoming a bag lady. I fear pain. I fear Alzheimer's disease. I fear broken bones.

Jesus asked once, "Why are you afraid?" (See Matthew 8:26) and then he answered His own question by saying, "You have so little faith!" So, if I have faith in God and if I have my priorities in order, then I will fear God and be in awe of Him and Him alone, the one who can calm the wind and waves. I envision that if I fear God in this way, then this appropriate fear will replace all the other fears. And as to those other fears, the Bible has something to say about that and it says it often. It is:

Fear not... Luke 2:10 (NKJV)

Lord God, I believe but help my unbelief. Help me to let go of every fear except the awe I have of you. Help me to trust in you to calm all other fears that are like the wind and waves in my soul. Amen.

June 18

Sacrificed Things

When my husband and I came home after a year in Taiwan, we brought with us several items made in Taiwan. One of them was a small, carved wooden Buddha. This I displayed in a China cabinet and I never thought much about it until one day I knew I was supposed to get rid of it. It was not pleasing to the Lord to have this image in my home. I obeyed and threw it out. This need to sacrifice a belonging didn't recur until many years later. While I was praying, the Lord brought to my mind a picture of a particular item and whispered "unclean" to me. It was a book of songs that a man whom I had once loved had written. In it was a song he said he had written to me, so I had kept it as a memento of him. But I had sacrificed my love for this man to the Lord years before He pointed to this final vestige of that relationship, and when He did, I immediately threw it out, in obedience.

When we become Christians and repent of our sins, the Lord does not always point all of our sins out to us at one time. They may be intricately woven into the fabric of our inner beings. To tear them out would be too injurious to the whole person, so, one by one, God, throughout our lifetime points to these things in us that He wants — the areas where we did not allow Him to be Lord — just yet. When God tells us to surrender something, we need to obey.

Why don't you, dear reader, stop for a moment and meditate. Give the Lord an opportunity to softly tell you if there is anything He is asking you to sacrifice. He may "keep" this thing (this person, this item, this dream, this habit, this talent) forever. He may replace it with something else more valuable, or even return it to you, transformed in some way, with His blessing. That's up to Him. The sacrifice is up to you.

> *But He said,* [to the question from the farmer's servants, asking if they should go take out the tares sown into the good field by the enemy] *'No, lest while you gather up the tares you also uproot the wheat with them. Let both grow together until the harvest....'* Matthew 13:29, 30 (NKJV)

Lord God, thank you that you gently weed our hearts of evil things. Right now, is there something in my life that it's time for me to surrender to you? If there is, speak to my spirit and I will obey. Amen.

June 19

In Search of Courage

After some dramatic events in my life, I had posttraumatic stress disorder. I suffered from panic attacks. During that period I felt that almost everything I did was dangerous and life threatening. When I went for a walk with our dog, Lucy, I thought a car would probably strike us. When I drove less than a mile away to the grocery store, I feared I would be in a deadly car accident. Every insignificant thing I did took tremendous courage. I had to talk myself logically through each move, telling myself that my feelings and so-called premonitions of evil were not based on reality, so I went against my feelings and into the fear-laden future every day, day after day. Gradually the fears subsided and after about a year I no longer suffered from the severe panic attacks.

I feel I am not a woman of courage, but yet, if courage is doing things in spite of fear (not fearlessness), then I was indeed brave after all!

Have I not commanded you! Be strong and of good courage;
do not be afraid, nor be dismayed, for the Lord your God is
with you wherever you go. Joshua 1:9 (NKJV)

Lord, help me to remember that, no matter how afraid I am, I am not alone. Amen.

June 20

The Queen of Courage

An excellent model of courage is found in one of the most heroic figures in the Bible — Queen Esther. The people of Israel were in danger of being destroyed, because Haman, the King's most trusted servant, had plotted genocide against the Jews. The news of this plot came to the man who had raised her, Mordecai. He informed Esther about the conspiracy through a messenger and said to her, "Who knows but whether you have come to the kingdom for such a time as this?" (Esther 4:14 NKJV) She had not been called to the king for 30 days and to enter the inner courts without being called was against the law; she knew she might be killed. However, she determined to go so as to save her people.

How her heart must have been pounding as she stood in the inner court where King Ahasuerus could look down and see her from his royal throne. She was a beautiful woman, which may be one of the reasons he decided to hold out his scepter to her. It was through her courageous efforts that a tragedy was averted and we are left with a rare and satisfying taste of justice, for Haman was hanged on the very gallows he had prepared for Mordecai.

How I long to be a woman of courage like that. I'm certain God has placed within us the seeds for just such greatness, even though the world may not ever see it, for we are destined for royalty and I believe it starts right now.

> *Go, gather all the Jews...and fast for me; neither eat nor drink for three days, night or day. My maids and I will fast likewise, And so I will go to the king, which is against the law; and if I perish, I perish!* Esther 4:16 (NKJV)

Lord, help us to have the courage of Queen Esther when we need it, for who knows but what we are on the earth for just such a time as this? Amen.

June 21

So Greatly Loved

Shortly after I became a Christian, I used my imagination to do an experiment. I knew that God loved me and had shown me His mercy and I was deeply grateful. However, I wanted to experience God's love for me in a special way. I sat on the top of our outdoor staircase at the old house on South Euclid in Pasadena, California. Gradually, in my imagination, I un-peopled the world until there was no one in the world but me. Oh! How much God loved me as the only human being on Earth. I could experience that free love so generously poured out upon me, just God and me. Then gradually I re-peopled the world. It was then I noticed an amazing and wonderful thing: The love stayed! That love from the Father for me had not altered, and I knew then I didn't have to ever imagine that it would deplete as the world continued to grow in population, even to the 6.8+ billion that now inhabit its surface.

God is capable of loving each of us as though we are the only person in the world. Unlike a human parent, He has all the "time" in the world for us. What a wonder this is!— Beyond our comprehension, but as we take in that love, it works a powerful transformation within us. Our part is to just be receptive to what is already there.

But God who is rich in mercy, because of His great love with which He loved us...made us alive together with Christ. Ephesians 2:4, 5 (NKJV)

Dear Lord, we are amazed at the mercy and love that you have shown us. Help us to open up toward Heaven each day and sense you pouring your love into the center of our beings, and then let that love we have received be poured out to those around us. Amen.

June 22

The Speaking God, The Silent God

I believe God speaks to different people in different ways. In this book I've occasionally mentioned that the Lord has spoken to me or given me a dream. I know that not everyone experiences God's communicating in these ways. It is not something that I chose, and it has nothing to do with my being more spiritual than anyone else, though I'm thankful God uses this way to talk with me.

There have been many times, however, when I have longed for Him to speak and He has not. I've gone for extended periods in which I neither heard nor sensed God's presence. My life in Him was completely based on faith during those months or years, not on feelings, and then, finally, the "silent" dark nights of the soul would pass and I would feel His dear presence again.

God knows each of His children intimately and He knows how and when to best communicate with us, or when to be silent. Dear reader, I believe that if you take time to listen, you will find the ways in which He speaks to you.

I will hear what the Lord will speak... Psalm 85:8 (NKJV)

Lord, teach me how to listen to you when you speak, and how to wait when you do not. Amen.

June 23

The Tree of Sorrows

Where or when I heard the story about the sorrow tree, I don't recall. Nor do I know its source. However, I've thought of it often, especially when I'm tempted to indulge in self-pity. It seems that there was a tree somewhere in the Heavenlies. On it, hung like Christmas tree decorations, were bits of paper, and on each was written the description of trials and tribulations of every human being on the earth. There were many people surrounding the tree, and they were all given a choice. They could select which sorrows they wanted, exchanging sorrow for sorrow, leaving their own on the tree. The people began to circle the sorrow tree, looking at the different kinds of hurts and pains that others knew — the curse of prejudice, homelessness, the pain of rheumatoid arthritis, the loss of a child, poverty and hunger, being the victim of war or criminal violence, a life of defeat, etc. The amazing thing is, or so the story goes, that all, without exception, found upon comparing their suffering with that of others, that they would choose to take their own sufferings back, instead of someone else's.

I know this principle to be true in my own life. When I compare what others go through, I will choose the lot appointed me.

What unhappinesses have come about in your life — those things over which you have no control? What are your sorrows? What have you suffered? With what sadnesses has God entrusted you? All suffer; no one is exempted from some form of pain. When the cup of sorrow or pain or grief comes to you, will you drink of it? I believe that if you can make but one adjustment, you will be able to — it is to not accept that cup, except as though it comes from the Father's hand. Ask God to help you not to see it as from Satan's hand, or from an earthly enemy's hands, nor from the hands of fate, but see it from the hand of Father, who can bring meaning into your suffering and comfort and strength for you to endure.

Shall I not drink the cup which My Father has given Me?
John 18:11b (NKJV)

Lord Jesus, enable me to follow you and, just as you did, drink the cups of life, bitter though they are sometimes are, choosing them as from the Father's hand because I know He loves me and wants the best for me. May You in some way be glorified through my suffering. Amen.

June 24

One of the Ugliest of Sins

He was friendly and warm toward me and hired me after two interviews. It was a job I was looking forward to. Then he invited me and another secretary out to lunch to celebrate. We had a great time and I was even more enthusiastic; I assured myself that I was going to enjoy working for my new boss.

However, as we were driving back to the office, everything changed. He, a Caucasian, made a derogatory statement about another race. My blood turned cold. The other secretary laughed. I was silent, but I was sitting in the back seat and I don't think he noticed. It was as though he had proudly announced that he was a bigot. He seemed to think he was being funny and clever. I knew immediately that I could not work for him, but I was too cowardly to tell him then. Later I called to say that I would not be taking the job after all. I don't know what excuse I gave. I know I didn't take the courageous step of being honest. Looking back, I'm as ashamed of myself as I was shocked at him! If this kind of thing ever happens to me again, may God give me the words that I need and courage to speak them.

> [Spoken of the Jews whom he hated, by Haman] *There is a certain people scattered and dispersed among the people in all the provinces...; their laws are different from all other people's.* Esther 3:8 (NKJV)

Lord God, examine my heart and reveal to me where my prejudices lie. Help me to root them out. And help me to be courageous to speak out against ignorance and injustice. Amen.

June 25

Sins of the Past — Part 1

I was told when I was a child that my great great-grandfather on my mother's side held slaves (He owned a plantation in northern Georgia). She did not tell me this in pride, but with shame — the shame I now feel when I think of it. As an adult I found the story confirmed in my great aunt's memoirs.

What do we do with such sins in our family histories? First, it is OK to take these things to God. Even though we are not personally responsible, if we feel shame and guilt, we may take that shame and guilt to Him and ask for forgiveness. Next, we need to guard against the kind of prejudice that allowed such things to happen in the past. Then we (I speak as a mostly Caucasian woman) need to be sensitive to others of any ethnic group other than our own, in our country, especially, the African American community that carries the consequences of the woundedness incurred upon them by our ancestors.

> *...the bondage was heavy on this people.* Nehemiah 5:18 (NKJV)

Lord, forgive the sins of my ancestors that I seem to carry in my own soul. We pray for an end to the consequences of their transgression to come in our lifetime. Amen.

June 26

Sins of the Past — Part 2

As part Native American, I am aware of a history of the great suffering that my ancestors experienced and the sins committed against them. Knowing this, Katie, a Christian woman and a dear friend, at one time knelt beside me and asked forgiveness from me for what the forefathers of this nation had done to my Cherokee (Tsalagi) ancestors in broken treaties and the abomination called "The Trail of Tears." I was deeply moved and received this offer of reconciliation. This was important to me, for it meant that I would have to give up the bitterness that I was carrying. Her taking this sin on is called by some "identificational sin." I'm certain this is one of the answers to the woundedness that our nation now suffers from — acknowledgment of the sins committed against Native Americans and Black Americans, among others, and the desire for true reconciliation.

On whichever side you find yourself, there is a moment of choice that is available to you now. If your ancestors were victimized in this way, decide to offer forgiveness should someone come to you seeking reconciliation and let go of the bitterness. If you decide to acknowledge identificational sin (of slave ownership or other offenses in the history of our nation) and seek reconciliation with a black friend (or any other ethnic group), wait until the Holy Spirit speaks to you to do so; I cannot stress too much the importance of waiting for His prompting. Only He knows the perfect timing!

You, O Lord, are our Father, Our Redeemer from Everlasting is Your name. Isaiah 63:16 (NKJV)

For those who have personally been sinned against, or those who are of an ethnic group which has been sinned against, past or present in this country (African Americans, Jews, Japanese, Mexicans, Irish, Native Americans, Armenians, Iranians, etc.): Father, help me, if I am ever approached with someone willing to repent of the sins of the fathers of this country, to receive this offer of reconciliation, that our country may be in the process of long-awaited healing. Amen.

For those willing to reach out in reconciliation: Father, give me the courage and wisdom to reach out in reconciliation at the right moment, that I may be part of the healing and redemption in this great country of ours. Amen.

For those who do not feel called to either side at this time: Lord, supernaturally help those who are part of reconciliation of any kind anywhere in the world. Amen.

June 27

Legalism

She was the widow of a police officer in a small Arizona town. She had lost her husband and, on a technicality, had been denied all benefits. The technicality was that her husband had been killed on the way to work, not on his job as a police officer. The article in *The Arizona Republic* on November 24, 1997, put it this way: "...the bean counters scurried away...it was the sort of hair-splitting that only a bureaucrat could love... [the] decision was mean-spirited and sharply unfair."

This is precisely the rigid Pharisaical attitude that Jesus encountered on earth. He was too spontaneous. He was too real. He was too filled with joy. He was too close to His Father. He was too compassionate. He was too free! Can't you see him speaking out His wise responses to the scribes and Pharisees? Or that joyful expression of utter freedom on His loving face when they criticized His disciples for plucking heads of grain to eat? Now that's the grace, that's the freedom I want more of. I know there's this little disapproving Pharisee in me, the one who wants it (whatever it is) done right (There is only one right way, of course — mine!). Don't you want to be free like Jesus, in such a close relationship with the Father, that you are not bound by the laws of anyone on earth but are free to obey the Heavenly laws of love and grace? I know I do.

> *...if you had known what this means, I desire mercy and not sacrifice, you would not have condemned the guiltless, for the son of man is Lord even of the Sabbath.* Matthew 12:7 (NKJV)

Oh Lord Jesus, set us free from legalism and immerse us in your gracious freedom of living! Give us unencumbered and joyful hearts. Amen.

June 28

The Art of Rocking

Grandma used to sit in a little rocking chair, which I still cherish. It is by the window in our living room. Any time I'm in a rocking chair or a back porch swing, I take advantage and do some rocking. Once I read that rocking stimulates the lymph system. But there's yet another reason to rock — according to a two-year study at Kirkhaven nursing home in New York, it was discovered that rocking brings peace of mind to the elderly people with dementia. Well, I'm not there yet, but a preventive exercise of rocking can't hurt, eh?

Daddy told me that when I was a baby, he had to get up every night with me after I came home from the hospital, a preemie with colic. One night he thought he had a solution. He put me in a rocking chair and put a cord around the arm and reached out and pulled the cord back and forth from his warm place in bed. His great idea didn't work. I knew the difference apparently, between the warmth of human arms holding me, and that of the cold, impersonal chair, even if it was moving.

Well, why do I share this? I don't know, except that rocking apparently reaches us in some deep place. We need to be rocked sometimes whether we admit it or not. Is this a spiritual discipline you need to develop? Can you imagine that you are a baby and that Jesus is rocking you, that He loves you, that He has the time for you, that He cherishes you, and that He holds you? This exercise of the spirit is one worth working on, but needs to be done in faith in order for the benefits to accumulate over time. You may be one of those whose little "inner child" needs to reach a place of being able to receive the truth — that he or she was wanted and welcomed into the world by Jesus Christ himself.

Hide me under the shadow of your wings. Psalm 17:8 (NKJV)

Lord, teach me how to let you hold my spirit. Let me know that there my soul may be in perfect safety. Amen.

June 29

Reconciliation

Once when I did something I felt was right, it turned out to offend "Joe," someone who had been a good friend up until that point. I wrote a note of apology, but there was never an answer. There were occasions when we would run into each other, but he would look the other way. It hurt my feelings, but each time it happened, I would need to forgive him again. Months passed.

Then something wonderful happened. Joe changed toward me. I had been asked to substitute for some sopranos who, at the last minute, were not able to sing in a choral group. I said I would, even though I knew that this particular man and his wife would be there. But instead of ignoring me, when he saw me, he said, "Pat, let's have a proper hello. It's been a long time." He got up from his seat, came over to me with a big smile and gave me a wonderful, warm hug. He had forgiven me too. That hug healed our relationship, but if I had not forgiven Joe already, I don't think I would have been able to receive that hug with such joy!

Is there anyone you need to forgive? Maybe you don't have to personally tell them, "I forgive you." Maybe they don't even know they need to be forgiven; lots of time folks don't. But if, when you see them, you communicate genuine caring, that will make the healing happen, for both of you!

Then Peter came to Jesus and asked, 'Lord, how many times shall I forgive my brother when he sins against me? Up to seven times?' Jesus answered, 'I tell you, not seven times, but seventy-seven times.' Matthew 18:21, 22 (NIV)

Lord, give me the fortitude to forgive indefinitely and the grace to let go of offenses, so that I may obey your command. Amen.

June 30

A Crown

One day when I was in my early teens, my brother did something that upset me terribly. I can't remember what it was but I knew of a hiding place, a kind of alcove in the long cypress hedge that went the full length of our property. I hid in there and I cried. My mother was worried about me and she looked for me until she finally found me in there, sobbing my heart out. I wouldn't leave until she coached me out by telling me that she wanted to share a secret with me.

I was curious. I left my hiding place. She said, "The secret is that some day you will be the Rose Queen!" Wow! What a prediction! I wondered if there was some supernatural way that she could know this. Could this be true? It gave me something to hope for.

Well, the years went by and finally, it was my turn to try out for Rose Queen of the famous Pasadena Rose Parade! However when I went forward to be interviewed by the Pasadena High School judges, I was so nervous I could hardly speak. I didn't even make it into the first round! Oh! What a letdown! Even though by that time, I had realized that Mama could not have known such a thing about the future, there was still that hope of a young girl who had wanted it to be true!

But my Lord saw that broken hearted little person and He had something else in mind for her. Many years later, I wrote a monologue for Queen Esther. I got to play that role in Toast Masters and at churches and at social events! I loved it. I got to write and act and be a queen! It was a dream come true. Then one day a Christian friend came to my house to give me something. She said, "The Lord told me to give this to you." She held it out; it was a little pink crown. Oh, it was not gold and inlaid with diamonds, but it was worth more than that to me. I knew what it meant!

For I have satiated the weary soul, and I have replenished every sorrowful soul. Jeremiah 31:25 (NKJV)

Lord God, you do restore the years the locusts have eaten again and again. Help us to recognize when you do this for us. We praise You for your compassion and everlasting kindness! Amen.

JULY

July 1

My Very Own Tomatoes

Daddy had a green thumb. On our property, he grew a full vegetable garden, plus walnuts, pecans, persimmons and grapes. He would spend hours out there in the garden — all in a world of his own. I didn't go with him, ever; there was something so private about his approach to the land and the things that he grew. He was in his element. He had a special gift that I didn't have, and I knew it.

However, this year I bought some tiny tomato plants. What was I thinking? Almost everything I try to grow dies. But I would try again. I planted them in a large planter (We don't have land suitable for planting here in our desert home.). I watered and fed them. I watched them grow. I was thrilled. They were my babies. Tiny green tomatoes finally became plump and bright red and then one day the first one was totally ripe, ready for picking! I was so proud. I cut it in two and shared it with Don. It was juicy and sweet and had a real tomato flavor, much better than the supermarket variety. Maybe I had a little of the gift of growing things after all.

The Lord God planted a garden... Genesis 2:8 (NKJV)

Father, thank you that you allow us to share in the growing of the green things that you have created. Amen.

July 2

Dreams, True and False

Aunt Didi was my mother's younger sister. Her given name was Elizabeth Katherine. She was tiny in stature and delicately boned. Her hands and feet were fragile and slender. She had black hair that had just begun to gray when she died at the age of 42. Her eyes were gold with black and red flakes — what were called "calico" in color. Her eyelashes were so long that when she looked up they touched her eyebrows. Her fingernails were sharply pointed and white-tipped. She told me she never cut them. This gave her something of a supernatural quality. It wasn't until years later that I realized she had filed them instead of clipping them.

She made the fluffiest, whitest divinity candy that I have ever tasted. And her chocolate chip cookie recipe could have been patented — a secret that she never shared. Those cookies were large and cake-like, running together and cut apart on the cookie sheet, stuffed with fresh-shelled walnuts and filled with chocolate chips, more than any ordinary recipe ever called for. I can still enjoy them where my taste bud memories live.

Oh! How I wanted to be like her when I grew up. But alas! At the age of 12, I realized I was not going to be like her; it was too late. I was much taller and had large hands and feet. There was nothing delicate about me. It gave me a terrible sinking feeling to realize that my dream of being like her wouldn't, couldn't ever come true.

No, I did not consider reality to be my ally in my early years. But over time I've come to believe that reality is my greatest friend. It can be anything from "beautiful" to "horrible" as one faces the circumstantial evidence. But as we invite God into whatever reality we find ourselves, He adds the even greater realities of grace and goodness, peace and joy; these are truer, eternal in value, and more real than whatever sinful, tragic, temporary "reality" lies about us! So, some dreams may die, but that which takes their place is everlasting as we seek God's will.

But where sin abounded grace abounded much more.
Romans 5:20b (NKJV)

Lord, we offer to you a sacrifice of all of our dreams that did not come true and we praise and thank you for all the undreamed dreams that have come true for us because of what you planned for each one of us. Amen.

July 3

The Magic of a Smile

I have a photo of my aunt Didi that my grandmother kept as her most prized possession. It is a tiny right profile picture in a gold-framed broach. It is surrounded with a delicate looped design and protected with a crystal. Her black hair is short and curled tightly. As small as the photo is, you can see those long black eyelashes!

What I remember most about her is how it felt to be near her. Aunt Didi always made me feel loved. One time we went to pick her up on a Pasadena street at a bus stop. She didn't drive and she had come all the way on a bus from Manhattan Beach. She was leaning against a black marble wall and reading a newspaper. I was disappointed when I saw her. She looked so old. Her face was marred with worry lines. But then, she saw us. Her countenance changed magically, gloriously. Our presence in her world seemed to totally alter her appearance! She smiled the most radiant smile you can imagine and it transformed her tired expression into the glowing countenance of an angel.

There are times when a smile from us can encourage the downcast heart of another human being. Even more, knowing that the Lord smiles as He looks on us, and sees us as precious and dear to Him. Such knowledge can make the expression of our face change and glow in reflected joy!

Hope in God; For I shall yet praise Him, the help of my countenance and my God. Psalm 43:5 (NKJV)

Lord, as I wait silently before you today, may I sense your smile shining upon me. May that smile change my countenance so that in some mysterious way, you will smile on others through me. Amen.

July 4

Independence Day

The Fourth of July! What does it make you think of besides remembering those who gave their lives so that our country could be free? I think of picnics, sitting on blankets or lawn chairs, resting under the stars on a warm summer night, with fireworks exploding overhead.

But what about other kinds freedoms? Is there anything to which you are in bondage? Are you addicted to alcohol, drugs, sex, pornography, food, or an unhealthy relationship? These are the kinds of things from which Jesus Christ desires to set us free. Some people, through prayers of the faithful, are set free miraculously and once and for all from unhealthy desires. Most need to pray *daily* for the strength to be free of whatever has captured them. Yes, most of us who have such attachments need constant, ongoing help. It's a day-by-day trusting, but it is through Him, our Higher Power, that we can find freedom!

One psychotherapist taught me that addictions may involve the need to run away from feeling what you don't want to feel, which is a kind of a way of "self-medication." Most often addictions take on a cyclical form. The "need" increases until you give into the temptation, which offers a brain chemistry altering "high" and release, which when it wears off, produces shame, which produces a need, which causes you to give in, and on and on it goes. Oh, dear reader, if you need help with an addiction, don't be too ashamed to go out and find it. There are doctors, therapists, 12-step programs and many specialists who devote their lives to helping others be set free from a variety of enslaving habits. Most of us can't do it on our own. I encourage you to find the help you need, so that you too may have your own independence day!

Suddenly, there was a massive earthquake, and the prison was shaken to its foundations. All the doors immediately flew open, and the chains of every prisoner fell off. Acts 16:26 (NLT)

Lord, shake the foundations, the roots of our addictions, loose our chains and set us free. Amen.

July 5

The Mountain Top

Summertime, standing on the very top of Mammoth Mountain in Mammoth Lakes, California, we looked down at the views from all sides. Stretching out in every direction was the beauty of the green forests, spotted with many lakes, sparkling in the sunlight. Even this time of year, the wind blew cold and hard and we tucked our hands into our pockets to keep them warm. I felt like the most blessed person in the world to be way up there that day, and I thanked God for the marvelous privilege.

Then my thoughts wondered. I thought about the fact that I was chosen by Him before the foundation of the world, that He knew me even then, and that, in some distant past, the earth was formed and also this dormant volcano mount on which I stood. I realized that as it was formed God knew that someday I would be standing up here thanking and praising Him for it. Now, isn't that a wonder? What a God we have: all knowing, existing without the limits of time, preparing for us a world that He knew we would wonder at someday in our brief lives upon the earth.

...he chose us in Him before the foundation of the world...
Ephesians 1:4 (NKJV)

Lord, I am incapable of comprehending how you not only know all things from beginning to end, but are also are with us in each moment. Thank you for times of glimpsing some glorious reality about your omniscience. Amen.

July 6

Grandmother Sarah's Album — Part 1
A Treasure Found

Long after my grandmother died and shortly after my father died, I found a small album — obviously quite old. Since my Dad had owned an antique and "junk" shop that was called "Harper's House," I thought it was something he had collected, so I didn't' look at it very carefully for a number of months. Then one day I took the time to examine it more closely. As I opened it and began to read, I realized with wonder that it had belonged to my great grandmother, Sarah [Sallie] Hicks Stephens. I also realized that it had been a family secret; no one had ever told me it existed. So much of a sacred treasure it was that it was never shared and could have easily been lost!

Entered on the now aging, fragile pages were poems and remembrances throughout a span of several years, from those who had known and loved her. Entry dates range from 1853 to 1883.

In the coming days I will share with you the entries I have found to be most precious. Here is the first, which speaks of friendship in a sweet way, in bold words of devotion written to a dear friend:

Morning Thoughts of Sallie

The rosy morning is round me now,
I feel its fresh breezes fanning my brow;
I think of Life's morn and its beautiful light —
And would ask that for thee it may ever be bright.

Not bright with the beauty of Earth alone,
Though its dazzling splendors around may be thrown;
Earth's brightness, if trusted, is doomed but to fade
And leave the heart lonely midst night's deepest shade —

But the radiance that beams from Heaven above
Flowing out from the fount of a Savior's love
Is a light undimmed by the falling tear,
A light which ev'n the Dark Valley can cheer.

Oh, may it be with thee on Earth below,
A solace, a guide, where're thou shalt go,
Till, led by its beames resplendent, divine,
You dwell where its glories forever shall shine.

Charlotte E. R., Cherokee Female Seminary.
Written in the 'cupola', Thursday Morn. March 24 1854

Some might say upon reading these last lines, "How quaint, but isn't it just another version of 'pie in the sky by and by?'" But think of it. In life, yes, there are joys, but there are also great sorrows along the way, and it is such thoughts as these writings express that bring to us, even in the midst of suffering, hope that there really is a better Tomorrow, a time when we will be safe in the place our Lord Jesus has prepared, one resplendent with glories we can't even envision.

In my Fathers house are many mansions: if it were not so, I would have told you. I go to prepare a place for you. John 14:2 (NKJV)

Heavenly Father, when times on earth are hard for me, help me to remember that you have prepared a place for me to live in Eternity with you, where there will be joys and wonders I cannot now even imagine. Amen.

July 7

Grandmother Sarah's Album — Part 2
A Love Never Lost

These words perhaps speak of unrequited love, sweet and sentimental. Such tenderness is so seldom expressed today. It would not be considered "realistic," but note these words and judge them only by the place in your heart that is "old-fashioned."

In this album there are written verses both old and new;
Most of those who've written have been smitten,
And some, perhaps, with you, Sarah.

Oft times the noblest hearts are doomed,
To feel the madd'ning glow,
Of unrequited, hopeless love,—
A lifetime load of woe, Sarah.

For what avails the stricken heart,
Where mortal charms preside?
Bold arrogance and vanity,
Stay close by beauty's side, Sarah.

And oft they trample in the dust,
Affection's warmest beam;
And drive from out the bosom's cove,
Love's first and holy dream, Sarah.

But where a noble intellect,
O'er sentiments hold sway,
Light vanity and arrogance,
Can never win the day, Sarah.

O, blest, indeed, the happy twain,
Where love pervades each breast;
Who love through honor and through shame,
To their eternal rest, Sarah.

Tahlequah August 24th, 1854, {Dr.} J. P. E.

There is seldom a love that does not in some ways disappoint or hurt, but through it all there is a love that is always returned and will not be taken away, no matter what. It is the love of Jesus, the one who comes to comfort through the Holy Spirit, the one who won't leave us, ever, no matter what. In this gentle Friend, we have one who will be saddened when we are disappointed or hurt, who will let the hurt come anyway, but who will not leave us without comfort in the midst of it, and who will draw all the more nearer if we will but let Him.

He healeth the broken in heart, and bindeth up their wounds.
Psalm 147:3 (NKJV)

Jesus, there are times when my heart has been broken. Please help me to remember that in such times you will give to me all I need to be comforted if I will but let you in. Help me not to shut you out, ever! or "punish" you by withdrawing from you or feel so sorry for myself that I can't let you lift my face upward to see the tears that stream from your eyes for me. Amen.

July 8

Grandmother Sarah's Album — Part 3
The Faithful One

This writer knew the Lord; there's no doubt of that. Her writing is heartfelt and, therefore, heartwarming!

When sorrow's hand is near thee,
And friends are thine no more;
Where none in fifty hear thee
A helping hand implore;

When helpless in thy sorrow
On nature look abroad—
Mourn not nor trouble borrow;
But put thy trust in God.

For He who tints each flower
And feeds each bird on high,
Possesses will and power
To hear thy pleading cry.

Then ask, and God will bless thee!
In faith, rest on his word;
Dire want may not distress thee
If thou trust in the Lord!

Janet Williams, 1863

Draw near to God and He will draw near to you. James 4:8
(NKJV)

Call upon Me in the day of trouble; I will deliver you, and you shall glorify Me. Psalm 50:15 (NKJV)

Lord, in the past I have called on You over and over and you have delivered me every single time! I know that You, the One who tints the flowers and feeds each bird on high also care about me and will take care of me every day of my life, including today. Oh Lord, may I glorify You for ever and ever. Amen.

July 9

Grandmother Sarah's Album — Part 4
The Greatest Treasure

The writer of this entry encouraged my Great Grandmother to cherish the Bible, the Word of God, and to use it as a faithful companion all along life's way.

The dim, dangerous and often lonely highway frequented and traveled by man, can only be lighted, made more peaceful and pleasant by brilliant beams of eternal truth, found in one Book alone. Oh! Be this valuable Volume thy constant companion, peruse it and learn its pure precepts to wield, to make you happy and safely lead you to that fair Land, where youth fades and dies not, but blooms in endless life. Early and oft remembered friend, Gre-te-hi [Cherokee name], I would thee naught save contentment now, and a home in Heaven!

Yours very sincerely,
F H P A P [Cherokee language, written]
[In pencil: Josh R]
Blome, March 3, 1854

As far as I know, Great Grandmother Sarah took this advice and, having been given the very same advice by her daughter, my grandmother, so have I. The Bible is the one book that is an absolute authority on life. I've read other religious writings and some have some truth, but this one book has every bit of information we will ever need to know about our relationship with God, our relationship with others, how to live a godly life, and how to plan for our eternity. It has a life of its own, for it was and is continually inspired by God. The Lord spoke to me once long ago and said, "The more you read it, the more you will learn to love it." I read it every day. It has changed my life, and it's true; I do love it more and more. We all need to take this advice from wise "Josh" and use this book to teach us, to heal us and to lead us.

For as the rain and the snow come down from heaven, and do not return there until they have watered the earth, making it bring forth and sprout, giving seed to the sower and bread to the eater, so shall my word be that goes out from my mouth; it shall not return to me empty, but it shall accomplish that which I purpose, and succeed in the thing for which I sent it.
Isaiah 55:10, 11 (NRSV)

Holy Spirit, I thank you for your great gift to the world of the writings known as the Bible with Old and New Testaments, that you inspired. I promise to glean from it teachings for the rest of my life. I promise to read it often. I know that as I read, I will come to love it more and more because its words bring me closer to you. Amen.

July 10

Grandmother Sarah's Album — Part 5
A Too Hasty Judgment

This writer loved words and had a unique way of expressing himself. Was he trying to impress her? He calls her Cousin Sally, but this does not mean that they were related by blood because she had been adopted.

For Cousin Sarah,

The spark that kindling abates the rage of contending monarchs bids the blackened story of war to cease that hushes the din of opposing metal or changes to illusions a sombre and frantic universe into one of mutual love is the cogent spark of friendship that now propels my pen. Yes cousin Sarah, it is that which makes it write thus — when thou art alone beholding with adoration the effulgent chariot of Phaeton as he drives her down the declivity of the western arch lending richness and splendor to the clouds that hang in melting beauty upon the brow of that horizon may the consciousness of my friendship augment the pleasure that thou dost derive from thus looking upon the true emblem of all the combined beauty of creations wondrous works.

O would I could write as bards of yore
Could have enclosed in mental store
The riches and sweets that would natural flow
To please my cousin Sallie

Or were I blessed with modern might
Could read in smiles, could read aright
The index of mind at single sight
I might please cousin Sallie

But humbled frail, insubstantial mind
It begs excuse to its sickly line
Conscious that it is not the best kind
that would please my cousin Sallie

Williamsville Park Hill, C.N. [Cherokee Nation]
July the 8th 1854
DLV

I've no idea who DLV was, but he certainly loved words, perhaps his own too much. At least that was my first take on this album entry! But who was he? And who am I to judge him? How do I know his spirit or the intentions of his heart? How easy it is to look at a few words and come to some conclusion that cannot possibly be correct! Perhaps it was not so much that he was in love with his own words as it was that he was in love with her, and was trying desperately to find a way to express his feelings to her. I shall never know.

Let us not therefore judge one another any more... Romans 14:13 (NKJV)

Lord, it is so easy to judge others, finding fault, when I cannot possibly know the truth about someone's inner character or motives. I leave that kind of true judgment with you. Help me to be discerning as needed, but guided by your Spirit and not by my own self-oriented human judgment. Amen.

July 11

Grandmother Sarah's Album — Part 6
Through the Years

The name of the writer of this entry is not legible, and yet I feel a kinship with this individual. He or she knew the same Lord I do and meditated about His agony in Gethsemane, the night that even the physically strong carpenter, Jesus, became weak and sweat great drops of blood. We too need to pray that same prayer when we are faced with a terribly difficult choice, a major fork in the road, or an illness unto death.

He knelt — the Savior knelt and prayed when but his Father's eye
Looked through the lonely garden's shade on that dread agony,
The Lord of all, above, beneath, was bowed with sorrow unto death.

He proved them all — the doubt, the strife,
The faint, perplexing dread,
The mists that hang o'er parting life,
All gathered round his head.
And the Deliverer knelt to pray,
Yet pass it not — that cup away.

It pass not — tho' the stormy wave
That sunk beneath his heart
It passed not — and was his to grieve
With tears a part of what He knew
But there was sent him from on high
A gift of strength, for man to die.

And was the sin bought thus best
With anguish and dismay.
How may we meet our conflict yet?
In the cost that comes that way?
Through him, through him that faith we trod
Save, Lord, we look to the Son of God.

O my Father, if this cup may not pass away from me, except I drink it, thy will be done. Matthew 26:42 (NKJV)

Father God, when the time comes when I must pray this dreadful prayer and knowing all things are possible with you, still hear that inner voice that shows me a road on which I do not want to walk, give me the courage that my Savior, Jesus, had that night. May this be so for me even though my friends forsake me as His did, even though I suffer, may I suffer for your sake and endure out of love for you. Amen.

July 12

Grandmother Sarah's Album — Part 7
Fond Farewells

Here's a selection of some simpler messages:

- Remember.
    Mary. Covel

- Sarah, Farewell forever.
    Leibbie Stephens
    Fort Scott, August, 1868

- A place in thy memory is all that I claim.
    Carie
    Cher Fem Semy, Feb 13th/55 [Cherokee Female Seminary]

- Sarah, 'Tis said that absence conquers love but oh! Believe it not,
    Your old friend and schoolmate, N.J.R.
    Cher. Fem. Sem, Feb. 13th, 1855

As I read these bold expressions of devotion to a friend I find them moving, and I feel nostalgic for a day when to express oneself in this way was perfectly acceptable. I don't hear such words any more, do you? We would be thought strange and overly sentimental, to use these quaint phrases. But surely we can find ways to tell our loved ones how we feel. Instead of "remember," we can tell a friend we won't forget! In those days it was not so easy to travel and when one said good-bye to a school friend, chances are that "Farewell forever" was indeed just the way it was going to be. And the sweet plea to be remembered — there is such gentility and softness there. Is it too late to go back to such a day, a day when gentle words came softly from unguarded hearts?

Greet ye one another with a kiss of charity. Peace be with you
all that are in Christ Jesus. 1 Peter 5:14 (NKJV)

Dear Lord, I have within my power to speak or write words of appreciation and kindness to those in my life. Help me to remember to do so often. Amen.

July 13

Grandmother Sarah's Album — Part 8
For a Grieving Wife

As I look at the entries under "Deaths" in the old family Bible, I find that there were three babies who died one after another. They were the children of my great grandparents. I can't imagine what it must have been like in those days to lose so many children. And then Delia came along, and she lived to be only four. After her death, my great grandfather, Spencer Stephens, wrote these words to his wife in her album.

For Sarah

Never more on life's current shall rise the sweet form — Delia.
If I could only now and then see a presentiment
From the skies, I could say that a bright angel still
Dwells in my heart.
Though her form like a lily
Was cast upon this uncharitable world, yet the season
of Life is but past. It is now in full bloom in
Eternity's prism.
I observe the different changes
Of Nature, the simple rose tells me that beauty
Has been.
Oh! Delia! Oh! Delia! It seems that
You should not remain but give to array for
The grave, thy short life was like that of the
Flowers and it's close like the flow of a wave.

Yours, Spencer S. Stephens [Delia's father]
Fort Gibson
June 30th, 1864

As I read the words of this grieving father, I find myself wiping away the tears. He seems to be able to express his feelings so well! He is not ashamed of his emotions. How precious to my heart to know this good man, my great grandfather, lived, so human and so sweet a man he must have been, and though I, of course, never met him, I hope I have perhaps a little bit of him in me and that one day I will meet him in Paradise!

But, beyond that, I am part of the family of God. I have been adopted into His family. I am the sister of Jesus! Jesus expressed emotions without shame and I know that by His Spirit He can feel in and through me and He can understand and feel my emotions and know why I feel as I do. Jesus came to earth and became a man and was like us, a little lower than the angels. Yes! He too experienced an array of emotions and He knew how to express them in perfect and appropriate ways. Our emotions are a gift from God!

Jesus wept. John 11:35 (NKJV)

Lord Jesus, thank you for so freely expressing your feelings when you were on earth. It seems to give us the right not to be ashamed, but to express ours as well. Give us discernment and courage to share our feelings in a way that is truthful and real in safe places with safe people, who will allow us that freedom and not judge us. Amen.

July 14

Grandmother Sarah's Album — Part 9
Giving What We Have

Here another dear friend writes to Grandmother Sarah:

I ask for thee,
So much of earthly happiness
As safely may be given,
Without unlinking the bright chain
That fastens thee to Heaven

Your aff. friend and old school mate
Abbie L. Britler
Mt. Hol. Fem. Sem. Dec./53

That which stands out most in this entry to me are these words: "...so much earthly happiness as safely may be given..." What a strange thing it was for such a very young woman to say and yet how wise. In this day we so often want it all, and right now! Instant gratification without waiting seems to be part of my rights! Remember the soda pop ad, I want a [soda] and I want it now!" That has come to be a way of life for many in this affluent society. Afraid to say *no* to ourselves, we are afraid to believe it's possible that having it all is not even good for us. Have we become a nation of haves, never satisfied and always wanting more? Let's look at our own lives. Is there some area in which we are bottomless pits? Spoiled and out of control, do we take for granted that all we have has been earned? It makes me sad to say these things and almost afraid to look at my own life. The starving children in China have become a cliché and yet are there not still starving children in the world? I put it to you and to myself, that with all we have, even if that is little, we must be giving out to others somehow, in some way, no matter how small those ways may be. We must, we *must* for the sake of our souls and for the sake of the world, lest we become like dead statues, lifeless, empty shells.

...Freely you have received, freely give. Matthew 10:8 (NKJV)

Father, you have given us all gifts — some with material things, others you have blessed with many spiritual gifts. May I give out of my blessings, to others that they too might be blessed and that you might be glorified. Amen.

July 15

Grandmother Sarah's Album — Part 10
No Time Limits in Eternity

Acrostic to Sarah

Should fortune fail, and friends indeed be free
And hollow hearts all wave their last adieu
Remember me; and know, that I will prove
A friend of friends, and worthy of thy love.
How sad, indeed, my pilgrimage would be
'Reft of thy smiles, and all I love in thee.
Oft in my day dreams, have I thought, of one
Sincere as thou; and by all smiled upon;
And thou, hast formed that thought and kept it there
Lest I should find the false as well as fair
In this frail book may words be found sincere
Each word when false, be blotted with a tear
Heavens blessings rest, on all whose names we find
Inscribed on pages, spotless as thy mind.
Calm be thy life, at early morn or even;
Kind be the Spirit; that to thee is given
Safe be thy passage to thy home in Heaven.

"Nems", Tahlequah, Aug 11 1854

Now here was a clever one, Nems, who wrote this acrostic. The letters that start each line spell her full maiden name, Sarah Rosalie Hicks. When I read the words, it's as though they were written only yesterday and I could have known this writer or the one to whom these words are written. What about it? Is this your picture of eternity? To God, all is flowing at once, there is no beginning or end to Him as there is to us who dwell in time on earth. And so, as we touch the One who dwells in Eternity, we may in some mysterious way, find in that eternal now where He resides, a way to touch, if only for a moment, the lives of those who lived before us.

The Lord is high above all nations, and his glory above the heavens, Who is like unto the Lord our God, who dwelleth on high. Psalm 113:4, 5 (NKJV)

Lord, you are everywhere and yet are no longer an earth dweller, nor confined by the chiming of the clock. May we realize that as we are in you, we find life Eternal, for you share your life with us. Amen.

July 16

Grandmother Sarah's Album — Part 11
Lessons from Long Ago

Here, her cousin, Ahmaisu (I don't know if this is a man or woman) wrote with such great wisdom that even in today's world we too might learn from these words.

"Life is made up of trifles." — so it is. Few circumstances are so trivial that we may not learn a lesson from them. A word from a friend: If in the right, feel not sad because you are misunderstood. Let your position be which it may, repine not. No one could fill it but yourself or you would not be placed in it. Be resigned to meet those who call out unpleasant feelings — They may under some circumstances, teach you better your own nature then even the angels could — They bring forth all that is evil that you may know and conquer. Be patient then — and live for something worthy a creature God has made. Then be the clouds that float o'er thy soul bright or dark, the star of holy trust will linger near, ever bringing to thy bosom peace.

> Your friend
> Ahmaisu Ross

Hidden in this paragraph are three precious pieces of advice. What the writer seems to be saying is: (1) If you know yourself to be right, stick with your guns and don't let anyone else pull you off center or cause you to suffer; (2) God has placed you where you are so don't complain; just do what He's called you to do (3) The world is filled with sour people who enjoy saying mean things; Listen to them just long enough to check out if they're right. If they are, then work (with God's help) on the problem in yourself that needs to be overcome. If not, let it go.

Do not be overcome by evil but overcome evil with good.
Romans 12:21 (NKJV)

Lord, so often I fear I am wrong and it's only the others who are right; help me to know the difference between right and wrong, no matter what others say. And so often I find myself wondering if I'm in the right place at the right time; help me to know by faith that I am where I am because you have placed me here. Also, Lord, people can be hateful and critical. Help me to listen to what they say; judge it correctly; and act on it or not, according to the wisdom you give me. And last of all, Lord, help me to overcome, by your strength, every evil that is set in my path. Amen.

July 17

Grandmother Sarah's Album — Part 12
Losses from the Past

This entry is in the handwriting of an older person — one who must have known that Sarah's mother died on the Trail of Tears and that her father, William Abraham Hicks died at Oothcaloga Creek, Georgia before the Removal at age 68.

To Sarah Rosalie

Blest be thy passage, o'er the changing sea of life; the clouds
be few, that intercept the light of joy:
The waves roll gently on beneath thy bark of hope
and bear thee up to meet a Mother and a Father and to
meet thy other Father, God.

Tahlequah, Aug, 1854, Mrs. M Augusta P, A Stranger/Friend

In 1838 the Cherokees were led from their homesteads in the east. My great aunt, Florence Stephens Lennon Evans, wrote about this in her memoirs in the late 1940s. In them she says: "Missionaries with land had been given notices that read: 'It becomes my duty to give you notice to evacuate the lot of land #____ in the ____ district of the third section and to leave the house now occupied by you to Col. William Handen or whoever he may put forward to take possession of the same and that you may have ample time to prepare for the same, I will allow you until the 28th day of this month to do the same. Given under my hand this 15th day of February, 1834.'"

She writes on, "There was some resistance but fighting was futile. It seemed better to sacrifice their home than their lives. Those who resisted were taken to concentration camps under military guard built for that purpose. Dr. Evan Jones, in Tennessee, wrote: 'Cherokees are nearly all prisoners...they are prisoners without a crime to justify the fact.' Uncle Stephen Foreman was in charge of the last 13,000 in the moving caravan. Progress was slow on account of sickness and rainy weather, with the resulting bad roads. They moved slowly on, weeping over the ruins of the past, enduring the tragedy of futility and anguish, looking back as long as they could see the landmarks of their beloved homes that they had lost. Their farms, mills, missions, and churches were a living monument to their industry and integrity. Sixteen thousand started. Four thousand fell by the wayside."

It is my opinion that what happened to the Cherokee tribe and other Native-American peoples, with the Indian Removal Act of 1830, is a blot on our country's history. I believe that God sees and remembers all of the Native American nations that did and do dwell in the midst of this great land.

When the Son of Man comes in His glory and all the holy angels with Him then He will sit on the throne of His glory. All the nations will be gathered before Him, and He will separate them one from another, as a shepherd divides his sheep from the goats. Matt. 25:32 (NKJV)

Heavenly Father, forgive us for our arrogance when we are so sure that our country is blameless. I confess when I think of the sins of our nation, past and present; I do not know how your Son will judge us as a nation when He returns to Earth. I ask that you have mercy on us and help us to do what we can to make this nation holy and righteous and pleasing in your sight. Amen.

July 18

Grandmother Sarah's Album — Part 13
A Sad Message

This short, sad message below seems to be from one who is so very tired. "Affection spilt with care" is perhaps speaking of one who has grown so tired that they have nothing left to give. We all have such times in our lives. Nowadays it's called "burnout" — something caused by too much stress, over commitment, over work and under nourishment of soul. I am convinced that if we follow the voice of God and join Him in what He is doing, and that only, we will not be burdened beyond bearing and any exhaustion we feel will have a sense of deep satisfaction attached to it.

> Forgive one whose affection is spilt with care
> Whose heart is chilled, but remembers thee.
> > J. Ross [this, in pencil by another hand]

Let me share here something that is remarkable about this entry. This individual, J. Ross, may well have been the great John Ross, Chief of the Cherokees in the 1830s, and our son, Daniel, married one of his descendents. This means that more than one hundred years ago the ancestors of Dan (including Cherokee Chief William Hicks) and the ancestors of Becki, his wife, knew one another! In a smaller place this wouldn't seem strange, but in this grand land of ours, it seems like a miracle to me. I was thrilled to learn of my daughter-in-law's heritage and it gave me one more reason to believe they were meant to be together! (I know — perhaps just an old romantic talking here!)

And He said to them, 'Come aside by yourselves to a deserted place and rest a while.' Mark 6:31 (NKJV)

Lord Jesus, sometimes I feel overwhelmed. Help me to remember to come to you, the one in whom I can always find rest for my soul. Amen.

July 19

Grandmother Sarah's Album — Part 14
The Little Things

And here is the final selection from my great grandmother's album written by her daughter, Florence (My Great Aunt Flossie). It speaks of "little things":

> Oh, what is life? Drops make the sea;
> And petty cares and small events,
> Small causes and small conquests,
> Make up the sum for you and me;
> Then, oh, for strength to meet the stings
> That are the points of little things.
>
> Flossie, June 12th [18]'83

In the El Nino winter of 1998, a small enemy came to California, one by one to find safe, higher ground. Oh, just a few at first, but then more and more. Driven from their homes by a rising water table, ants, ants and more ants entered homes in water-soaked areas and were found in places such as freezers, laundry baskets, coffeepots and, even ice cubes.

Ah, yes, it's often the little things that get to us, isn't it? Or, to reverse the picture, that we can do to get to others — the same old little annoying habit? The chip, chip, chipping away at someone's patience! Until they explode! Or cry! Or yield! I remember as a child hearing about a terrible method of torture. It involved the drip, drip, drip of water on one's forehead until the victim is driven insane! This reminds me of a Proverbs 19:13. It reveals how I behaved during a certain period of our marriage, nagging my husband over a particular issue. It makes me ashamed and embarrassed to remember how I carried on in this power struggle that went on for months!

> *...the contentions of a wife are a continual dripping.* Proverbs 19:13b (NKJV)

Lord, when people don't do what I want them to or don't change the way I want them to, please give me courage to find another way rather than nagging, or give me grace to forgive, or give me the fruit of patience to endure, which ever it is that I need most. Amen.

July 20

Gruesome Secrets

In June of 1998 a body of a woman dead for 11 years was finally found. She had killed herself but the husband didn't want to report it; he was afraid of being blamed. This is a sad story because the man himself finally attempted suicide too — a way to get rid of a secret that was kept for so many years that it ate away at that man's soul!

Secrets can be horribly dangerous. They can take on a life of their own. They can grow and become distorted and corrupt our souls. Things need to be revealed, yes, even the ugly things. The "bodies" need to be discovered and given a proper burial.

During one especially difficult challenge my husband and I found ourselves judged for exposing a family tragedy that we had experienced. This was met with strong disapproval from a group of people who had a philosophy of silence and secrets. We had broken their code. We realized that they believed in sweeping everything under the carpet where it should stay! In more than one of these families, there were hints of secrets of abuse and great childhood suffering. If exposed, such things could have been healed, forgiven and transformed, but as far as I know, to this day the secrets remain, and there they may stay until judgment day when every secret thing shall be exposed. Do you want to reveal such things now or have them revealed later? My option is to get it out into the open right *now*!

I have chosen to share my personal secrets with a few special friends and professional counselors. How blessed I have been to meet with compassion, healing and forgiveness. Dear friend, if you are holding onto a dark secret, one that remains powerful in its isolation, know that to open these doors to a *trustworthy* confidant, will be the beginning of bringing light into the deepest darkness and peace into a tortured soul.

The Lord my God will enlighten my darkness. Psalm 18:28 (NKJV)

Dear Lord, out there among the readers are some who have chosen to keep powerful and harmful secrets. Set them free to share with a safe listener, so that they may find peace and healing. Amen.

July 21

The Death of a Beloved Parent

When Mama died, I became deeply aware of how special her life had been. Oh, she was not rich or famous or successful in the world's eyes. She was not a "church" person for some of her life. But when she died, I knew the Lord came to us in a special way to remember her life with us when we said good-bye to her. After the funeral, family and friends got to together at our home. We rejoiced together and told stories about her and looked through family albums. It became a celebration, but what was unmistakable was that this life was extraordinary, and what was even more extraordinary was that I knew it is so with the life of every beloved child of God. I could even sense the presence of angels in the house. To God, my mother was of great value and special. I discovered anew that day that no matter how little known by the world, all, even the most "invisible" lives, are seen and known and cherished by God.

Precious in the sight of the Lord is the death of His saints.
Psalm 116:15 (NKJV)

Dear Lord, thank you for the special lives of the ordinary "saints" who have gone to be with you — unknown and yet loved and cherished by you. Help us to know that though we are not special in the eyes of the world we are, each one, in life and in death, special to you. Amen.

July 22

Seeing God

There is a story about a little girl who wrote a letter to a cosmonaut who had reported that while he was in space he had not seen God. She wanted to ask him if he was pure in heart. I don't know if this anecdote is true. I do know that it is true that the pure in heart will see God (See verse below).

If we want to see God we need to be willing to make the sacrifice of being purified in order to do so! How does one become pure in heart? I think that the first step is to accept that we are not pure. There is a problem in the world and it is called sin. It is a state into which every person is born, a state out of which there is only one door and that door is a person and that person is Jesus Christ. So the first step to seeing God is to recognize our own sinfulness. If we feel no sense of sinfulness and therefore believe we have no need of forgiveness, there is Someone who will help us; One of the Holy Spirit's jobs is to bring our sinfulness to our awareness. When we are made mindful of our sins, then we will ask for forgiveness. The ancient prayer: "Lord Jesus Christ, Son of God, have mercy on me a sinner," is sufficient.

Once this is done, life becomes a series of times of work and times of rest. During the work, we will find that life presents us with "challenges" and these challenges do a work within us that will purify our inner life (new born-again self). The more purified our inner selves, the more easily we will see God. So there are two disciplines: (1) Be pure (in Christ) and (2) Look for God everyday and everywhere.

Blessed are the pure in heart, For they shall see God. Matthew 5:8 (NKJV)

Lord, make me pure and give me spiritual vision so I can see You many times every day. Amen.

July 23

The Simple Moments

A book that has been my daily companion for years is "God Calling," a collection of messages from the Lord that were given to two English women during their times of prayer together. (The works were compiled by A. J. Russell and published by ©Barbour and Company, Inc. 1985) Time after time, day after day, I've been encouraged by these daily messages.

My favorite lesson from this little book has to do with Jesus being the Lord of the little things. It says that nothing in the day is too small to be a part of His scheme. It is the little stones placed together that finally create the lovely mosaic.

That's what most of life is built of, isn't it? The small things, the little moments, one-by-one, that will build my life into a precious mosaic. I want to have a quietly faithful, moment-by-moment life, believing God is with me in all of the common things, the seemingly insignificant moments, the quiet words and deeds that are combined to create the pattern that becomes each of my days.

Here a little, there a little. Isaiah 28:10 (NKJV)

Lord, help me to learn to love the little things, the little moments, and fill my heart with gratitude for all that you have entrusted to me. May I be a faithful servant, creating along the way something that will someday be beautiful and bring glory to You. Amen.

July 24

Living Sacrifices

In Old Testament times the priest offered animal sacrifices but in the New Testament we are asked to offer our own bodies as living sacrifices. How do we do this? I've heard it said that the problem with living sacrifices is that they keep crawling off the altar.

Yes, it is possible to crawl off of the altar. One time I did it because I didn't like living in the desert and I wanted to leave. Since God had called us to be there, and we had decided to follow Jesus and our lives are not our own, I had come, but I didn't like it — well more to the point, I literally hated it! I couldn't imagine that the Lord wanted to put me in a place where I was so miserable! How could He? Perhaps He had just forgotten me. So I crawled off, so to speak, and then found myself in what I can only call unsafe or unholy ground (spiritually speaking). I was not protected from the torments of the demonic! Yes, I know it sounds bizarre, but when I rededicated my life and determined, that no matter what, I would obey, rather than make happiness my goal, though the physical environment did not change, I found that I was "safe" and at peace spiritually and the torments ceased! This was an absolutely amazing lesson to me, one that I had never heard about from any other source (except my own life).

> *I beseech you therefore, brethren by the mercies of God, that you present your bodies a living sacrifice, holy, acceptable to God, which is your reasonable service.* Romans 12:1 (NKJV)

Father, help me to stay still and quiet on the altar of sacrifice. Amen.

July 25

One of Life's Good-byes

There was a special place my husband and our boys and I lived for nineteen years — my favorite home. When it was time to leave and move to Arizona, Don went ahead of me. One last night in the home alone was more than I could bear and my son, Dan, and his wife, Becki, insisted that I sleep at their place.

The next morning Dan drove me through parts of L.A. back to South Pasadena to the address on Mission Street. I was deeply sad but also accepting of what was happening. We had made this choice because Don felt called to the ministry in the small town of Goodyear, Arizona. That early morning sky was filled with the "after clouds" of rain — the whitest of whites, against deep, dark grays. In the center of that skyscape, from cloud and into cloud sprang forth a rainbow, radiant and luminescent as rainbows are, but also it carried, as always, a promise of life for me, for my future.

As we drove up to the old California bungalow for the last time, perched on top at the south end of the roof was a mourning dove and on the north side sat a squirrel. It was as though they were waiting for us to return, co-inhabitants, aware of change in the air. It seemed that nature around us knew and grieved that we were leaving. After all, hadn't we enjoyed this green place, this gentle space together? And now we would go, yet here they were, these kindly creatures appointed by God to tell me good-bye. God knew the ache in my heart. I truly believe this was not a coincidence; the fruits of this sweet display of condolence was that I was comforted and isn't that the work of God — our Companion through the hard times — to comfort and to encourage? Yes! That is your God and mine.

> *All praise to the God and Father of our Lord Jesus Christ. He is the source of every mercy and the God who comforts us. He comforts us in all our troubles so that we can comfort others. When others are troubled, we will be able to give them the same comfort God has given us. You can be sure that the more we suffer for Christ, the more God will shower us with his comfort through Christ.* 2 Corinthians 1:3-5 (NLT)

Dear Holy Spirit, help me to see those times when you reach out through your creation and say that you care and that you love me and that you will comfort me when I am sad in the midst of one of many of life's good-byes. Amen.

July 26

Knotty Situations

Have you ever wondering how the threads in sewing kits get completely tangled up? This has happened to me so often that one day I wrote, just for fun, an explanation. Here it is:

The Mystery of the Tangles

There is, I'm told, on a chilly night,
A tiny, little goblin sprite
Who comes when all are warm in bed,
In search of things like yarn and thread.
He tiptoes passed a sleeping mouse,
And looks and skulks through all the house.

Except for chains, he'll pass up jewels.
He's much more interested in spools.
He jumps into his task with glee,
Indulging in a joyous spree,
To tangle, snarl, to entwine and twist
There's not a thread he's ever missed.

And if you should wake up and catch his act
It's a jig and a song, and that's a fact.
A somersault here, a whirligig there,
And he'll make those threads just like matted hair.
And listen closely and you will hear,
The silliest words ever touched your ear!

Like the dig dig diggy of the dew dew dew
And the flip flip flippy of the flu flu flu
To the tig tig tiggy of the two two two
And the rick rick riggy of the rue rue rue.

And so he goes as he turns and sings,
And it's like his legs were made of springs,
And yet if you think you really know,
There's never a bit of proof to show,
Who comes in the dark and unfixes things
Like yarns and thread and cords and strings.

How is it that all of life seems to present us with different forms of tangles? — the strange entanglements of relationships with their invisible bonds that hold us trapped, unable to extricate ourselves can be worse than the tangles of yarns and thread and cords and strings! Think of the hold an abusive husband has on his wife (or vice versa), or the hold a possessive mother has on her son who can't seem to break free and move on with his own life, or the trap of an extra-marital love affair, the desire to break it off because it's wrong, and yet....

Aren't these the kind of tangles that Jesus Christ can not only untangle but break? Of course, if we are willing. Oh, that's not to say it's not painful or difficult. But to break such ties we must depend on the supernatural power of God; we need to reach a place where we admit that we cannot do this for ourselves and then, as we humble ourselves under the mighty hand of God, that hand will reach out and untangle that which has become entwined in our souls, in our lives. Ask Him. I know He can do it. He's done it for me on more than one occasion.

> *But remember that the temptations that come into your life are no different from what others experience. And God is faithful. He will keep the temptation from becoming so strong that you can't stand up against it. When you are tempted, he will show you a way out so that you will not give in to it.* 1 Corinthians 10:13 (NLT)

Lord, there are entanglements of sin in my life that I can't undo. Please help me acknowledge them and then help me escape from them. Amen.

234

July 27

The Tongue's the Thing

Gossip — that old, pugnacious demon that loves to destroy friendships, undermine professional careers and ruin reputations; how do we curb our lust for such tantalizing tales? I wrote the following after being educated by becoming the victim of rumors:

Gossip

Murmurings, whisperings, sour or sweet?
Is their gossip? Do words have feet?
Is there error told as truth?
Do the lies fly through the roof?

If I tell, will my tale will be told,
And will it haunt me when I'm old?
If, for fun, I add some spice,
Will someone else pay the price?

Am I sure all my facts are straight?
Or, if spoken, then checked too late,
Will my cute, twisted version yield
The kind of pain that can't be healed?

If I speak secrets for personal gain,
Will a fond friendship survive the strain?
Or will I have cashed in on another's terrain
Bringing a friend's heart far too much pain?

If I hear words I should not speak,
But more than just listen, and no secrets keep,
Will I be able to soar above
The kind of crisis spun by unlove?

And when I whisper, if words creep out
Under closed doors and grow to a shout
Will their shame greet me on a public street
And make me wish they'd dropped dead at my feet?

Teach me then, Lord, control of my tongue,
When I am teachable, while I am young
That all words I speak, loud or soft, good or ill
Have power to wound, have power to heal.

Fire goes out for lack of fuel, and quarrels disappear when gossip stops. A quarrelsome person starts fights as easily as hot embers light charcoal or fire lights wood. What dainty morsels rumors are—but they sink deep into one's heart. Smooth words may hide a wicked heart, just as a pretty glaze covers a common clay pot. People with hate in their hearts may sound pleasant enough, but don't believe them. Though they pretend to be kind, their hearts are full of all kinds of evil. Proverbs 26:20-25 (NLT)

If anyone does not stumble in word, he is a perfect man, able also to bridle the whole body. James 3:2 (NKJV)

Lord God, help me to consider the consequences of "unlove" before I speak. Amen.

July 28

The Genesis of a Ghost Story

It was 1957. I was 18. It was a black, moonless summer night. I was in my room on the second floor of the old wood-frame house by Barnegat Bay, visiting our only rich relative, Florence Du Bosque. Dark and silent it was, and then I heard young men's voices, their low tones traveling easily across the quiet water to my listening ears. Dressed in a long, white flowing nightgown, I had an idea.

And so, all lights out, I lit a white candle, and walked, as in slow motion, back and forth, back and forth across the wide, upstairs bedroom window, holding the light in front of me as I glided.

Their voices suddenly stopped; were they watching? I turned and faced the window, and slowly, slowly sank beneath their view, brought the candle to my lips, and extinguished the flame.

Another moment of silence, and the voices, returned, excited and louder. Did they see that young girl that evening? Do they still tell of the night, when out fishing, they saw the ghostly figure of a young woman in the window of that old house, long since burned down, on Barnegat Bay, New Jersey?

But when they saw Him walking on the sea, they supposed it was a ghost, and cried out; for they all saw Him and were troubled. And immediately He talked with them and said to them, Be of good cheer! It is I; do not be afraid. Mark 6:49, 50 (NKJV)

Lord, most of us have some kind of "ghosts" in our lives that haunt us. Help us to identify them and trust you as you remind us not to be afraid. Amen.

July 29

To the Memory of Matilda, Cat and Friend

She had hidden on an open shelf in the closet. I discovered her there, and tenderly lifted her up and took her outside and placed her down gently. She moved quietly away — for the last time.

I found her in her final sleep five days later — under the house. Frailer and moving more and more slowly, I knew she was dying but I kept putting off saying "Good-bye" and "Thank you." And so she faded away and I robbed myself of one last moment of holding her tiny, furry self and running my hands through her softness.

But in that silence of the unsaid, and from that ghastly ache at the front of my throat, I vowed to never again regret other unspoken, simple, little words. And so in the memory of Matilda, I say now "good-bye" and "thank you."

The gifts that God gives us through our precious pets are indescribable. If you have ever had a beloved pet, you will understand.

> *The wolf also shall dwell with the lamb, The leopard shall lie down with the young goat, The calf and the young lion and the fatling together...* Isaiah 11:6 (NKJV)

Lord, you have brought into being and love all of your creatures. Thank you for those little lives that you have created to be our companions. They have taught us unconditional love and faithfulness and acceptance of the cycles of life and death. Amen.

July 30

Invisible Surprises

On our return trip from Europe in 1981, we had a smooth flight. Everything was fine, that is, until we hit the air above the Rockies. Don had just gone back to use the rest room when it hit! It was clear air turbulence. It was a shocker! It was a rocker! Where was Don? Overhead compartments flew open, sending some lighter weight baggage through the air. The refreshment cart, not "moored" kept leaving its spot. *Where is Don? He should be here holding my hand.*

He had a different story to tell. Sitting on the commode, he was just about finished, when he discovered it was impossible to get up off the seat. However, he is quite tall and it was not difficult for him to unlock the door, open it and sort of stick his head out to see what was happening. Under the circumstances no one cared, or even noticed him. It was worse back there, in the tail of the plane, of course. It went on for perhaps five minutes. When it was over a flight attendant had a sprained ankle from her wrestling match with that refreshment cart, people were grabbing for the little white barf bags, and children who had been playing cheerily, were silent.

Well, life is full of such times of unexpected "turbulence." It's invisible; we don't see it coming! But there is — the thing that throws us for a loop. What to do? Emergency prayers. "Help" is a good one. God is there. He's not surprised by anything that happens. He'll help us through the unexpected. Keep in touch with Him in the good times and it will be easier to receive His help during the surprise visits in the bad times.

> *For in the time of trouble He shall hide me in His pavilion; In the secret place of His tabernacle He shall hide me; He shall set me high upon a rock.* Psalm 27:5 (NKJV)

Lord, help me to keep in touch with you all the time, so when the surprise visits of life's turbulent moments come, I will know without a doubt that you are right there with me. Amen.

July 31

How to Help Your Minister's Spouse

Well, it didn't happen until I was almost 60 — this new life of being a minister's wife. I didn't have a clue about what was expected of me and I could find no books on the subject. My heart would go thud when, added to my name in an introduction was these words: "Pat's the minister's wife."

For all those out there who don't know how to treat one of these people (a minister's wife or husband), here are some hints which I have learned the hard way during the past few years:

Introduce us by name, not by the profession of our spouses.

We may choose to join the church and that gives us the same rights and responsibilities as other members, no more, but no less.

Don't expect us to do everything. We know what our gifts are and will seek to find a way in which to use them.

Don't expect us to come to every single function. We're not going to.

Don't expect us to be holier than thou. We're not.

Do take time to find out if we're human. We are.

Well, there you have it. I hope it helps you to help your minister's spouse.

Oh, yes, and there's one more thing: Pray for both your pastor and his or her spouse every day. It's a hard job and they need God's help, help that will come as you support them in prayer.

> *The elders who direct the affairs of the church well are worthy of double honor, especially those whose work is preaching and teaching. For the Scripture says, 'Do not muzzle the ox while it is treading out the grain,' and The worker deserves his wages.'* 1 Timothy 5:17, 18 (NIV)

Lord God, have mercy on ministers and pastors of churches, both small and great, around the world. They need your empowering, the fullness of your Spirit, and the support of their flocks as they seek to follow that to which you have called them. Thank you for their obedience to you. Amen.

AUGUST

August 1

Tumbleweeds — Part 1
A Safe Place

For the next few days I will be quoting a few paragraphs from my Aunt Hortie's (Hortence Harper Simpson) memoirs, *Tumble Weeds on Barren Prairies*, a book written and self-published, about her days in Waurika, Oklahoma Indian Territory. Following is her recollection of Oklahoma weather.

> *I remember my Mother telling of the terrible storms that came. The old school house we lived in wasn't very strong on its foundation. She said the strong winds would rock it. She was alone many times with my brother and me* [as small children]. *The lightning was very fierce and she was awfully afraid of it. She would put us in the middle of the feather bed. It was her belief that the feathers would keep the lightning from striking us. No family in those days was without feather beds. I can still feel the warmth they gave us during the awful cold winters.*

I love to read about that comforting scene — those little children placed in that plush bed and protected by the feathers! Aren't there times such as this in your life, when you feel that you want a featherbed to hide in so you will be protected and warm during the cold, harsh storms of life?

> *Be merciful to me, O God, be merciful to me! For my soul trusts in You; and in the shadow of Your wings I will make my refuge, Until these calamities have passed by.* Psalm 57:1 (NKJV)

Father, when I am overwhelmed and feel powerless and in danger, help me to remember that there is a place where I can find refuge, that hiding place under the shadow of your wings. Amen.

August 2

Tumbleweeds — Part 2
A Childhood Fear

Aunt Hortie shares a terrifying experience:

> *I believe one fear that really scared me was when Haley's Comet appeared in the sky. I could hear the people* [talking about it], *"It is the end of the world!" And our family was all scared, as we looked skyward. We had no warning, like people do nowadays of things to come. We were numb with fear. The whole sky was lit up with this "monster" looking thing with a tail trailing. I ran into the house to hide, so afraid that it really was the "end of the world."*

Grandma, my mother's mother, also spoke of the "end of the world." This was a way of describing judgment day when Christ would return to earth. As a child my heart beat faster when she spoke about this even though it was frightening to hear about. I longed for Jesus to come back — I wanted it more than anything! I had a dream that I looked up and saw Him coming out of the sun with His arms outstretched. He landed in my neighbor's back yard. I ran into my house to tell my family. My Dad lit a cigarette and said, "I'm not ready."

The words of Aunt Hortie and the description of my dream sound quaint as I read them now, but there is such a day coming. Jesus Christ, when He left His followers and ascended into Heaven, promised to return. If He should return today, would you or I have to speak the words that my father spoke, "I'm not ready."

Think about it. What do we do to *get ready*? Are you ready today? Do you know how much Jesus loves you? Do you know that you are in need of a spiritual rescuer, a Savior? And even though you know Him as Savior, do you know that you need Him every day as the one who gives grace and mercy, strength and comfort? I've been a Christian for more than fifty years and I still need spiritual help every day and every moment of my life. Without Him I can do nothing! I can't even "be ready" without Him teaching me how. Let's make a goal to, together, "stay awake" and to be ready spiritually by seeking God's guidance so that we will be doing whatever we are called to do, day by day and moment by moment, up until the hour that He calls us home or that He returns!

Watch therefore, for you know neither the day nor the hour in which the son of Man is coming. Matthew 25:13 (NKJV)

Dear Lord Jesus, you who are the Alpha and Omega, someday you will come back to Earth; we know this because you have promised it. May we be ready for you on that great day and greet you, not with fear and guilt, but with joy and victory. Amen.

August 3

Tumbleweeds — Part 3
The Simple Things

Here Aunt Hortie tells of a special outing she took in her teens.

I went with Aunt Dora and Uncle Tidwell in a covered wagon to Spanish Fort, Texas. It took us quite a few days to cover the miles, but we had fun. We would sleep in the wagon at night and cook our meals over a fire outside. I remember the cool, dewy mornings when we cooked bacon and other foods over the fire. How good it tasted! Simple life was fun and the beautiful world God made for us, we enjoyed!

Reading these words of such joy over simple things gives my heart such a sense of nostalgia — "the good old days." But the simple life can still be ours if we make it so, enjoying the things that belong to everyone — a starry night, a radiant sunrise, a cool, dewy morning, a breakfast cooked outside over an open fire, a glorious sunset, a cool breeze, these have not changed; they are even enhanced by the contrast with the complexity of the age in which we now live.

Then, as soon as they had come to land, they saw a fire of coals there, and fish laid on it, and bread. Jesus said to them, 'Bring some of the fish which you have caught...Come and eat breakfast.' John 21:9-12 (NKJV)

Dear Lord, I wish I could have been there at that breakfast you served. There you were, after your glorious resurrection, preparing food for your disciples who had been fishing, so that you could have breakfast together with them. What a fun time you all must have had. May I create times such as this for my friends and family — simple food, prepared with love to start a day filled with appreciation for all the simple joys. Amen.

August 4

Tumbleweeds — Part 4
The Healing Waters

About the Waurika Harper land she tells us:

...my father had bought a farm about a mile northeast of Waurika. Here, we had a large house with room for all our family. The porch encircled most of the house. The water well on the farm had a mineral taste. My Father had it analyzed and was permitted to sell it for health purposes. Many people came with jugs and other containers to buy the water.

Perhaps that old well is still there, flowing out its life-giving springs. I would like just a sip, wouldn't you? Are you thirsty — oh, not for that kind of water — but for *spiritual* water? If you are not, there is something wrong. Pray to be thirsty; pray to be hungry. For how will you be filled, if you do not know that you are empty?

Ho! Everyone who thirsts, Come to the waters; And you who have no money, Come, buy and eat. Yes, come, buy wine and milk without money and without price. Why do you spend money for what is not bread, and your wages for what does not satisfy? Listen diligently to Me, and eat what is good, and let your soul delight itself in abundance. Incline your ear, and come to Me. Hear and your soul shall live... Isaiah 55:1-3 (NKJV)

Lord God, if I imagine that I am satisfied when I am not, make me thirsty. Help me find in You the water of spiritual life so that I may come and drink, and my soul might come to life. Amen.

August 5

Tumbleweeds — Part 5
Waurika Floods

When the floods came:

I can remember when the creek running through Waurika became a raging river covering the main street. It came across the railroad tracks and partly up the hill. We were living a mile from town when the flood came. People came to our house to stay until the waters went down and they could go back to their homes.

This is a picture of higher ground, a safe refuge in a time of severe and unseasonable flooding. That old home was a place where neighbors were welcome. No doubt coffee and food were served 'round the old fireplace and everything was shared. I want my home to be like that, oh, not necessarily just in time of physical disasters, though that could happen, but I want our home to be a safe place where people can come share their fears and cares and feel safe.

Deliver me out of the mire, And let me not sink; Let me be delivered from those who hate me, and out of the deep waters. Let not the floodwater overflow me, Nor let the deep swallow me up... Psalm 69:14, 15 (NKJV)

Lord, let my home be a place where those who feel they are "drowning" can come for a safe spiritual refuge. Give me the grace to pass on to them so that they might receive the comfort they need. Amen.

August 6

Tumbleweeds — Part 6
The Good Father

Here's a report of more Oklahoma weather phenomena:

In the springtime the cyclones and tornadoes kept us watching. They could come up in the middle of the night. Many times we were awakened by Father; half asleep; we got into some clothes and ran to the storm cellar. In those days, no house was built without a storm cellar. We knew when Father said, "to the cellar," we should not tarry, because Oklahoma storms didn't give you time to tarry. I was almost as afraid of the inside of the cellar as of the storms. The lantern was lit and carried into the cellar first. Then we went down. There had been places cut out of the walls where we could sit, but I was always afraid of snakes that might be coiled in the shadows or a spider would jump on me. Father would stand at the door, on the steps, holding the door ajar so he could see out. He would watch and it amazed me that he knew exactly when the storm had passed over and it was safe for us to go back into the house. How wonderful it was to hear him say, 'We can go back to bed now!' We would run for the house, although the wind was still blowing. We could trust our Father to know it was safe, and pile back into bed to fall asleep without fear.

Here is a beautiful example of a good father, playing the role of protector of his family. I love this story because it gives us a picture of how our Heavenly Father looks after us. Not all of us have had good, protective fathers that we could trust, but we all have a good Father in Heaven. Let's look for similar picture stories in our lives and in the world, that show us who the Heavenly Father is.

The Lord is my rock, my fortress and my deliverer; The God of my strength, in Him I will trust, My shield and the horn of my salvation, My stronghold and my refuge... 2 Samuel 22:2, 3 (NKJV)

Lord, help me to learn how to hide in you even in the midst of storms. Amen.

August 7

The Glories of the Sea

When we moved to the desert, I longed for the sea. I missed the Pacific Ocean that we so often visited when we lived in Southern California. We took it for granted and I didn't know just how dearly I relished that special gift of just walking along the shore, until it was six hours away. I wrote this poem to help remind me.

Spirit Me

Come brave riders on the wistful wind, soft walkers on the summer storm,
Whisk me away, across yellow sands, and over playful gusts of warm,
Above dusty planes, far, far, and farther away,
Let me dream a soft night, let me laugh a sweet day,

Beside, above and under my ancient mother sea,
Who, glistening, by moon or sun, rocks and lullabys me.
It's there I'll freely soar, I'll dance and sing, I'll laugh and play
With albatross and gull of sea until the break of day,

Where great whales, singing, beckon me and dolphins bid me stay
And ocean breezes whisper and teach me the white foam's way.
It's there I'll fish and catch each picture in a thankful heart
Of swirling greens and blues in magic mixtures that will dart

In many shades of healing cool and scents of blissful blue.
So, swimming in these memories, I'll then return to you:
My fair, but naughty sands that cause bare feet to prance and burn.
To you, twisting angel winds that ever twirl and turn.

Yes! Carry me far away, but bring me back again,
New portraits trapped forever in my hungry soul and then
When comes the time of blowing sands that bring the stinging pain,
And threatening laughter in the clouds that bear an angry rain,

Let these scenes remind me, with this constant rainbow scroll
Of fond memories that calm and gently soothe my thirsty soul.
So, please — just this once — quench my longing for the gift of wings
And gladly take me to the sea's bubbling spouts and joyful springs.

To happy, giggling children chasing crabs and saving shells,
To strolling lovers, captured by the seaside's mildest spells,
Yes, come friends, riders on the sky, and carry me away,
For just one more gentle night, for just one bright, dancing day.

Let the Heavens rejoice, and let the earth be glad; Let the sea
roar, and all its fullness... Psalm 96:11 (NKJV)

Lord, thank you for wonders of this world that you have created, especially the oceans and seas. Help us to take care of them and remember that it is you who are the Creator of all such beauty. Amen.

August 8

A Visitation of Hope in Time of Sorrow

I've mentioned her before — my friend, Suzanne, who died from cancer. I looked for her healing, but it did not come. As she neared the time of her soul departing from her body, I had an experience of realizing God's presence, even if He was not healing her physically. The day I finally accepted the truth, she said to me, "I guess I need to tell you that I know I am dying." I didn't want to hear these words; I was hanging on to every hope. I had prayed continually for two years for her healing and had believed for it, but that day I faced the fact that she was truly dying and that God was not going to work the longed-for miracle.

As I left her house, I heard a mocking bird singing and turned and looked up at her two-story home. On the topmost part of the roof, there was that bird singing its heart out! Had I not noticed that, I would have missed something else — beyond her I saw a whole flock of geese, something I had never seen in Southern California during my entire life of over 50 years of living there! They moved silently, gracefully southward, but one broke formation and came in my direction and dropped lower and honked, and then returned to its station in the sky. I was spellbound, standing there in wonder as I watched them. Somehow in that moment, I knew that, no matter what happened, God was in the midst of our circumstances, and that day, by way of those Snow geese, I knew that truly God had come near. I hadn't gotten my way; but God had gotten His, and my hope was still in Him.

For You are my hope, O Lord God... Psalm 71:5(NKJV)

Lord God, I acknowledge your presence in all of life, even when it seems my prayers are not answered. I proclaim you to be Sovereign God. Just like that mocking bird, proclaiming forth its territory, you call out above me, "She is mine." I am in your territory. The fact that ultimately you are in charge means that you are still my hope, no matter what seems to be happening around me. Amen.

August 9

The Rainbow's Promise

When living in Arizona, Don and I saw many rainbows, but one day we saw a RAINBOW — Oh! Not just any rainbow! This rainbow was different. It was, within the single ribbon of color, a double rainbow, twice through the entire spectrum! Then, outside of that, in portions of the late afternoon sky, was another rainbow, making it a triple rainbow in places. I was transfixed; it literally took my breath away. Yes, it was more than an ordinary rainbow (though I doubt that there is such a thing as an "ordinary" rainbow). It was saying something to me. It was promising something to us. Our time in Arizona had been rocky, heart breaking, and spiritually discouraging, but there was a promise in the sky, waiting for me to take it: *God is not going to let us be destroyed here. We will survive in His care.* I received this miracle in the sky very personally, no matter how "natural" an event it might have been, or, for that matter, no matter how many others, in faith, looked heavenward, and said, "Lord, I take your promise for *me* today." That day that rainbow and all it promised belonged to me!

> *The rainbow shall be in the cloud, and I will look on it to remember the everlasting covenant between God and every living creature of all flesh that is on the earth.* Genesis 9:16 (NKJV)

Creator God, thank you for your gifts of signs in nature that remind us that you keep your promises forever. Amen.

August 10

A Case of the Gets

We hear a constant bombardment of "Gets" these days: Get a life, get real, get a job, get a grip, get over it, get on with your life, don't get mad — get even; get with it; get happy! A bumper sticker I saw today on a four-wheel drive vehicle, said, "Get in, shut up, and hold on!" But wait a minute. With all this free advice coming at us, let's look at what the Bible says about getting:

> *Get wisdom! Get understanding!...Wisdom is the principal thing; therefore get wisdom, And in all your getting, get understanding.* Proverbs 4:5, 7 (NKJV)

> *How much better it is to get wisdom than gold! And to get understanding is to be chosen rather than silver.* Proverbs 16:16. (NKJV)

> *The fear of the Lord is the beginning of wisdom.* Psalm 111:10 (NKJV)

Lord, to be in awe of you, to acknowledge your greatness, to believe in you, is the beginning of wisdom, and therefore, it must be the end as well. May I above all else, then, *get* this one thing: wisdom. Amen.

August 11

What's Missing?

In art of any form, what is missing can be as important as what remains. The selective choice is also the selective omission. In writing a novel, what are left out are the simple, mundane things of life. In a piano composition too many harmony lines will camouflage the melody. In a painting, the choice of not only the object painted, but the space between objects is part of the composition, as well as certain colors and the omission of others that create the desired illusion.

When I think about Jesus and his life, what was missing? Was it a full life? What did He leave out? A few things come to mind: He, after a certain point, left his profession as carpenter. There is no record that He ever had a romantic interest and certainly no wife or children of His own. He forfeited, as well, a long life, for it is believed He died around the age of 33. He forfeited honor and glory, which He could have chosen, but instead chose servanthood and poverty. He laid aside the

Heavenly glory He had known before, and became a man whom He himself described as having no place to lay His head. Jesus missed much in his life, so that we might, now and Someday, miss absolutely nothing!

> *And Jesus said to him, 'Foxes have holes and birds of the air have nests, but the Son of Man has nowhere to lay His head.'*
> Luke 9:58 (NKJV)

Lord Jesus, I cannot help but love you as I am reminded of how carefully you chose what to leave in, but also what to leave out, of your own experience here on earth. Amen.

August 12

Food for the Heart

Food! It's a friendly word, isn't it? It's always much more enjoyable to eat with others than to eat by yourself. So, here's my very own recipe for my favorite tuna salad.

    1 3 1/2 oz. can white chunk tuna (dolphin safe)
    1 apple (Gala is best); reserve 4 wedges and chop remainder
    2 Tablespoons mayonnaise
    1 Tablespoon honey mustard
    1/2 tsp. curry powder
    1/4 tsp. grated orange rind or orange marmalade
    Hand full of currants (or raisins)
    1/4 cup chopped celery
    1 1/2 Tablespoon sweet pickle relish
    1/4 cup of walnuts for crunchiness (optional)

Mix and add low fat yogurt, low fat sour cream or more mayonnaise if more moisture is needed. Serve, using a round scoop, on a bed of greens and garnish with remaining apple slices.

Suggestion: Now, call someone and invite her/him to lunch. Maybe you could make it a person who needs spiritual nourishment too and you can witness to them or pray for them. Then serve the tuna salad and with a bran muffin or a cranberry scone, iced tea and love. "Enjoy!"

The little girl got up at once and began to walk out...and [He] told them to give her something to eat. Mark 5:42, 43 (NKJV)

Lord, is there someone you would like for me to invite to lunch? Put that person on my heart and make this time with her (or him) and with You something special. Amen.

August 13

Out of Joint

I was making coffee and noticed that the plastic lid on the glass portion of the pot was not on straight. I looked at it from different angles, trying to figure out what was the matter with it, but I couldn't see anything wrong except it was slightly askew. Still, I could fit it under the rest of the coffee maker, but I had to kind of force it. I took it out again. I put it up to eye level and looked carefully at the plastic hinge. Aha! I saw what was wrong: the hinge was not quite in straight. I applied some carefully aimed pressure and pop! Just like a chiropractor working on a bad back, it snapped into place. Just as I did that, it was as though the Lord was saying to me: "That's the way our relationship has been [yours and Mine] lately; everything was working; we were not completely out of fellowship, but until you forgave Me two nights ago, we just weren't quite in sync." Now, I didn't actually hear those words with my ears; I just heard them in my heart. I understood!

Sometimes God hurts us or disappoints us by just being God. I read an article some time ago by an eminent theologian about how we should not even speak about forgiving God because He doesn't sin. But that isn't the point! Sometimes we need to forgive God for our own sakes because we don't like something He did or didn't do. I was carrying resentment in my heart against God! At that moment two nights before, laying awake in the dark, I suddenly knew that I must forgive Him. The Lord had taken something away from me and I felt I could not bear it. I felt betrayed and deeply hurt by Him and I said it to Him, "I forgive you Lord." Two days later, the Lord showed me a real life picture of what had happened by the *parable* of the coffee pot lid! I needed to know that — that even though things were not perfect, somehow His and my relationship had not been entirely broken, just badly "out of joint!"

> *The Lord gave and the Lord hath taken away; blessed be the name of the Lord.* Job 1:21 (NKJV)

Lord, I know that everything I have is really yours and so am I. You bought me with a price and I have said, "Not my will but thine be done," but then sometimes when your will is done, it seems so horrendous and I just don't want to embrace it. Help me to let go of my will and way and to say with Job, no matter what, "Blessed be the name of the Lord." Amen.

August 14

Other Eyes

As I walked toward the Acacia tree, it looked beautiful, filled with yellow blossoms, almost serene. As I got closer, I heard something! What was that sound — a decided hum? The tree was full of life. It was filled with — Yikes! — bees! Needless to say, I didn't stay long. However, those bees were properly and proverbially busy! I thought of the times in my life when I've looked at a group, a person, a church, and thought nothing much was going on! But how deceived I was. When I got closer, I found that all kinds of things were happening — underground labors for the Lord — not big bright, well-advertised work. No, just little quiet deeds with the work coming out of compassionate hearts and souls, and individuals — quiet on the outside, but on the inside, aflame with desire to serve others and aflame with love for the Lord, just not showy, not obvious! So, let's take time to find out about these things! It's worth it. There's a lot going on everywhere! We can ask God to help us see with eyes and ears that are inspired by His all-knowing spirit.

...His eyes behold.... Psalm 11:4b (NKJV)

Lord, when it pleases you, give me eyes to see what you see. Amen.

August 15

The Sea in Autumn Light

As I shared before, I love the sea. I have always felt a yearning to be near it — something in my soul responds to whatever it is that the sea gives. Many years ago I wrote a letter to the Lord about my feelings as I basked by the sea on a fall day.

Dear God, this is so beautiful. Thank you. When I arrived by the sea shore I was anxious and worried, but then I saw the ocean, and she seemed to say, "Welcome, darling; everything is all right now." Oh, the sea is in my soul. I think of her as "Mother Sea," and I hate being far away from this "mother." It's almost as though I can't breathe if I am too far away from here.

The Ocean. Today it is difficult to describe. I've never seen it quite like this before. The sun is hitting the waves from a different angle. Underneath, they are black-green, out further there are dark gray valleys and shining peaks. There is a strip of foggy, smoky haze above the horizon but in front of that there are a few white — no, more than white — sail boats spot-lighted by the sun, the same brilliant white as the foam.

The Sky. White cumulus clouds, streaked across with gray by Your giant paintbrush. Yes, it looks like a painting — unreal — yet no it's not! It's just one of those so very real offerings of life that catch you so totally off guard that at first you doubt its reality, and you have a "This-can't-be-real" feeling. It is the unexpected that captures you in a most wonderful way. You think, "Am I dreaming?" And yet deeply you know that it is that intense, static moment that is screaming louder than anything "This is reality."

The sea is His, for He made it... Psalm 95:5 (NKJV)

Creator God, thank you for the beauties of the oceans and seas that you have created; they remind us of the depths of your love. Amen.

August 16

The Outside Vs the Inside

As I write this, there are those around me who are suffering from many physical ailments. Not to overburden you, but here is a partial list: One dear lady has severe leg cramps and is unable to determine the cause; another just fell and needed several stitches in her scalp; a little child has what appears to be a life-threatening illness, but doctors are not sure what it is; a man with diabetes just had to have a finger amputated; two women are just recovering from surgery; another...well, I'll stop there, but there are more.

I should not to be surprised at such things; they are to be expected as part of our lives on the earth. We are not to allow ourselves to become discouraged. Why is that? Because whatever our physical suffering, it is "light" and though our physical beings are aging, our inner selves are growing, being built up daily! Just read these verses and be encouraged:

So we do not lose heart. Even though our outer nature is wasting away, our inner nature is being renewed day by day. 2 Corinthians 4:16 (NRS)

Lord, teach me to count any physical suffering as a temporary thing that even in itself will, by your grace and mercy, be building me up in my inner person. Amen.

August 17

Encouraging the Children

Which kind of friends do you like most — those who say kind and encouraging words, or those who withhold their encouragement and praise and make critical remarks, with sourpuss expressions of disapproval? I read somewhere that we must hear something good about ourselves many times before we believe it, but that most of us accept without question, the critical thing said to us just once. I know this is true of me. I am easily discouraged, but this was especially true of me as a child. Children need encouragement and praise from the adults in their lives.

As adults it is within our power to encourage the children we are so fortunate to have in our lives. We can acknowledge the gifts we see in them. On my desk is a colorful bookmark card published by ©The Positive Line. Printed on it is a list of 101 Ways to Praise Kids. Here are a few: That's incredible! Far out! Great! Terrific! You tried hard! You made it happen! Fabulous! Bravo! Dynamite!

And the list goes on! What a great idea, this card is. (Thank you, Positive Line!). Let's learn how to praise the children in your life. If we smile and *encourage* them (cause them to be *courageous*), they will flourish in the atmosphere of strength and nurture that you create!

Be strong, and let your heart take courage.... Psalm 31:24 (NRS)

Lord Jesus, lover of the children, help me to be the one who brings encouragement to the little ones with whom you have entrusted me. Amen.

August 18

The Poustinia

In Catherine Doherty's book, "Poustinia," she speaks of that place where the Russian Poustiniks (or hermits) would go to find their dwelling with God. The place would be as simple as possible, the only furniture a chair and a cot, the only book, a Bible.

In Russia when a Christian received the calling of God to be a Poustinik, he or she would sell all their worldly goods and go to the woods near a community and build a little hut. The community would always welcome the presence of the Poustinik because they knew that he or she would pray for them and would be there to help them when any need presented itself. The villagers would bring food to the Poustinik. They were not hermits, as we know them, because they were not recluses but were always welcoming any and all to their little domicile. Their door was to be locked to no one (only the wind) and whatever they had would be shared with any guest even if it were only water.

The rest of his or her time would be spent reading and placing the word of God into their hearts. A Poustinik was always to tell whatever he had heard God speak to him while in the poustinia.

What Catherine Doherty brings to us in the West is a new kind of understanding of this calling. We can then, have within us a Poustinik of the heart.

When God asked me to go on an 18-day juice fast, it wasn't until I was in the middle of the fast that I realized He was calling me to the poustinia *within* and that He had some things to teach me. It was not until the last day of the fast that I was able to get to that poustinia within myself through the vehicle of my imagination. I went through the darkness of my own soul and had much pain and suffering and "saw" my flesh as pulverized. I reached that place (inner poustinia) where I asked Jesus to come. Of course, I had asked Him there before, but this was truly the inner center of my being and I asked Him again, just in case I had not been clear in the past. I did not know how dusty it would be. I imagined it was full of cobwebs and spiders and bats. I was not pleased to ask my Lord into this place but I knew I had to because only His light could make the darkness flee.

When I "saw" my little hut in the mountains, it was quite plain but I was excited because I was going to have a special guest. I got it all ready as best I could and found some olives and figs and wine and bread to feed my Lord when He would come to "dine" with me. I wanted Him to be comfortable, but I knew he was happy with simplicity. And He came! I was greatly pleased to serve Him, but in the midst of this visualization, I was called away, either by external or internal distractions and then when I returned, I saw myself go up the mountain path to the door where I saw Jesus standing in the doorway, looking at me with great anticipation and joy that I was coming "home." I knew with all the delight of a child in my soul — I had asked Jesus to come and He had moved in. It was now His place. He welcomed me in and He had made the hut all that I wanted it to be. There were wild flowers on the little wooden table, picked from the meadows nearby. There was food — fresh fruits and vegetables and nuts. There was a little braided rag rug on the floor and a comforter on the cot where He asked me to rest and He wanted to rub my sore, tired feet. The Servant of all was now serving me. What a truly humbling experience this inner journey was.

I came to realize that this is what we all need: that center, that lovely, comfortable place where Jesus dwells, *always*: He does not leave. He is at home there and all the time, and even when we are "gone," He is praying for us and waiting for us. We need to know that wherever we go, no matter what chaos there is about us, there is that quiet center where the Lord of Heaven and Earth dwells. How can we possibly become the servant of others without it?

It was difficult for me to find that place and maybe you already have access to it easily and at all times, but if not, I hope that you're able to find it there, in the center of your being, the home of the indwelling Christ, so that you might at any time draw water from that well, light from His light, peace and joy and love from His presence within.

You, Father are in Me, and I in You; that they may be one in Us... John 17:21 (NKJV)

Lord, help each of us not to only invite you in but remember that you are there and that together we go about our lives and invite others to be part of this family of love. Amen.

August 19

The Touch

I shared with you before how I fell in love with my piano teacher at the age of 13. I built my life around the days that I would go for my music lesson. Every week I spent time in his presence and those moments together fed something in my hungry, young soul. Then one day, when I was 16 we had a "date." It was my birthday and he took me to the Griffith Park Observatory — one of my favorite places. We learned magical things about the moon and spiraling galaxies and planets in their orbits. Walking beside him was my glory and my heaven. As he drove me home, I feigned sleepiness so I could lie on the seat next to him, my hand could rest toward his leg and my little finger could touch his knee. This way I could draw part of him into me — without him even knowing it. I stole a part of him silently and secretly that night and I received a healing. I wonder if he knew.

There is a story about a woman who did something similar with Jesus. She knew that if she could only touch the hem of his garment she would be healed. She thought she could do it without anyone knowing. She was wrong. Jesus called out, asking who had touched him. Maybe He already knew who she was before He asked. Maybe He knew also that she needed to acknowledge her healing before others and she needed a word from Him that she might receive more than she ever dreamed possible. That's the way Jesus is — giving other than, and more than, we ask, often in ways that we do not recognize at first. We ask for a job and He gives none for a while, so that we may spend more time with Him and learn the secrets of poverty. We ask for a mate and are given none, that we may find in Him our all in all. We ask for a healing and receive none, that we may learn patience and obedience and how to receive Him in our suffering. When we know that He is our best friend and that we can trust Him utterly, we know that He will be there in every circumstance of life, forever.

If only I may touch His garment, I shall be made well.
Matthew 9:21 (NKJV)

Lord, I reach out to you to touch you today, knowing that by so doing, there is some way in which I will be made well. Amen.

August 20

The Strongest of Hands

Mei-leng, originally from Mainland China, was our amah during our term on the mission field in Taiwan. One day she told me in her broken English how she became a believer: "I no good, Missy! I go here. I go there. I play má jiáng (Mahjong). I no good [person], Missy. One time I dream I stand on high, high up place. Looky way down all around. I on tiny island with cliffs." She turned all around indicating the vast chasm below her, "Way down here, way down there." I scare, Missy. I cannot get across [to a safe place]. Then man come. He big, strong, have long hair and he dress long white robe and he have big, big hands. He reach hand across to me and lift me over [indicating abyss]. Her face changed from the acted-out fear to one of radiance. "I safe. I happy. I wake up. I think *I now takey Jesu into my heart.*" Her face beamed with joy as she covered her heart with both of her hands.

I knew that she understood that the man in her dream was Jesus, but she had never seen a traditional Westernized portrait of Him. One Sunday sometime later, after returning from church service, I left the church bulletin on the kitchen table. Mei-leng gasped and picked it up. "Missy, who jissy man?" She pointed to the conventional likeness of Jesus depicted on the front cover.

"Why Mei-leng, that's Jesus. Haven't you ever seen a picture of Him before?"

"No, Missy. I no see. I take, keep, OK?"

"Yes, of course, Mei-leng."

She smiled in ecstasy, as she clutched the picture to her heart, "Missy, this is same man I dream who come with big hand and save me. Jissy [this is] my Jesu."

Is my hand shortened at all that it cannot redeem? Isaiah 50:2b (NKJV)

Lord, we are all in need of a rescuer and we know you are the only One who can save us. Reach out your mighty hand to us and we will take it! Amen.

August 21

A Place of Rest — Part 1

Did you ever try so hard to do what you thought you should that you exhausted yourself, and then found that God wanted you to give up because then He could start working?

My salvation experience was similar. As I shared with you before, I tried being a Christian for about a week. My goal was, I thought, simple enough: I would say nothing bad, do nothing wrong and think nothing evil. You can't imagine how shocked I was that I couldn't follow through! It was not until I despaired and gave up that I discovered that there was another way: asking Jesus Christ himself into my life to do it for me. That was more than 50 years ago and the process is still going on.

That was the beginning of my understanding of what "resting in the Lord" means. But God does things in His own way, using His own timetable and He works from within. In 1985 one of the hostages from Flight 847 shared how he had impressed one of his captors by explaining that he was not afraid on the outside or on the inside. When God works in us to create us in the likeness of Jesus Christ, He does it from the inside out and what happens in our hearts shines through to the outside.

But does "resting" mean that we just sit around passively waiting for God to do His perfect work? I don't think so. It is said that Einstein had the happiest thought of his life when it occurred to him that a person falling was both at rest and in motion at the same time. Existing in the element of God's grace is similar to that. We can enjoy the free fall of the skydiver or fight all the way down; it's up to us.

Letting go and letting God may sound easy, but it is not. It's not being passive; it's about the most active thing we can do. This is not only because it involves will and practice, but because just the other side of rest is trust, and just the other side of trust is love and love implies relationship — one that is intimate at that, and which, just as in marriage, takes work, time and energy.

Aspire to lead a quiet life... 1 Thessalonians 4:11 (NKJV)

Lord, help me to understand about the kind of rest that you require of me. Amen.

August 22

A Place of Rest — Part 2

But how do we rest? There is nothing quiet and passive about relationships and love. Love is active, caring, doing, and giving. It is involvement. But if we attempt actions of love before basking in the presence of the King of Love, it is apt to be laborious, dutiful and wearisome. If however, we take time to partake of the Source, soak up that love and life and grace, believe it, receive it, and become filled with it, then we may go out into the world, and we won't have to try; it will happen; it will be spontaneous and it will be joyful because it comes from the overflow.

This does not mean we don't get tired, or have empty days, even times when we find we must give out of our need. That is part of the process, but the goal, the ideal, is to find that place of constant rest. It is possible.

When Peter exhorts us to humble ourselves under the mighty hand of God so that we might partake of grace, he also presents to us a God on whom we may cast our cares — because "He cares for you." (I Peter 5:7) When Jesus told His disciples not to be anxious, He was speaking to us as well. Jesus meant what He said — I'm going to start believing that; I don't think I've taken it seriously enough before. What about you? Do you know this kind of rest? Do you realize that God wants us to abide in this place constantly? This is His vision for His people — that we might abide in Him, not just occasionally, but every single moment.

Remain in me, and I will remain in you. For a branch cannot produce fruit if it is severed from the vine, and you cannot be fruitful unless you remain in me. John 15:4, 9 (NLT)

Jesus, teach me about that kind of abiding so others can see fruits of the Spirit in my life. Amen.

August 23

A Place of Rest — Part 3

Evelyn Underhill, in discussing Abbe Henri De Tourville's inner life style, says that this complete confidence in the divine generosity "is of all methods the most exacting because...it must be applied at every moment." Tourville himself said, "A perfect childlike simplicity puts us at once into an intimate relationship with God without hindrance."

Brother Lawrence found this same rest by practicing the continuing presence of God and doing all that he did, not for the praise of men, but out of his love for God. This is why he could claim to be "in as great tranquility" in his kitchen working as he was upon his knees "at the blessed sacrament."

Perhaps this life is a little like sailing. When we go sailing, we don't fight the wind but we do make sure our sail is set so that the wind can do the rest. I believe that is the way it can be when we are in the center of God's will, abiding in Him and doing all for the love of Him. What a wonder to have this available to us, not a dutiful, driven life, but a life filled with expressions of love we have for the One who loved us so much that He, upon the cross, gave His life for us.

This is the law of love; this is the kingdom of God; this is the life lived in the restfulness of the wind of God's will.

The idea of resting in the Lord is, of course, not new. It seems to have been Jesus' idea.

Come to me, all who are weary and heavy-laden and I will give you rest. Take my yoke upon you and learn of me for I am gentle and humble of heart and you shall find rest for your souls, for my yoke is easy and my load is light. Matthew 11:28-30 (NKJV)

Lord, when I am weary in my soul and think that I can't go on, help me to remember that you are my place of rest. Amen.

August 24

The Dress Rehearsal

Don Richardson, one of my acting coaches, directed many episodes of the TV western series, *Bonanza*. One of the actors was Dan Blocker who played the character of Hoss. Don told how Dan, who had a photographic memory, could memorize his lines in one reading, and then would totally throw himself into the part — it was as though he became that person. In a discussion of the plot, if he (the actor) heard of some dastardly deed done by a villain, he would exclaim, "Oh, no. He didn't do that did he?" — never out of character, even off camera.

That's what we need to do, isn't it? — To totally throw ourselves into this backstage drama of life. We are given a role to play, our very lives, servants of the Most High God. After all, in some ways the curtain hasn't even gone up yet. That will happen when Jesus Christ returns — the dawning of a new age — the time when God's purpose will be done on Earth as it is in Heaven, and then we will see what the "show" is really about! Meanwhile, we prepare, and hoe our row, as the farmers do, and know that, someday, the spiritual reality will come upon us. And if we've learned our part, we will know how to play it once the next curtain goes up.

Remind them to be subject to rulers and authorities, to obey, to be ready for every good work, to speak evil of no one, to be peaceable, gentle, showing all humility to all men. Titus 3:1, 2 (NKJV)

Lord, help me see clearly the role that you have appointed for me today. Amen.

August 25

Dyslexia of the Spirit

In first grade, I was in a fog. I didn't understand what was going on around me. I recall looking up at a picture of Little Boy Blue asleep against a haystack. I understood that picture well. I can see his sleepy little face, his horn beside him, the haystack, the blue sky dotted with the whitest of clouds. I wanted to be there. The memory of that picture resides clearly in my soul.

My mother would call the teacher to see how "Patty" was doing. The teacher would say, "Oh, just fine." However, the teacher was talking about the other Patty, the bright one, not me. But in time, it was discovered that I could not read. Whatever method of teaching was being used in that class was not working for me, so Mom wouldn't let me pass first grade and she, evening after evening, after working all day, would sit down with me and teach me to read, using phonics. I finally learned how, but it didn't come easily.

At that time the term "dyslexia" was not used but years later I was tested and found to have a moderate degree of dyslexia. I can confuse two of anything, for instance: North/South or left/right or 21 and 12. When it comes to words, an example would be that the liquor Grand Marnier was to my eyes named for an old sea captain (Grand Mariner). Recently I had a chance to play with a flight simulator. To pull forward was to make the plane climb; to pull back was to make the plane go lower. I couldn't get it! I continually confused the two directions. So I crashed landed the plane off the runway! Mmm, perhaps I'd best not try to learn to fly after all.

Is it possible to be a spiritual dyslexic? Can I get confused about my belief system and believe that faith is trying instead of resting? Of course; I've proven that in my own life. But there is a way that is straight and there is a path that is the way, and that way is a Person. Let's keep focused on Him as He goes before us. This way we won't get confused and go in the opposite direction.

The eye is the lamp of the body. So, if your eye is healthy, your whole body will be full of light; but if your eye is unhealthy, your whole body will be full of darkness. If then

the light in you is darkness, how great is the darkness!
Matthew 6:22, 23 (NRSV)

Lord, help me to have clear and healthy inner vision so I may be filled
with light. Amen.

August 26

More Than One Kind of Thief

When I was around nine years old, I was taking a walk down our 300-
foot old, dirt driveway. Along the side of the drive were some
beautiful, red Pyracantha berries hanging seductively over a neighbor's
fence. *Might they be mine, since they are on our side?* I wondered. I
didn't know for sure. But I wanted them. I picked a bunch and decided
to give them to my mother (This "generosity" of course, was to keep
me from feeling so guilty about picking someone else's berries.). I
stood before her with my hands behind my back. She asked what I was
hiding. I smiled and said I had a present for her and handed her the
berries. Guilt must have been written all over my face.

She didn't smile. "Where did you get these?" she asked. I told her.
She said "These are not our berries; they belong to [our neighbor] Mr.
Post. You will need to go to him and apologize and give them back."
Thud went my heart. Oh, how humiliating! I didn't want to, but Mama
insisted and I went down our old drive, and up his, and stood shakily
on the porch steps and knocked. I could hear him limping to the door,
using his cane. He was in his nineties. "Here, Mr. Post," I poked the
berries at him. "I stole these from you. I'm sorry." He frowned at me,
took them and grumbled, "Well just don't do it again." *Slam!* went the
door. Such humiliation and such a response was indeed a great
deterrent. Thievery would not one of life's options for me!

But what about stealing other kinds of things? What about stealing
someone's heart, their affections that rightfully belong to another? We
can deeply hurt someone by doing what seems like a "harmless"
flirtation. If we are tempted, we need to back away immediately, before
we hurt someone and, in the end, ourselves and our relationship with

the Lord. It's not too late. We can ask for God's strength in the midst of such temptations. He will make a way to escape!

No temptation has overtaken you except such as is common to man; but God is faithful, who will not allow you to be tempted beyond what you are able, but with the temptation will also make the way of escape, that you may be able to bear it. 1 Corinthians 10:13 (NKJV)

Lord, keep us from giving into the temptation of taking anything that belongs to another. Amen.

August 27

Lost & Found — Part 1
A Spiritual Detour

There was a time when I believed in reincarnation. It was the western-ized version — romantic and tantalizing where a soul is reborn many times over, into a new body, and often travels through the centuries with the same group of friends or relatives. A more appropriate term would be "transmigration of the spirit." It is fanciful and not truly spiritual in concept but ever so tantalizing and romantic. For instance, when you meet someone to whom you are attracted, you can imagine that part of the reason for that so-called "mystical allure" is that you knew that person in a former life as perhaps someone you loved, but at that time, in that century, he or she was not able to return your love. This then becomes the making of a perfectly understandable passionate affair consummated after perhaps centuries of unrequited love. I believed such lies even after becoming a Christian. I thought they had just been left out of Scripture! I even went so far as to have what is called a "Life Reading" and found out all the *wonderful* people I had been, starting from the time I was a guidance counselor on the mythical continent of Atlantis!

After making this long and treacherous spiritual detour, as I was about to read the Bible one day, I realized that there was something wrong with my beliefs. I asked the Lord to show me if my concept of reincarnation was true. I then looked down to where I had already opened the Bible. There the words stood out as though marked with a highlighter:

> *And as it is appointed for men to die once, but after this the judgment, so Christ was offered once to bear the sins of many.* Hebrews 9:27, 28 (NKJV)

Lord God of Truth, if I am to die once, then I am to live but once and once only. Where I am in error in any of my beliefs, I ask that you bring the light of your sacred word to me, so that I may know reality. Amen.

August 28

Lost & Found — Part 2
A Return to the Path

In my thirties, I felt an emptiness inside and began to search for what I thought would be something "more." My spirit went after other gods, in a manner of speaking, and my heart after another man. I left my husband and in so fleeing, after some time, found myself in the incredibly dark world of the occult with nothing left but a broken heart.

How could I, a Christian woman, have wandered so far away from what the Lord wanted for me? It can happen when there are areas of darkness, when what psychologists called "the shadow" self has not been discovered or dealt with — so off I went in search of fulfillment that left me empty and wounded. My husband and I were divorced. My times with the children were limited, upon their request. Yes, my heart was broken and I knew I had believed lies, but what were they? Where was the truth?

What should I believe now? I asked the Lord. This was the reply He gave to me, *"Jesus Christ and him crucified."* (1 Cor. 2:2). That was it, and I heard those words as clearly as though an angel standing right there in the room had spoken them to me. So I started back at the beginning, back to the foundation of my faith, praising God and asking for His mercy. And He was there. He came for me and brought me back to Himself and His light!

Have you ever wandered off? Maybe you have and don't even know it. Take a moment and reflect. Do you feel centered — oh, not in yourself, but in Christ? If your center lies anywhere else, you are in need of correction; you've strayed. Come on back into the light.

At midday, O king, along the road, I saw a light from heaven shining more brilliant than the sun, shining around me and those who journeyed with me. [Words of St. Paul] Acts 26:13 (NKJV)

Lord, where I have wondered off, bring me back to the truth and yourself. Where I have been pulled off center, help me to center my life in you, and anywhere I am lost and in darkness, shine your radiant light on my path so that I may see. Amen.

August 29

Lost & Found — Part 3
The Healing of the Ring

During the process of healing I went through after this time away from the Lord, I found a prayer group which I began to attend every Friday night. It was at one of these meetings where the Lord spoke to me clearly in my heart and asked that I confess that I was in love with two men, "Ken" with whom I had become involved, and my (ex-husband) Don. I couldn't even comprehend what God was talking about. I had relinquished my love for Ken and I was certainly not in love with my ex-husband any longer! I argued with Him, *"I can't say that Lord. It's too humiliating."* But this gentle urging continued in my heart and so I obeyed. Those with whom I shared this that night did not make fun of me nor did they judge me; they prayed for me to know who God wanted in my life and what I should do.

My eyes were closed as they surrounded me in a blanket of prayer, but in front of me I "saw" a golden wedding band. It was about a foot in diameter, but it was not a complete ring; it was broken with a portion of about a third of it missing. However, as they continued to pray, I saw that gap bridged and it became a whole ring, round and complete! I was in a state of wonder! What could it mean? Was God going to heal my marriage? Was I, in fact, still in love with Don? And as I asked, I began to feel something — a love welling up in me for Don! I couldn't believe it. How could this be? A lost love restored? I felt a deep, secret place in me coming to life again and overheard myself wishing that my marriage could be saved! I was in shock. I still loved my former husband! How could this be? I still loved my Don.

Do not stir up nor awaken love until it pleases. Song of Solomon 2:7b (NKJV)

Lord, you promised that we would experience miracles greater than you performed when on earth. What could be greater than these inner miracles, where you change our hearts? Holy Spirit, where my heart is hard, soften it, where it is cold, heat it up, where it is shriveled, enlarge it, where love has slept, awaken it — for your name's sake. Amen.

August 30

Lost & Found — Part 4
A Marriage Restored!

For two weeks I prayed about the possibility of the restoration of our marriage every day and I felt more and more strongly that it was God's will for Don and me to be re-united. Or was it just another fantasy? I had to find out. I finally became courageous enough to call and ask him to come over for a cup of herb tea. I was ready to take a risk, knowing that the chances were that I would be rejected.

Don arrived, handsome as always, with his clear blue eyes that make me feel like I'm looking through him into the sky on a warm, spring day. We sat down on cushions (the only "furniture" I had) in my living room. I told him about the prayers I had received at the meeting and the vision of the gold wedding ring, and that I believed God wanted us to be together and so did I! He listened to all of this silently. When I had finished I asked him how he felt.

"I still love you, Pat, and if this is what God wants for us — to be together — then that's what I want too!" He touched my hand. We had just experienced our own quiet miracle.

We both cried and felt that what was happening to us was almost incredible, but it was just sweet and simple enough for us to know it was real. Don then did the perfect thing: He got up, kissed me on the forehead and said good-bye.

Within a few weeks, on a beautiful summer day under the gazebo on a cliff overlooking the Laguna Beach shore, we joined hands and became husband and wife in front of witnesses. And I felt just what all brides are supposed to feel: It was the happiest day of my life! That was 33 years ago, as of this writing. The second time around, though not without some hard times, is successful because this time Jesus Christ is truly the center of our life together.

Our favorite verse throughout the years has been the one quoted below. God has given us to each other as gifts. We are unspeakably grateful that he restored, healed and made our marriage more beautiful than it was before. And we have lived "happily ever after," loving each other more and more as the days and years go by.

My beloved is mine and I am his. Song of Solomon 2:16 (KJV)

Lord, sometimes life, when we obey your leading, gives us the happy endings we long for. Thank you for such times. Amen.

August 31

Depression's Depths

Many people suffer from depression. It is difficult to explain what it is like, but a friend of mine wrote a poem that describes the experience with insight and expertise. I know everyone does not experience depression is the same way, but for some his description may be nearly perfect. I include this poem, because if you too suffer from depression, you will find you are not alone, and if you do not, you will discover something of what it is like to find yourself in that dark world. I appreciate Zhenya Kovalenko's allowing me to use this for the sake of the readers.

Night

The North is silent
Uneasy lull awaits as darkness gathers
Dry rot unseen in lofty places
Unshored structures hid by Blackness
Sand and stone appear as one

Who beckons travelers?
Whose voice is clear?
Why are the sounds unsure?

Gusts disturb this tortured sleep
Words in flooded streams still rage
And desperation strips my soul
Before abyss...or hope

San Diego, April 1965

LORD, hear my prayer! Listen to my plea! Don't turn away from me in my time of distress. Bend down your ear and answer me quickly when I call to you, for my days disappear like smoke, and my bones burn like red-hot coals. My heart is sick, withered like grass, and I have lost my appetite. Because of my groaning, I am reduced to skin and bones. I am like an owl in the desert, like a lonely owl in a far-off wilderness. I lie awake, lonely as a solitary bird on the roof. Psalm 102:1-7 (NLT)

How long, O LORD? Will You forget me forever? How long will You hide Your face from me? How long shall I take counsel in my soul, Having sorrow in my heart daily? How long will my enemy be exalted over me? Psalm 13:1, 2 (NKJV)

Lord, for those who suffer from depression, I ask for your comfort to come to them. Help them to know that you remain with them through the darkest night, and that some day the Morning will come when there will be no more tears. Amen.

SEPTEMBER

September 1

A Close Call

In 1957, when I was 18, I had the following dream:

I was in the neighbor's garden. I looked up in the sky and I saw a huge, gray rug unfurl and roll down right to my feet. My heart stopped. My blood turned cold. I knew I was to walk up onto the carpet, and that this meant I was going to die. I took a step back, looked up and called out, "But I don't want to die yet. I'm too young." There was a pause, and then I knew my plea was heard because that rug that had come down from Heaven, rolled silently up into the sky and disappeared.

Still within the dream, I went back into our yard and Grandma was sitting there sewing. I told her what had just happened. She said, "This means that you are going to have a very close call with death. But you have been spared. You have something to accomplish. You will be allowed to live." I woke up.

Shortly after this, I went to a graduation party at a friend's house. Many of the graduating students were drinking. Several of us didn't have a ride home and "Harry" offered to drive us. He started out driving safely, but then we realized he was drunk. He began to speed, going east on California Street in Pasadena. We were screaming at him to stop, but he only went faster. I was sure we were going to die. Suddenly I felt as though I had been removed from my body. I was aware of another being beside me floating up there with me. I looked down from my place above the car, a blue convertible with the top down. I could see all of us, our hair blowing madly in the wind. I saw that we were coming up on Lake Avenue and that the light was red. There was no way we could stop. Mary, who was sitting in the passenger seat by Harry, suddenly jerked the wheel from his hands and pushed his foot off the gas peddle, so we could stop, but at that moment there was a car coming through the intersection. At this point I felt I returned to my body, though I won't make any certain claim that I actually left (See 2 Cor. 12:2.). Somehow, truly miraculously, the car missed us — just barely, but the next moment we were headed straight toward a light pole. Suddenly the car straightened out; I don't know how. We were safe, no accident, no deaths.

Was this the fulfillment of my dream? Whether it was or not, we had all been spared. And I was grateful to be alive!

O God; I will render praises to You, For You have delivered my soul from death. Have You not kept my feet from falling, That I may walk before God In the light of the living? Psalm 56:12, 13 (NKJV)

Lord, thank you for delivering us from danger, even those times when we don't realize that you are miraculously intervening. Amen.

September 2

Angels — Part 1
Michael's Visitor

There are times when I believe I've experienced angels. I'll share some examples of angelic encounters in the next devotional readings.

When our son, Michael, was a baby about seven months old, I heard him "talking" (the way babies talk, that is). He would say something and then laugh. One day I quietly crept into his bedroom where he lay in his crib. He was supposed to be taking a nap. I got the distinct impression that he was looking at something, or, more precisely, someone — invisible! He would wait, appear to be listening, and then laugh, or wait and then say something in baby talk. He seemed to be focusing right in the spot where someone would be if they were leaning over the crib gazing at him. But there was no one there — at least no one that I could see. I tiptoed out of the room where I felt that there was a lovely, warm presence. I didn't want to interfere with this wonderful exchange between two different kinds of God's creatures — a human child of the earth and an angelic being sent from Heaven.

See that you do not look down on one of these little ones. For I tell you that their angels in heaven always see the face of my Father in heaven. Matthew 18:10 (NIV)

Father, encourage us to believe in angels, just as the children do. Amen.

September 3

Angels — Part 2
Mrs. Lindsey's Angelic Vision

When I was about ten years old our family lived next door to an elderly couple, Mr. and Mrs. Lindsey. They had a big, white house with a rough stone walk that led through a white wooden arch with pink rose vines growing on either side and up over the top. Sometimes my brother, Preston, and I would go over and visit them. On one such visit (I don't know how the conversation began) Mrs. Lindsey began to relate a story to us about the time she had seen an angel. Following is as much of it as I can recall.

> *"It was during the First World War," she said. "We had friends whose son had gone overseas. Word had come that he was missing in action. His parents were terribly upset, of course. At the very moment that they were getting this news, I looked up and saw an angel standing in the corner. He told me to tell the boy's parents that they were not to grieve or worry — that their son was safe. I went to see them right away, and told them what the angel had said. They found it hard to believe, but I insisted that it was true. And at the end of the war, he came home without a scratch on him!*

We were amazed. I'd never heard an angel story before. We both asked her, "What did the angel look like?"

"Oh, I can't describe it."

"But you said you saw it."

"Yes, but it was a presence there — not a form that I could possibly describe."

"Well, can't you remember *anything* about it?"

"No — no more than I've told you!" She stopped talking and frowned at us. I could tell she was miffed with us for insisting she tell us more, but she wasn't going to make up something just to ease the insatiable curiosities of two youngsters!

Then the angel of God said to me... Genesis 31:10 (NRS)

Lord, thank you that sometimes you send your angels to come and deliver messages to us and through us. Amen.

September 4

Angels — Part 3
A Supernatural Intervention

My dear friend, Birgitta, tells this story that seems to without a doubt involve the intervention of an angel. See what you think.

It was Saturday mid-day and the first really warm spring day in Sweden, 1986. I had dressed in a white pants suit and was on my way home through the center of Stockholm on my just-purchased new bicycle. (My old bicycle had been stolen earlier that year.) Unbeknown to me, the man who sold me the bicycle had left the extra key unsecured in the lock, so that the bolt was swinging back and forth with the movement of the bike. The traffic was very heavy, parked cars on the right, and two lanes in each direction. I was in the right lane between two cars going about 20 - 25 miles an hour. The left lane was full of cars. Something caught my eye at the right and I must have wiggled the front wheel. Suddenly the bike came to a screeching stop. I lifted up and was catapulted over the front of the bike. While my mind told me my life would come to an end in the next instant, my body made a somersault in the air. I landed on my feet and the bike landed on its side in front of me. Car breaks screeched. I grabbed the bike and made off to the right between two parked cars as two men on the sidewalk came running toward me and grabbed my arms as I was trying to stay upright. The traffic had stopped right there and everyone was looking at me. One of the men asked if I was okay. It all happened so fast I still wasn't sure. I didn't know yet if I was hurt. The two men said I had made a perfect somersault. I touched my head and checked my white suit. Everything seemed to be unchanged. No dirt on my clothes, no blood and no bumps on my head or anywhere. The new bike was all crooked, the seat broken, the front light cracked, and the front wheel and the handlebars bent. Then I discovered the unsecured lock, and I understood what had happened; it had swung into the wheel, causing the bike to stop suddenly.

The two men left. On shaky legs and still trembling, I started walking slowly toward home with the bike that now had to be lifted up in front in order to roll forward on the back wheel only. I felt terrible about the expensive bike. But as I was walking, I realized, the store had made a mistake and I turned around and started walking the many blocks back to the bicycle store. On my way I realized what an incredible situation it was. It dawned on me that I could have been killed. How could I have made such a perfect somersault and landed on my feet without divine intervention? My guardian angel must have been right there to protect me. I began to rejoice and thank God for his protection. My step got lighter and lighter and my spirit soared as I walked into the store and told the sales person, who happened to be the manager, what had happened. His face took on a mixed expression of horror and awe and he apologized profusely. Then he gave me an identical new bicycle and I was on my way home again rejoicing and praising God. But I also realized that I had been over-confident and foolhardy taking the short route in the heavy traffic, so I chose another way home.

They shall bear you up in their hands, Lest you dash your foot against a stone. Psalm 91:12 (NKJV)

God, thank you for the times you have sent angels to silently, invisibly, intervene to rescue my friends (and me). Amen.

September 5

Angels — Part 4
An Angel to the Rescue

It was a beautiful summer morning on the island of Gotland, Sweden. Birgitta and I were taking a walk on the high cliff area above a cathedral ruin in the ancient town of Visby. As we strolled along, picking wild strawberries, she told me the following angel story.

A young family with a little girl, no more than two years of age, had rented a home near this precipice overlooking the Baltic Sea in the distance. Since the property was fenced, they believed it to be quite safe, and had left the child to play in the yard. Later they looked for her, and found to their horror, that the gate to the yard was open, and the little girl was nowhere to be seen. There was a long, steep stairway to the left across the road that led down to the cathedral, and the parents ran down, desperately calling for their daughter, fearful that she must have fallen to her death. However, when they reached the foot of the cliff, they found their little girl happily playing in the cathedral garden. They asked her what had happened. She explained in baby language, smiling, "The nice (or pretty) white lady [lady in white], the white lady."

The town's people were convinced it was an angel who caught her, one the little girl could only describe in this simple manner.

I too believe this was an angel. The angel took on an appealing, non-threatening appearance, that of a beautiful lady in white. I suspect that angels appear to us in forms that we can accept. They may appear to be human, or angelic, with wings, or without, large, or small, depending on what we need at the moment.

For He shall give His angels charge over you, To keep you in all your ways. Psalm 91:11 (NKJV)

Lord, increase our faith so that the angels will be more and more free to intervene supernaturally in the world around us. Amen.

September 6

Angels — Part 5
A Few Words of Advice

I had some words of advice from an angel once. I was driving my car east across Walnut Street in Pasadena, and the brakes went out as I was trying to stop at a signal light on El Molino. I tried to stay calm and managed to turn the car to the right so I wouldn't go across the intersection and be in the middle of cross traffic. I kept going south on El Molino, my foot was off the gas, and I was slowing, but the car wasn't stopping. I decided that in order for no one to be hurt, I should hit a tree so I could stop the car. I aimed for a thick date palm tree and was already up on the curb when a voice said to me, "The emergency brake." That hadn't even occurred to me; I reached for it and the car stopped a foot or two from the tree. I wasn't hurt at all, not to mention the tree!

Just a few words spoken in time of need made all the difference. Don't doubt it. God sends messengers to help us in innumerable ways throughout our lives. We don't always know. We don't always hear. But in some way these busy angelic beings are doing what they were appointed to do — minister, guard and give us urgently needed messages.

> *Then an angel of the Lord said to Philip, 'Get up and go toward the south to the road that goes down from Jerusalem to Gaza.' (This is a wilderness road.)* Acts 8:26 (NRS)

Lord, give us all the faith we need to believe that you work in many wonderful ways, including through your messengers, the angels. Amen.

September 7

Angels — Part 6
The Sound of the Golden Trumpet

One morning when I was still in my teens, I was awakened by the clear, beautiful sound of a trumpet. It went something like: "Da, da, ta DA!" I almost flew out of bed. That last "ta DA" was not only loud, but piercing. The sound was so real that I was sure someone must be playing a trumpet in the neighborhood. I got up and opened the French doors leading out to the balcony and listened, but there was no trumpet or any other music, except for the songs of the birds on that clear, fresh morning.

I don't know how, but I felt I knew that, without a doubt, it was the music of a *golden* trumpet. I thought at the time that, since it was obviously not 'real' — not in the physical world, nor of an earthly origin, that it must be from a heavenly source, and if from a heavenly source, then it must be the trumpet of an angel.

I remember that exquisite, clear, golden sound today as though I had just heard it. But what did it mean? Now looking back on that shy young girl who didn't yet truly realize that Jesus loved her, I believe that God allowed her to hear the sounds of a supernatural musical instrument played by an angelic being. What I now suspect is that God was calling me to himself, calling me to be one of His elect. He knew I needed extra encouragement.

And He will send His angels with a great sound of a trumpet, and they will gather together His elect from the four winds, from one end of heaven to the other. Matthew 24:31 (NKJV)

Lord, you are still gathering. By your Holy Spirit, call the young people to yourself today. They need you so much; help them to turn to you. Amen.

September 8

Angels — Part 7
The Memory of His Face

I believe I have a memory of seeing my own guardian angel. I don't know when it was, but I suspect that babies are sometimes able to see their angels so perhaps my babyhood is from whence this memory comes. It is only the face I so clearly remember, as though it is imprinted indelibly on my spirit.

This is what I recall: The face was more male than female. The substance of the face reminded me of translucent candle wax with a kind of defused soft light glowing from the inside. His eyes could be described as somewhere in between tender and mischievous. I don't recall seeing any teeth, but his mouth was small with upturned corners in a continual expression of delight. It makes me smile just to think of it. I believe this is a genuine recollection, stored in my spirit where it can never be erased. And one more thing — there was a sense of pure joy that came with that guileless "archaic" smile. It reflected the Father's joy and I know its purpose in my life and yours is for our strength.

> *...for the joy of the LORD is your strength.* Nehemiah 8:10 (NKJV)

Lord, help us to receive the joy that you so freely offer to us because we need supernatural strength this day, and every day. Amen.

September 9

Angels — Part 8
The Angel's Song

I was awake early that morning. It was still quite dark out. But I couldn't get back to sleep so I stayed in bed and prayed for a while. I told the Lord that I would like to be able to sense His Spirit more, but also that I would like to be aware that there are angels present in my life.

Lucy (our dog) stirred and I got up to let her out. On the way back through the living room, I heard a single tone, ringing clearly. There was a pause. Then it continued — a familiar melodic phrase. It was coming from the angel music box that was on the table behind our sofa. I had not handled it recently — not even to dust it. Nor had I touched the table on which it stood as I walked by it that morning. But there it was — slowing spinning on its pedestal as the melody from the Christmas carol, "Silent Night" rang out. I could hear the words clearly in my mind: "All is calm. All is bright!" I was absolutely dumbstruck. It was a direct and immediate answer to my earlier prayer. I knew without a doubt that real angels were around me, helping me, guarding me, ministering to me, whether I could see them or not. What a wonderful encouragement to my fearful heart on that cold winter morning!

The angel said to them, 'Do not be afraid....' Luke 2:10a (NCV)

Lord, thank you for sending these special messengers to us. Help us to have faith that they are here to help or minister or guard when we need them. Amen.

September 10

Angels — Part 9

I said something to one of my dearest friends that hurt her deeply. She said something back that hurt me deeply. The experience wrenched my heart and soul. I was effected both physically and emotionally. I had always worried that her death would be one of life's hardest blows should she die before me. But now our friendship, as we knew it, had died, and we both realized it could never be the same. *Oh, Lord, please make something good come out of this,* I prayed. I forgave her and I believe she has forgiven me, and I think that in time we will have a new friendship that will prove to be even better.

However, during that time of grieving I had to be in constant prayer for several weeks to allow God to heal the wound, but it turned out it was not just this wound. God showed me in my mind's eye that her words had pulled a scab off of an *old* wound and that there was an old infection there that needed to be drained, so I let the Great Physician do His work and it took months for the healing to take place. But it did! One marvelous night, in a dream, God took me back in time to a place when and where I had believed a lie, and He set the record straight. It was as simple as this: Someone, whom I thought had *not* loved me when I was quite young, had indeed loved me very much! That was it.

During this time of waiting for the healing to come, I felt very unsafe. That is why the Lord sent His angels. I saw them only with my eyes closed, but I also felt their presence. The first took the form of a German Shepherd/husky mix. He was huge! He sat by my bed all night long one night, never going to sleep, just watching over me. The second (a different night) took the form of a German Shepherd too but this was a pure bred, and he stayed right beside me on the bed, also watching over me through the night. I immediately recognized both as angels, but they took a form that was a symbol of their angelic duties — to guard me and to help me to feel safe. They only needed to be revealed to me twice because I knew that, by faith, they would be there as long as they were needed.

For he will order his angels to protect you wherever you go.
Psalm 91:11 (NLT)

Dear Heavenly Father, thank you for the times that you send guardian angels to us. We know, that even when we do not see them and sense their presence that you will send them to us, as needed! Amen.

September 11

The Spirit of Joy

In the 1960s *Charisma* magazine made its debut. On the front cover was the Lutheran pastor who was one of the Pioneers of the Charismatic renewal in the historic churches, The Rev. Herald Bredesen. When I saw his face on the cover, it appeared to glow! I thought to myself, "I must meet him." It was a prayer/wish that I almost forgot.

Some months later, we were in Taiwan where we attended a luncheon sponsored by some local missionaries and the speaker was — you guessed it! — Herald Bredesen. I was smiling from ear to ear! He spoke about the baptism in the Holy Spirit (Some call it the filling of the Spirit.), and the gifts of the Spirit. He came over to us afterwards and said to us, "You know exactly what I'm talking about don't you?" We said, "Yes!" and that was the beginning of our friendship. He ended up staying with us for a few days and what a treat that was!

While in Taiwan, Herald visited and prayed with Madame Chiang Kai-shek. He went by taxi, and his window was rolled down. Suddenly, as if out of nowhere, someone flicked a cigarette and it hit him in one of his eyes. He said it was as though it had been diabolically aimed; he didn't even have a chance to blink. But then, Madame Chiang Kai-shek and her prayer partners prayed for him, and by the time he got back to our home, his eye was completely healed!

It was a pleasure and an honor to meet this man of God. What a gift it was to experience a personal encounter with someone so filled with the Spirit of God, so filled with joy!

And the disciples were filled with joy and with the Holy Spirit. Acts 13:52 (NKJV)

Lord, help us, like those in the early church, to be filled with the joy that only the Holy Spirit can give. Amen.

September 12

A Needed Ingredient

One day shortly after Don and I moved to Arizona, we were driving along Glendale Avenue near Goodyear when we passed a walled in area where we could see mounds several feet high. They were sparkling white. It looked like snow, but in the middle of Arizona, in the spring? I don't think so. What could it be?

When we passed a sign that said "Morton Salt Group," my question was answered; it was salt! Salt — not so costly these days, but what a valuable commodity it was during the days of Christ.

I have heard ministers preach about salt — as a preservative, and that it is — to this day. Ever had any cured Virginia ham or smoked Alaskan salmon? I've heard it said that it is those in the world who are Christians who are preserving the world! Perhaps that is true, but Jesus made it clear that He called us to be the salt of the earth because of something else — flavor. Human beings use salt to add flavor to the foods that we eat. Imagine a bag of potato chips — without salt? How about saltine crackers — sans salt!? Pickles without salt would be, well, just cucumbers. Popcorn would be, well, I'm sure you get the point. But the scary thing about what Jesus said was that salt could lose its flavor.

Is the world a tastier place because of you or me? Do we have flavor and savor, making life around us, no matter how difficult, truly palatable? I think that is one of the reasons we as believers are needed in the world — to bring hope where there is despair, to bring meaning where life seems to lack significance, to bring to everyday occurrences flavor, so that the quality of the inner life is raised and enjoyed — just like a piece of that Virginia smoked ham!

You are the salt of the earth. But what good is salt if it has lost its flavor? Can you make it useful again? It will be thrown out and trampled underfoot as worthless. Matthew 5:13 (NLT)

Lord, make me a savory seasoning in the world, not bland, boring, and without flavor. I want others to see me and then want to taste and see that the Lord is good. Amen.

September 13

The Salted Sacrifice

In the Old Testament book of Leviticus, we find that along with grain offering, salt must be added. Salt is part of the sacrifice. In Mark 9:49, Jesus tells us that we will be seasoned with fire and every sacrifice will be seasoned with salt.

How do we season our sacrifices with salt? How can I offer up myself as a living sacrifice and with that, make sure that salt is added? I don't know for sure, but I have a theory, and what I suspect is that we are told to add to the sacrifice of ourselves, a sprinkling of salt and I think the salt is our praises to the Lord, so that as we go through the seasoning process in the refining fires of life, we will not emit the sour smell of self-pity or the cynical smell of bitterness, but we will carry with us a lovely, flavorful fragrance that others around us will "smell" and be drawn to. Can't we all do that? — Praise God, as we make ourselves a daily living sacrifice to Him? I don't always remember to add praise, but I'm going to try to do it more, because I know from experience that every day to which I add praises along with my talks with God[3], I find myself moving more and more into a place of grace and joy that just might be noticed by others around me.

Let them sacrifice the sacrifices of thanksgiving, and declare His works with rejoicing. Psalm 107:22a (NKJV)

Lord, help me to remember to praise you and may my praise be a sweet savor to you. Amen.

---

[3] The books that have helped me understand the wonder and power of praise more than any others are "From Prison to Praise" and "Power in Praise" by Merlin Carothers.

September 14

A Letter to Selden

After my brother-in-law died in September of 1994, I needed to write the following letter to him. It helped me get through the sadness of losing him.

Dear Selden,

On the day of your death, but before we learned that you had died, I was walking among arts and crafts booths at a street fair in Hermosa Beach. In front of me in the crowd there was a man wearing a T-shirt. Written on the back of it were theses words, "Jesus Christ is Risen from the Dead." It gave me goose bumps! It is the ancient Christian greeting for Easter morning and to it is traditionally replied the words which I spoke as I walked by him, "He is risen indeed."

Later that day when we heard the news about the heart attack that had taken you so suddenly, these words came back to me with such power and force that I received them as a direct message from the Lord to me for comfort and hope. And so you, our dear Selden, will one day be risen from the dead, for Christ is risen indeed! I love you and miss you, but we will see you again. Yes! That is the Christian hope. We will see you again!

I am the resurrection and the life. He who believes in Me, though he may die, he shall live. And whoever lives and believes in Me shall never die. Do you believe this? John 11:25 (NKJV)

Lord, I believe that you are the resurrection and the life. Amen.

September 15

The Guard Dog Died

Do you know the old joke that starts with the question, "What's new?" The answer is, "Oh, not much, 'ceptin the dog died." This is spoken with a drawl of undetermined origin, and continues like this:

"The dog died! Oh, no! How did that happen?"

"Well, it heppined when der barn burnt down."

"The barn burned down! Oh, no! How did that happen?"

"Well, it musta caught fire ferm de hourse!"

"The house burned down too. Oh no! How did that happen?"

"Well, it caught fire ferm the candile aburnin' on the coffin."

"Coffin! What coffin! Who died?"

"Oh yeah! I furgot to tell ya! Old Great Grandma Oona died."

And so it went. Well, I had a bad summer — "the summer that was," I call it. During that summer things got out of control and well, you might say, "The dog died." In my case it was an inner guard dog that protected a big door with the "big secret." When the dog died, I could finally get to the door and open it and behind was something I hadn't wanted to remember. However as I did so I was able to put some pieces together in my own heart, by the grace of God. And so, I want to tell you that sometimes the pain and the death of a part of ourselves (like the guard dog) is necessary in order to get to the truth that will set us free.

Perhaps that's part of God's plan for you too. Oh, I'm not suggesting that you go digging around for those old memories, but when the time comes, go through the doors of the memories you need to, in order to get cleansed of any root of bitterness! Just consider it "house cleaning" time. The Savior is coming and He wants a bride without spot or blemish.

See to it that no one fails to obtain the grace of God; that no root of bitterness springs up and causes trouble.... Hebrews 12:15 (NRSVA)

Would not God search this out? For He knows the secrets of the heart. Psalm 44:21 (NKJV)

Lord, you are the Guardian of my secrets; if any need to be revealed, I trust you to be the Revealer that I might be free of any inner bitterness, unforgiveness or wounds in my heart. Amen.

September 16

Anger, Friend or Foe?

I was loaded down with luggage on the way to our hotel room. The handle on my cosmetic bag broke and the case fell open. Cosmetics and intimate items fell across the carpet right in front of the elevator. I said a word that would shock my children and then to myself I said, *never again.* I quickly collected the objects strewn about in front of me. *Next Christmas when they ask what I want, I will remember what I need: a new overnight case.* I did remember. I did get a new cosmetic case. My anger motivated me to do something about the problem. That was the first time I saw so clearly how anger could be used constructively. It was also then that I realized that I needed to look at the anger I carry so that I will be able to understand it in others. Anger can be terribly destructive or, if contained; it can be a source of energy to use as a force for change where change is needed.

I've struggled with anger much of my life. Once the Lord showed me a picture in my mind of a river. He said that anger is like a river that needs to be contained and not overrun its boundaries (flood surrounding areas and doing damage). He said that when it is contained it can become a powerful source of energy for doing good, not harm. That's a discipline most of us can work at — learning to contain the energy of anger and the using it in a creative, constructive ways.

> *When you are angry, do not sin, and be sure to stop being angry before the end of the day. Do not give the devil a way to defeat you.* Ephesians 4:26, 27 (NCV)

Dear Lord, you know that I am capable of anger and sometimes speak thoughtlessly. Other times I see something that angers me and I keep it in and don't do anything about it when I should. I ask your help in these times, first, to curb angry outbursts, so that I will not say anything that would grieve your Holy Spirit, and secondly, I ask that, when something I see makes me angry, I would use that energy, contained and controlled, to do something creative and constructive about the problem. Amen.

September 17

Beauty for Ashes

It has gone through a time of rebirth — the area around Mt. St. Helen's, where trees and all living things were destroyed by the devastating eruption of May 18, 1980. My husband, Don, our son Mike and his wife, Karen, and I visited the site in the summer of 2000 and there we found that amid the fire-ravaged land, life has begun to return. Instead of the gray fields of ashes, new growth, fresh and green has sprung up. The sight filled me with a sense of hope. Even in a place that once looked like a moonscape, life has emerged anew. I bought a memento of that disaster. It's a little carved bird. I am reminded of this miracle of new life each time I hold it in the palm of my hand, this piece of ash from that dreadful day that has been transformed by an artist's hands into a gentle dove.

In the same manner, God can take our lives and transform them. What may seem to us like nothing but a pile of ashes, in His hands, can be turned into something beautiful. We need to remember that — when all seems lifeless and hopeless around us, God, the miracle working One, can take the remains and make them spring into something alive and new, full of vitality and hope, proclaiming the glory of the Lord!

To give them beauty for ashes, the oil of joy for mourning, the garment of praise for the spirit of heaviness; That they may be called trees of righteousness, The planting of the Lord, that He may be glorified. Isaiah 61:3 NKJV

Lord of miracles, wherever in my life there are ashes, I sacrifice them to you. I ask that you turn them into something beautiful. Where there is mourning, help me to await with anticipation the season of joy that is to follow. For any spirit of heaviness upon my soul, grant me a spirit of praise, and do all this for your name's sake so that you will be glorified in my life. Amen.

September 18

Inner Healing — Part 1
A Time for Waiting

In the entries for the next few days, I will tell you a little about my experience in what some call "inner healing." I want you to know, right from the start of this section that I am aware that this kind of healing is not for every hurting person because God does not use the same method of healing for everyone. He who is the Author and Finisher of our faith, generously and mercifully reaches out and heals each of us in a myriad of ways throughout our lifetime walk with Him. The kind of inner healing that I will be writing about is only one of those ways. So approach these next days' readings with expectancy, open to see just one more way in which God works healing in the lives of His children.

In the fall of 1964 I attended a small prayer meeting in the home of a friend. It was there that for the first time I was the recipient of inner healing prayers. I had never heard of "inner healing" but as I experienced God's deep, profound caring for my inner life, I felt the longing to be called into that ministry. Years passed but no such opportunity presented itself. It was one of those things I couldn't forget but I just put it on the "back burner" and went about with my life, trusting God to bring it to pass if it was part of His plan for me.

Twenty years later, (Yes! I said 20 years!) I received an invitation to be on the Board of Directors of Diakonos, of a nonprofit inner healing organization based in Pasadena, California (now located in San Dimas, CA). I accepted immediately. I had the privilege of being under the teaching of Susan Highleyman, MFCC, the Director and Founder of Diakonos and her mother, Joy Highleyman. This afforded me the incredible opportunity to pray for the inner healing of others — that is what I had so deeply desired.

It is this experience that makes me say to you today, whatever your deepest desire is, if it has been planted in your heart by God, no matter how long you must wait, there will come a time for it to become manifested in your life. You've heard it before but I'll say it again, God's timing is perfect.

Delight yourself also in the Lord and He shall give you the desires of your heart. Psalm 37:4 (NKJV)

Lord, sometimes I don't know the difference between what you want for me and what I want for me, but if the desires that I have in my heart are placed there by you, then I believe that they will bear fruit, so I ask that you give me patience to wait for your perfect timing. Amen.

September 19

Inner Healing — Part 2
Old Memories, New Healings

On my first occasion of specific prayer-brought inner healing, a friend, David, prayed me for. As he did so, he had an inner vision of something that had happened to me at the age of seven or eight:

"Your brother," he told me, "had become enraged against you. He was chasing you with a board in his hand. You ran from him but he was gaining on you, so you crouched down, tensing your back to take the blow as he held the board over you."

I shook my head, "No, David, I don't think so. I don't' remember anything like that happening to me. You're wrong."

"Pat," he raised his voice, spoke with authority and grasped me by the shoulders, "the board had a nail in it."

I went limp in recognition. "You're right. It's true," I told him. The entire scene instantly crashed into my consciousness. "But he didn't hit me; he laughed at me and threw the board on the ground." It happened that this incident with my brother was at the root of my recurring back spasms. We prayed for healing of that memory and that was only the first of many such healings in my life.

That God cared for me so much that He would reveal to another person memories out of *my* past affected my profoundly. I realized He knows and loves us all like this — deeply, intimately, and completely.

It was a personal encounter with the omniscience of God and, instead of frightening me, as I might have suspected it would, I felt comforted and at peace in my heart, that there was Someone who knows all about me. I hope that the awareness of God's all-knowing power will be a comfort to you today too.

O Lord, you have searched me and known me. Psalm 139:1 (NKJV)

Lord God, today I acknowledge you as all-knowing. My heart, my past, my hurts, my dreams and longings, are all known to You. Help me to find comfort in your omniscience. Amen.

September 20

Inner Healing — Part 3
A Time for Truth

Once we become Christians and are a part of the Christian family, newborn spiritual beings, we are not only in need of healing in our lives, but we are also embarking on a life of spiritual growth. We find that there is a daily cross that we are to take up so that we might work out our own salvation. This is the work of God within us — to help us to die to areas of the old nature so that we can be transformed into the new life that is hidden with Christ in God. There is a self-discovery that is not narcissistic. It is a liberation that leads to transformation and it is a two-fold self-realization:

1. As you discover who you are, bit by bit, (in the old nature), you become aware of what needs to be forgiven (brought to the cross). As you do this, a part of you that needs to be brought to death, dies. It's the same with a seed; when it dies; it can then be planted and a new plant will come into being. I believe we as Christians go through many such little deaths and little resurrections. The old dies. The new is born. And so it goes as God transforms our entire personalities to become, each time, more and more like Jesus Christ.

2. On the other side of this transformation you discover experientially who you are in Christ Jesus and what it means to be born again, a child of the Heavenly Father, an heir of promise, a co-inheritor of the Kingdom of God.

Only the Holy Spirit of God knows the deep, complexities of our nature and only the Spirit can impart to us the power of patience that will bring us to the unfolding maturity of our inner (spiritual) person. This knowledge of who we are in Christ brings us into ever-growing fellowship with Him, the One who is creating us anew. We all need this work to take place within us and we need to be diligent to move toward learning how to receive the Holy Spirit's work in our innermost beings, so that this transformation of the inner person might take place.

We all need to, from time to time, take a look at our lives. Where are we in our spiritual journey? Are we stuck in the past because of frightening memories, not that we won't let go of, but that won't let go of *us*? Are we holding on to unforgiveness and letting that get in our way of receiving God's forgiveness for us? Can we cast ourselves on Him and ask Him to help us to be ready for the inner journey of spiritual encounter accompanied by a sense of adventure? What is the Holy Spirit whispering to you, to me today? There are new joys and new challenges and new mercies every single day! God wants to lead us into truth because He knows that it will set us free!

> *When the Spirit of truth comes, he will guide you into all truth. He will not be presenting his own ideas; he will be telling you what he has heard. He will tell you about the future.* John 16:13 (NLT)

Dear Holy Spirit, help me to face the truth that you would reveal to me about myself and help me be willing to allow you to reach down into my heart and heal me and move me on into the future adventures that you have in store for me. Amen.

September 21

Inner Healing — Part 4
The Challenge of God's Healing on the Inside

Inner healing can be difficult, painful and exhausting work. It involves something in us coming to a place of death. When we moved to Arizona, there was a time when I was sure we weren't meant to be here. How could God call us to be where a lot of people didn't even want us? Well, that people-pleaser in me had to die! That people-pleaser had been a tyrant, worse than anyone outside myself had ever been! I came to the place where I accepted that we were to be there and not to listen to what others said, but listen to what the voice of God was calling us to and, in this case, for those ten years, it was to *stay*! We were to be God-pleasers, not people-pleasers! I knew too that when the time came for us to leave Arizona, there would be those who would want us to stay. So, that time did come and when it did, once again, we knew we must not be people pleasers, but God pleasers and go where the Holy Spirit was leading us to go.

Is there something in you that needs a healing "death" today? You can start by just asking the Lord to show you. He won't "kill" anything that needs to stay. You can trust Him.

O wretched man that I am! Who will deliver me from this body of death? I thank God through Jesus Christ our Lord! So then, with the mind I myself serve the law of God, but with the flesh the law of sin. Romans 7:24, 25 (NKJV)

Lord, help me to allow anything that needs to die in me die, and bring to life that which is born of you. Amen.

September 22

The Praying Mantis — Part 1

While visiting our son, Michael, and his wife, Karen, in West Richland, Washington, in the summer of 1999, he told us that when he had begun to work on putting in his new landscaping, he and the gardener had almost accidentally killed a praying mantis. He had seen it just in time and had redeemed it from certain death. He placed it near his front door. From that time on, day-after-day, the praying mantis stayed at his door. It faithfully guarded it and did away with spiders and other insects that might have entered the house.

There are so many lessons here I don't know where to begin. But to me, the most obvious is that once we have received the guardian of our soul, the Holy Spirit, we are protected from the entering in of evil spirits. Of course, we have choices; we can still open the door to addictions and fears and resentments and say, "Come on in!" if we really want to, but we are protected by this presence within us in the sense, that though Christians may be oppressed by Satanic forces, they cannot be possessed. Upon entering the family of God, we become new beings and our lives are no longer our own, we are the possession of God the Father. Satan cannot claim us as His own; we belong to Another and we now desire to glorify God.

> *For you were bought at a price; therefore glorify God in your body and in your spirit, which are God's.* 1 Corinthians 6:20 (NKJV)

Father God, you have stationed guards inside and outside our spirits. Help us to, by supernatural vision, see that you have provided us with all the spiritual protection that we need. Amen.

September 23

The Praying Mantis — Part 2

Another lesson that I see coming out of the praying mantis example is the value of a redeemed life. God reaches down and picks us up and puts us in a safe place, just like Michael reached down and picked up that praying mantis. Then we, out of gratitude, become useful, doing a work for our Lord — whatever that is, even if it is just to be a doorkeeper.

> *I would rather be a doorkeeper in the house of my God than to dwell in the tents of wickedness.* Psalm 84:10 (NKJV)

Father, you see us when we are lost, and when we ask for your help you come and pick us up, clean us off and care for us, give us gifts and a calling, and place us in a safe spiritual place for all eternity. Thank you for your redemptive transforming power in our lives. Amen.

September 24

The Praying Mantis — Part 3

The third lesson I learned from the praying mantis has to do with something else, closer to a mother's heart. Michael and Karen have moved from Washington State to the California coast, so they are much closer now, but still miles away from us. We pray for him and for Karen every day but I am still comforted with the knowledge that God provided a little reminder for me (that praying mantis). I know that His eye is on Michael and Karen, and He, the Great Intercessor, also prays for them! What an encouragement to my heart. It increased my faith and awareness that my God loves our children more than we possibly can. Knowing this truth can help us to let go of worry.

> *Do not worry about anything, but pray and ask God for everything you need, always giving thanks. And God's peace,*

which is so great we cannot understand it, will keep your hearts and minds in Christ Jesus. Philippians 4:6, 7 (NCV)

Lord God, you are so good to us, always caring not only about us in all ways, but caring for our loved ones more than we ever could. Help us to leave them in your care, especially when they are far from us. Amen.

September 25

The Praying Mantis — Part 4

The other, and perhaps the most obvious symbolic meaning of the praying mantis, is that God has provided us with holy angels, guardians of our souls and lives. We don't see them (at least most of us don't) but they are there and they have been given work to do — to minister, to guard, to bring messages, to do battle for us. I believe that there are times when we may need to call on extra angelic help and, if so, we can be assured that it will come.

> [Following are the words of an angelic being.] *He said to me, 'Do not fear, Daniel, for from the first day that you set your mind to gain understanding and to humble yourself before your God, your words have been heard, and I have come because of your words. But the prince of the kingdom of Persia opposed me twenty-one days. So Michael, one of the chief princes, came to help me, and I left him there with the prince of the kingdom of Persia.'* Daniel 10:12, 13 (NRSV)

Father, thank you for the ministering spirits of the angels; I pray that you send them to those in need of them today. Amen.

September 26

A Mouse in the House

There is another story of redemption that I witnessed in Michael's and Karen's home that summer. One evening Mike and I were visiting in the kitchen. It was late at night. Out of the corner of my eye I saw a little movement — like a mouse. I turned to look but saw nothing. I said, "Mike, do you have mice here?" "No," he assured me, "we've never had any mice." "Well, I saw something move over there." I motioned toward the stove. He got down on his hands and knees, but saw nothing. I believed him — no mice. But he explained that they do occasionally get some "really big bugs." *That must be some big kind of bug,* I thought.

In the middle of the night I had to get up to go to the bathroom. I had a strange sensation as I walked in and closed the door — that I wasn't alone. I turned on the light. There by the door was something alive — could it be? I know there were no mice, but a bug that big? No, the thing I was trying to make into a bug in my mind's eye was no bug; it was a small, darling, horrible little mouse. I wanted to scream but I didn't want to wake the household up. I wanted to jump up on the toilet seat, but "Scooter," the mouse, far more frightened than I, had a panic attack and somehow managed to squeeze his way under the bathroom door and out into the hall. For a moment I was relieved, but when I came out I didn't know where Scooter had gone. I had left the door to our bedroom open.

It was dark. I slowly, step-by-step, made my way back to bed. There I lay, trying to go back to sleep. But it wasn't to be; *rustle, rustle* came a sound from the corner where we had piled our luggage. I woke Don, explained about the visitor, and he got up and moved the whole mess outside into the hall and closed the door. The mouse had definitely been in that pile because we didn't hear from him again, not that night, that is.

The next night as we sat in the living room, we all watched as Scooter reappeared, shamelessly running across the floor and hiding behind the TV stand. Mike was determined that he didn't want to have to kill the mouse so he got a clothes hamper and a piece of cardboard and managed to scare the mouse into it, covered it and carried it across the street, where he let it go and saw it run into a hole! Safely home at last!

Here it is again — a picture of the little people (us) running around where we could get into trouble and then someone, instead of destroying us, redeems our lives and takes us to a safe place! Isn't it wonderful — another perfect example of the work of our redeeming God?

> *Strengthen the feeble hands, steady the knees that give way; say to those with fearful hearts, "Be strong, do not fear; your God will come, he will come with vengeance; with divine retribution he will come to save you."* Isaiah 35:4 (NIV)

Lord, sometimes I'm filled with fear and run off trying to hide, but even so, I trust you to find me and give me the comfort I need to be a courageous follower of Jesus. Amen.

September 27

Bugs

Bugs. We had plenty of them in Arizona. There were cotton bugs, scorpions, ants, and a variety of cockroaches. One day I was washing my face in the bathroom basin and looked down to see two little eyes staring up at me. They belonged to a critter with a tiny body doing "pushups" on the drain stop; it was a cricket. There are also some unknown little beings that I don't like because — well, I just don't like the way they look. I've been acquainted with creepy crawlies since I lived in that old home in Pasadena, California. It was built so close to the ground that it didn't take much for living things to get in — lizards, black widow spiders, centipedes, and my least favorite of all, the potato beetle. I was taking a nap on our couch in the living room one day when I felt something tickling my forearm. I awoke and saw one of these (the latter) ugliest of creatures attempting to crawl up my arm. I shrieked and jumped at least a foot high.

The existence of these ugly critters makes me wonder: What spiritual lessons can we learn from such repulsive beings — still part of God's creation?

I decided that there are a whole group of beings in the animal kingdom that display many wonderful characteristics of the Lord God, but these ugly creatures, are symbolic, not of God, but of the evil in the world — I happen to believe that there are evil beings, called demons, that are despicable and poisonous to our spiritual lives, lying and stealing and killing their way through a fallen existence. But whether you think of them as literal beings or not, you have to admit that there is evil in the world beyond human evil and it is manifested in the horrors of earth life that we see in the news media every day. Just today: six deaths on the highway due to a drunk driver, a father killing his children and himself because his wife has left him, and the awful stories of children killing children! These evils are as deadly as the black widow, the rattlesnake, the killer bees!

So the Lord God said to the serpent: 'Because you have done this, You are cursed more than all cattle, and more than every beast of the field; On your belly you shall go, and you shall eat dust all the days of your life.' Genesis 3:14 (NKJV)

"...these are the birds you are to hate. They are hateful and should not be eaten. You must not eat...vultures; black vultures;...the jackdaw;...the carrion vulture; ...and the bat. Leviticus 11:13-19 (NKJV)

Lord, there are temptations and dangers that come my way that are of an evil origin. Help me to recognize their source, resist them and call upon the name of my God for help and protection. Amen.

September 28

Laughter in the Morning

I had just gotten up and was making my green tea in the kitchen area. Don was nearby having his quiet time.

"Oh no!" I said.

"What's wrong?" he asked.

"Well, I just put salt in my tea."

"Why would you do that?"

"Well, I put it in instead of cinnamon and turmeric."

"Why do you do that?"

"Because they're both good for your brain!"

"Well, I guess it's not working," he said without missing a beat!

I admitted he was right and we both had a good chuckle.

Then I sat down with him and we enjoyed the coolness of the morning as the fresh air softly blew the window curtains. We watched the sky. At first it was filled with dark clouds but these were suddenly tinged with glorious pink and gold! We read the Bible aloud and then we prayed together, thanking God for His grace and goodness to us, thanking Him for all that we have, knowing that all are gifts from Him!

Light is sweet; how pleasant to see a new day dawning.
Ecclesiastes 11:7 (NLT)

Lord, there is no better way than to start the day by spending time with you. Amen.

September 29

More Than One Kind of Freedom

On September 22, 1998, President Bill Clinton introduced Nelson Mandela to an audience at a meeting in the east room of the White House. He told the story of how he had on one occasion been walking with Mandela and he asked him if, after being released from prison after 27 years, he had felt anger against his enemies for even a short amount of time. Mandela had replied that he had — but for only a moment, for he had said to himself, "If I leave there and continue in anger, then I will still be their prisoner." What truth there is in those words! To retain anger and resentment is to keep us in a prison of our own making. But we have a choice. We can set ourselves free and say in our hearts "I forgive you," to any and all who have hurt us or harmed us in any way.

But what if we are continuing on in a situation or in a relationship that we cannot get out of, but in which we have taken on a victim mentality? We need to remember that even if we can't change a situation, we can change our hearts toward the person involved; that's where we have the power — in our wills. Please don't think I'm saying we can do this all on our own. We start with our wills, and then the Lord God empowers us. Yes! We need *supernatural* power, and it's available, anytime, anywhere.

> *But I say to you, love your enemies, bless those who curse you, do good to those who hate you, and pray for those who spitefully use you and persecute you that you may be sons of your Father in heaven; for He makes His sun rise on the evil and on the good, and sends rain on the just and on the unjust.*
> Matthew 5:44, 45 (NKJV)

Lord, even when I can't change my circumstances, you can help me change my attitude. I relinquish my anger and bitterness to you and in return, I receive your power and joy and peace. Amen.

September 30

Maybe it's Not Too Late

Is there something in you that wants to be a missionary — some lost dream, some seed planted long ago, and yet this dream has not come true — not yet anyway! Perhaps it's not too late. Now days there are many opportunities to go on short-term missions to some distant mission field where you can serve for a week or more.

Don and I have been on such missions twice. In 2003 after our church in Goodyear helped pay for a new translation of Campus Crusade's "The Jesus Film" into Lithuanian, we were invited to visit the lovely Baltic country of Lithuania. It was simply a mission of going door-to-door to pass out the video. I remember one young man on the street to which I gave a copy. I can still see him in my mind's eye, sitting on a curb and holding it in his hands and looking at it as though it were a treasure. He seemed poor and even now when I think of him, I pray for him, though I never knew his name.

We took another trip in 2004 when we traveled to Guatemala on a fact-finding mission to visit the work of the CRIS Foundation where field representative, Chris Halter, ran a clinic in Santa Caterina Palopo near Lake Atitlan in the highlands. We found the country lush, green, and beautiful, the people warm-hearted and welcoming. Both Don and I were humbled to have opportunities to speak at churches (with Chris acting as our translator). We found the churches there vital, the Christians motivated to share the Gospel with others in a place where the fields were ripe for harvest, the ministers anxious to disciple new believers.

In 2005 we took a trip to Italy. It was not a mission trip but we looked on line for someone who was doing mission work there and found a lovely couple from England who had a small group of students meeting in their home for Bible study. We arranged a meeting so they could share with us their particular mission. They were situated ideally in the middle of Florence, a city filled with many young people who had come to study there. It was a rich experience and we have stayed in touch with them.

We left each of these places with our faith increased and our hearts expanded and touched because of what we witnessed — Jesus Christ being shared by loving Christians, in both word and deed. Yes, there were physical and financial sacrifices but these were life-transforming experiences that changed the way that we looked at God's world forever.

And he said to them, 'Go into all the world and proclaim the good news to the whole creation.' (Mark 16:15)

Oh God, we call out to you today for that kind of love, and if it is your will for any of the readers to go on such a trip, help them to know where you are leading them, and give them the means to accomplish what you have chosen them to do. May they be used to be a blessing and to bring glory to you. Amen.

OCTOBER

October 1

Judgments

During a national political crisis, I was astonished to discover that one of my closest friends and I were in total disagreement when it came to our assessment of the issue. How could we both be Christians and believe so differently? I realized that the key to understanding this disparity in political beliefs was not the so-called facts, but the attitude of the heart, and the attitude of the heart is where the spiritual judgment is made, not from political biases. I saw many on *both* sides who were mean-spirited, judgmental and vindictive. At first I just thought it was the other side, but then I realized that many others, including me, were just like them. I too had given way to the temptation to judge and I was judging in just as mean-spirited a way as they were! I stepped back and asked for supernatural help with my attitude problem.

Sometimes we are absolutely powerless to change circumstances, but as we all know, we are not powerless to change our attitudes, even if we can't do it alone. So when I asked for God's help, I felt led to begin to pray for all parties on both sides of the issue. And then an amazing thing happened. I came to realize that the other side was not comprised of just a bunch of monsters; they were human beings who had opinions that differed from mine — that was all. As I prayed, I found I was no longer angry, no longer mean-spirited, but wished good and blessings on all. I had offered myself up to the working of the Holy Spirit to change my heart, and He had!

...He shall not judge by the sight of His eyes, Nor decide by the hearing of His ears; But with righteousness He shall judge... Isaiah 11:3 (NKJV)

Lord God, thank you that you are willing to help transform our attitudes. When mine is negative and selfish, cold and judgmental, or hateful and vindictive, come Holy Spirit and blow a fresh breeze across my heart so that I will be more like Jesus. Amen.

October 2

It's All in the Way You Look at It

As my husband and I were traveling in Idaho we stopped in the small town of Invermere. He had gone into a coffee house for a latte' and I sat outside at a sidewalk table. Across the street, there was a two-story building with a shop on the ground floor and an apartment on the second floor. In the window of the apartment were several artifacts, including a large ceramic Siamese cat. My eyes were still on it when a few cars drove by in both directions. The inanimate piece of porcelain, suddenly came to life, turning back and forth and watching the traffic on the street below. I laughed out loud. How sure I had been that that cat was not flesh, fur and blood! How wrong I was!

I was reminded that day about how often I've been sure I was right, only to find that I (of all people!) had thoroughly misjudged a person or a situation! It's not much fun to have our mistakes brought to our minds, but isn't is truly wonderful that we have a God who cares about our errors in judgments so much that He provides us with sources of truth, so that we may change our minds?

Let this mind be in you which was also in Christ Jesus...
Philippians 2:5 (NKJV)

Lord, send me the truth in whatever form you choose, and help me to learn to laugh at my errors in judgments. Amen.

October 3

Remembrance

There are times that I know I will never, ever forgot — times that when they occurred, somewhere in my brain, I must have chosen to "film" them. One such special occasion was in 1957. I had graduated from high school and my high school graduation gift from my second cousin, Florence DuBosque, was a trip to New York and New Jersey where I visited her and her husband, Steele.

During the weekdays we lived in a little apartment in Greenwich Village. The evenings were spent going to the finest of restaurants, but as exciting as it was to get a taste of an affluent life style, it was the weekends that were the best of all. They began on Thursday mornings. We drove down to Barnagat Bay, New Jersey, where they had a cozy cottage next to the shore. One day I counted 38 walking steps to the sea. The most magical of all nights was the evening that Florence and I went for a swim. The sea was filled with small phosphorescent jellyfish. Some were the size of silver dollars. Others were no larger than a pin head, but there were thousands of them. They did not become visible unless we touched them, so as we swam through the water, we would come upon them and they would light up, and we could see our own bodies glowing with a light green color. It was like a dream. I rolled over in the seawater and floated, looking at the heavens, green sea stars beneath me, and sparkling heavenly stars above me.

Later we took a walk along a path through a nearby meadow where the fireflies danced. I never experienced a more magical time in my life. I didn't think about the Lord then, but He thought about me. He was there in all His creative glory, speaking to me through His wondrous world. It happened over fifty years ago, or was it yesterday?

When we encounter these precious moments, we need to make a point of memorizing everything about them. How do we feel? What do we see? What do we hear? What do we smell? Then, when that time comes when we are lonely and longing for beauty, we can take a moment and remember — just remember, and in the midst of our remembering, remember God.

All the ends of the world shall remember and turn to the Lord... Psalm 23:27 (NKJV)

Lord, help me to store memories in my soul that will heal me in the time of spiritual drought, but most of all, help me to remember you, for you are always mindful of me. Amen.

October 4

A Maze Craze

In the fall, a gifted maze creator visits Arizona yearly and builds some fantastic mazes through which the public can stroll. They are made in a field of corn. One is in the shape of the state of Arizona. It's open for a couple of months in the fall and this amazing maize maze is just what families need to have a pleasant walk together. The longest anyone has taken to get through the current maze, which is designed by a horticulturist from Utah, Brett Herbst, is 3 1/2 hours. He says that if you make all the right turns, it only takes fifteen minutes, but that most people take an hour to escape from this life-sized game!

We human beings tend to like other kinds of mazes too — mysteries to solve. Challenges. I have a friend who one day walked through a large office going around desks and through aisles. When she arrived at her destination, her fellow office worker, said, "Do you know that you took the absolutely most difficult and longest route to get over here?" She realized that this indeed had been the case. This one observation caused her to take a look at her entire life. She recognized that she managed to create all kinds of difficult challenges for herself so she could solve them or overcome them. She's a bright, intelligent woman. I suspect she gets bored and so she creates puzzles to solve just for the fun of it.

But life can be a maze too. You turn a corner when you take a new job and you don't know what will happen — success and promotion, or a dead end job with snooty co-workers? Or could this be the church where you'll meet your spouse-to-be? Or the community where you're moving, will it be all that you had hoped for? Life is full of surprises. For believers it's a life of faith. We may feel as if we can't figure what turn to take next. We don't have a map of the maze of our lives. But the Lord does! If we prayerfully make our decisions, He will help us in all these choices and we will make it through our own personal life "maze."

The people who walked in darkness have seen a great light; those who lived in a land of deep darkness — on them light has shined. Isaiah 9:2 (NRSVA)

Lord, the Light of my life, sometimes I get lost along the way. I feel like I've made a wrong turn and that I'll never find my way out. But that's not true. You know the whole pattern and you knew I would take this way to begin with. Help me to thank you even for the times when I feel lost, because I know, in your sight, I'm always "found." Amen.

October 5

Victory

When we moved to Arizona, my husband and I experienced some severe difficulties including being accused of things of which we were not guilty. People that we thought were our dear friends inexplicably turned against us. The pain was almost more than we could bear. And this happened three times. But I remembered what God had told me as we were embarking on this mission and I finally understood. He said, "Golden, golden, golden." It meant that we would go through three refining crises.

One of the lessons I learned while there was how important it is to pray for and to forgive those who had made themselves our enemies. But I can't pretend that it was not a difficult time for me — the most difficult of my life. Then one day, I was sitting in my car, crying, and feeling sorry for myself. The Lord spoke to me and said, "Do you love me enough to stay in the desert forever for my sake?" I was shocked. How could He ask such a thing of me? I sat there, knowing this was a vital spiritual turning point. And then I discovered something I would never have guessed about myself. I knew the answer and it wasn't what I thought it would be. It was: "Yes, Lord, I will."

I thought that meant that we would stay in Arizona for the rest of our lives. But it did not. In time, we moved to Beaumont, California, which is considered "high desert." So I'm still in the desert! But this has been a blessed place for us, where we can both serve our Lord in a variety of ways. Then, once we were completely settled here and the morning after the day we knew that we had sold our home in Goodyear, the Lord awakened me with these words, "You have been through the dark night of the soul and you have survived!" I arose with a shout in my spirit, "Yes, I have survived!" I was filled with inexpressible joy. I praise God for helping me through that time of darkness and for bringing me into a place of victory!

These trails are only to test your faith, to show that it is strong and pure. It is being tested as fire tests and purifies gold — and your faith is far more precious to God than mere gold. So if your faith remains strong after being tried by fiery trials, it will bring you much praise and glory and honor on the day when Jesus Christ is revealed to the whole world. You love him even though you have never seen him. Though you do not see him, you trust him; and even now you are happy with a glorious, inexpressible joy. 1 Peter 1:7& 8 (NLT)

Lord, you know what we need and it is you who allow us to go through things that we find so terribly difficult. Even so, you can make something good come from what seems hopeless. Whatever happens to me in the days ahead, help me to overcome by the power that you give me, help me to receive your peace, and also help me to remember to praise you all along the way. Amen.

October 6

Mashed Meatballs and Skewed Plans

Tony brought in the huge casserole of Lasagna to share with the engineering department where I worked in Pasadena. It was absolutely delicious — the best I had ever tasted, so I was thrilled when he gave me his family's secret recipe. Then came the special occasion on which to make it. I carefully sorted out the ingredients, but I didn't read the recipe directions in advance. So, step-by-step, I followed along. One of the most difficult parts was to make meat balls. I carefully mixed the ingredients together and made cute little meatballs, which were then fried.

Later on, as I read along, the directions said to break the meatballs apart. *What*?! I screamed. *No! Not these beautiful little meatballs that I so carefully formed!* No one will ever even see them! I didn't want to, but I tore them apart. And wow! What praises that dish got! It was truly the best-ever recipe keeper you can imagine and those crushed meatballs were no doubt a big part of the reason.

I thought of this when, after coming to Arizona, I misread the meaning of a dream I had. In it I was told to roll up my sleeves and go to work! When I woke up the next morning I was sure that this dream meant that I would have my own ministry in Goodyear — most likely one involving inner healing. Shortly after that the Lord spoke to me and He said, "I will increase your gifts." Wow! Super deal! That must mean, I thought, that I would need these extra gifts for "my" ministry.

Well what I realized, as time passed, was that the work I would be doing would be on myself! I had to go into psychotherapy with a Christian therapist because of being traumatized by what was going on around us. And the additional gifts? Yes, there was an increase in my gift of discernment, which was greatly needed, and also, and even better, a call to be more of an intercessor, and even more amazing, the Lord led me to write. Somehow I imagined that part of that would mean I would become a well-known writer and I would be earning a substantial amount of money! But God never promised me that I would be rich or famous! However, I did obey and write, and this book is one of the results of that calling.

Well, as you can see, I had totally misread God's original intentions. Just like the meatballs in the lasagna dish, I felt my life was all mashed up for a while — totally useless I was, and in so much misery and pain. But in the end, the Lord helped me to come out a "tastier" and better human being and that is what He was after, not MY ministry, but HIS ministry to me and later (in intercession and writing) through me.

Do not boast about tomorrow, For you do not know what a day may bring forth. Proverbs 27:1 (NKJV)

Lord, sometimes I think you have shown me something about my future and then I discover that my interpretation is entirely wrong. But that's OK. I don't have to know the future, but I take heart in knowing that whatever I go through, joy or pain, you will be my companion all along the way. Amen.

October 7

The "Yes But" People

My husband who was a marriage and family counselor for a number of years in Southern California tells me that one of the worst clients to have is one who appears to listen to what you suggest, but then they say, "Yes, but...." They come up with excuses as to why they cannot follow through with the needed action. In other words, they are stuck, and something in them wants to stay that way!

A member of my Toastmaster's chapter shared with us about a call he received from a woman who had been a Toastmaster in Dallas. She moved to the Phoenix area and wanted to find another Toastmaster's division in which to continue her work on her CM (Competent Toastmaster). She was told about an early morning meeting place, "No," she replied, "I'd have to get up at 5:00 a.m. to go to that one. I don't get up that early." Another suggestion was made, "No, there you have to pay for lunch; I don't want to have to pay for lunch." A third suggestion was made; "No," she once again responded, "they meet for two hours and I'm willing to meet for no more than 1 1/2 hours!" My friend suggested yet another location. "No, I'm not willing to drive that far. Isn't there any place that I can go?" Having offered all the information he had about the local Toastmaster Club locations, my friend just gave up. I would have been tempted to suggest, in not so kind a voice, that she move back to Dallas. This is a perfect example of this kind of person.

I hate to admit it but sometimes I'm a "yes but" person. How about you? Are you allowing yourself to be stuck because there's something you really just don't want to do even though you know you should? Maybe it's time to "just do it!" You'll almost certainly discover that you are no longer "stuck" and that your life has been changed for the better! By the way, joining Toastmasters was just such a choice for me!

Deliver me out of the mire... Psalm 69:14a (NKJ)

Father, I admit I need help in helping myself sometimes. I want to see where I get myself stuck so I can just do what I need to in order to change what needs to be changed. Amen.

October 8

Songs in the Night

Don was at an elder board meeting and I was feeling lonely. I was sitting in the living room, not bothering to turn on the lights as twilight descended. And then, as if out of nowhere, came the beautiful songs of a bird. It sounded as if this warbler must be inside of the house. But how could that happen? I walked around trying to find the source of this wonderful, pure melody. Back where I started, I finally realized this music was being piped right down the chimney into the living room. *Was a bird caught inside there?* I wondered. *No, but perhaps one is on top of the chimney.* I walked outside and looked up and, sure enough, there on the edge of the chimney was perched a warbler, singing her heart out, just for me. And, so I received this as from the Lord — who didn't leave me alone in my sadness, but gave me the gift of a serenade from a California Thrasher, sent from on high!

> *Where is God my Maker, Who gives songs in the night...* Job 35:10 (NKJ)

Father, thank you for sending us messengers to cheer our spirits by singing songs in the night. Amen.

October 9

GODS4U

I was going to speak at Toastmasters the next day, but I had become extremely anxious. Don and I were driving along one of the thoroughfares in Goodyear, Arizona, and I was worrying and fretting.

How could I possibly do it? I was saying to the Lord, "Father, I don't know if I should even try if there's a chance I can't pull it off. Should I or shouldn't I?" Now don't laugh! Believe it or not, it was at just that instant that I looked up and saw a car in front of us with a license plate that said, "GODS4U". That's all I needed. God is for me. I received it as something that had been specifically planned by the Lord for me to see at that very second. I would give the speech.

The meetings were early (6:30 a.m.) and it was still dark when I left the house. After I arrived, I had to go back to the car for something. I glanced up at the desert sky; it was clear, immense, and beautiful. Just then a shooting star streaked across the heavens. It was the second boost I needed before I went in to give my seven-minute speech. I felt as if the Lord was with me all the way through and then the audience was encouraging with their comments. Yes! God was for me! What more did I need?

If God is for us, who can be against us? Romans 8:31 (NKJ)

Lord, you really are on my side, aren't you? Help me to never doubt it. Amen.

October 10

Wishes

There is a hope that, unsummoned, rises in me still
It is that some earthly soul will match this inner thrill:
Of sharing timelessness, magic, mysteries and tears,
That unalone I might know the longings, joys or fears
And not be thought silly or perhaps just simply mad
Or to be pensive, brooding but not thought morbidly sad.

To find escape: a space, a place without a door
Without a ceiling, walls or even floor
Yes, somewhere more than my own room
Where I might flourish, grow and bloom
To laugh or cry without someone to sneer
To be alone, yet have a friend who's always near.

To have all these wishes and yet even more:
Someone with whom my dreams to share, explore.
Not to be despised, belittled or a castaway
To feel as much a part of life as sunlight is to day
To be welcomed, understood, received
Loved, honored, heard, and most of all, believed.

For you are my hope, O Lord God. Psalm 71:5 (NKJV)

Lord, how long it took me to discover there is only One who could understand this field of wishes and it is you and you alone. Amen.

October 11

Mixed Messages Versus Truth

We were driving through La Canada/Flintridge in California when we passed a See's Candy Store. In one window was a large sign that read: "Closed." In another window was a sign the same size that read: "Open." What a great illustration of double messages. Psychologists tell us that those who give us these "double messages" are controlling people who are "crazy makers" — those who want to perplex us and thereby they, by keeping us guessing, make us confused. Another example: a young man tells his girl friend, "Well, as far as you are concerned, I haven't closed any doors, but I haven't opened any either." An unwise girl will stay around just hoping, but a wise woman will get out of such a relationship quickly!

How does this apply to our spiritual lives? Society will keep us guessing. Don't we get mixed messages all the time — no matter what the subject — everything from loose relativists to up-tight purists! Where does the truth lie? I remind you of this: there is only one ultimate source and it's in a person — Jesus Christ himself. There is no other embodiment of indisputable truth — His words are spirit and life. When He walked upon the earth He was filled with the overcoming Spirit that truly rose above all the other silly arguments that mankind has come up with since the dawn of civilization. So, when we are not sure of the truth, it is time to improve our relationship with the One who is the Truth.

> ...*Grace and truth came through Jesus Christ.* John 1:17 (NKJV)

Father God, help me not to be deceived by all the mixed messages around me, but help me to find my truth in the One through whom it came into the world. Amen.

October 12

The Dream Maker

Read this quotation. "I am moved to pleasure by visions of ineffable beauty which I have never beheld in the physical world. Once in a dream I held in my hand a pearl." These are the words of Helen Keller.

From ancient times, dreams and their interpretations have been of great interest to peoples from around the world. What about you? Do you remember your dreams? Do you pay attention to them? Do you know that if you learn to listen to your dreams and ask God to help you understand them, that they can dramatically change your waking hours?

From what I've learned, dreams fall into many categories and can be interpreted on many levels. So, what should we do with them? First, we can learn which dreams to discount. I believe that these are: (1) The ordinary dreams that are just our way of working through what happened the day before and will not have any deep hidden meanings for us; and (2) Dreams that are simply caused by something physical — we have to go to the bathroom, so we spend time looking for one in a dream, or we ate pizza just before we went to bed and we have a nightmare. Churchill called such dreams, "Children of the night, of indigestion bred!"

But, there are many kinds of dreams that need to be paid attention to. Here are a few:

1. Dreams that are extremely short often have a clear, important message.

2. Dreams that wake us up are saying, "Listen to me."

3. Repetitive dreams are trying to tell us something again & again and will continue to return until we "get it."

4. Dreams that have great emotional content. We need to pay attention to these because they tell us the truth — not necessarily about the characters or things in the dream, but about the way we *feel* about the things or people in our dreams. An example: I thought I had forgiven someone for offending me until I dreamed I told her to "drop dead."

Or dreams may present us with an idea that might help with a problem. A friend recently told me of having pain in a knee but discovered a possible solution when, in a dream, a little child tugged at the hem of her skirt and told her, "Your knees wouldn't hurt so much if you just lost some weight, lady."

Some people find it helpful to make an effort to remember their dreams and write them down right away. We can meditate for a moment, asking ourselves what we were dreaming and then ask, "What is this dream telling me that I need to know?" If we don't do this and just jump out of bed, most dreams will not make it into our long-term memory and they will be lost forever.

So let's make a point of not wasting our dreams. They are gifts from the Lord. To ignore them is like throwing away pearls. Most dreams are our own private creation (Supernatural dreams are, of course, the exception.). We write the script, design the set and play all of the characters. So before you go to sleep this evening, ask the Lord to help you to be open to these messengers of the night. Listen to them; learn from them and think of them as gifts that need to be unwrapped so that they may bring to you a new understanding of yourself — that fascinating person within you — the dream maker.

God gave them knowledge and skill in all literature and wisdom; and Daniel had understanding in all visions and dreams. Daniel 1:17 (NKJV)

Lord, give us wisdom to understand our night visions and dreams. Amen.

October 13

Dreams and Visions about the Future — Part 1
The Sickle and The Cross

The next few days I will be sharing with you some dreams that I have had over a period of many years. Perhaps some were supernaturally inspired, so just in case that's so, I pass them on to you, my dear readers.

The first dream I will share with you came in two parts. The first part was simply this: a red flag with a black sickle. As I watched, the sickle came to life with no visible hand touching it. It came out of the red background, and was swung through the air, going right through me (but not harming me) as though sent out to reap. I believe this is the symbol of the final spiritual harvest that will come upon the earth and I believe it has already started, but possibly not yet in the United States.

The second part of the dream: Immense angels (several stories high) swept down and destroyed man-made structures — skyscrapers! I was at first horrified at the utter devastation, but then I was filled with a sense of awe and glory because the angels tore down everything until there was nothing remaining standing except the Cross of Jesus Christ. Hallelujah!

May I never boast of anything except the cross of our Lord Jesus Christ, by which the world has been crucified to me, and I to the world. Galatians 6:14 (NRSVA)

Lord, you suffered and died on that cross. It is the center of history. I believe that man-made belief systems will one day be destroyed by whatever forces you send, but the Cross will remain forever. Amen.

October 14

Dreams and Visions about the Future — Part 2
The Beast

On January 1, 1980, I saw a vision. I was wide-awake, but my eyes were closed, and I saw it not just once, but twice. It was utterly silent except for two words at the end of it. I was watching as a ram with two horns came up out of the earth. Once he stood upon the earth, he changed into the form of a man; the only thing that remained unchanged were his eyes — which were radiating a penetrating hatred, and red in color. They looked directly toward me, but I felt completely safe because, though I could see him, I knew that he could not see me. I then heard these words, "The beast." That was all.

> *"Then I saw another beast coming up out of the earth, and he had two horns like a lamb and spoke like a dragon."*
> Revelation 13:11 (NKJV)

Lord, whether dreams and visions we have are personal or supernatural, I know that you reveal to us what we need to know day by day and I trust you with the future, both mine, and that of the world. Amen.

October 15

Dreams and Visions about the Future — Part 3
Much Work to be Done

I had been feeling without hope and the following dream began to heal my hopelessness. I had asked God to show me the meaning of the parable of the foolish virgins, and this dream, at least in part, seemed to be an answer. The dream came to me on May 18, 1994, and appeared to be revealing that those who are kept pure in their devotion to God and keep on obeying His direction in their lives now in this present age, will be those who do the works in the coming age.

Many Christians, including me, were still alive when the Lord returned to Earth. It was clear that Jesus had come back in a physical body and He went to a specific place on Earth (this may have been Jerusalem, but I wasn't sure). While others remained in their earth-bound bodies, we who were believers were in *new bodies* that were strong and able to do much work, and there was a keen awareness that there is much work to be done. We were given the Spirit to go with us. We knew where and when we were to go to certain places to minister, one assignment at a time. We were transported (like Philip) in these supernatural spiritual bodies to places on the Earth where we were needed to minister, and we were given supernatural abilities to work the works of God including healings and miracles.

There was an amazing sense of continuity from the present life into this new life that the return of Jesus Christ would usher in. We are now being prepared and should be preparing ourselves. I saw the world as a whirling mass of blue — and with eyes of faith, saw spiritual activity everywhere over the world as the believers swiftly went from place to place in their ministries, bringing the power of the living God with them wherever they were called.

This dream renewed my faith and my hope that Jesus is indeed returning, and that there will be magnificent and marvelous changes taking place on the Earth, that may even happen in our life time!

...Blessed and holy is he who has part in the first resurrection. Over such the second death has no power, but they shall be priests of God and of Christ, and shall reign with Him a thousand years. Rev. 20:6 (NKJV)

Even so, Lord Jesus, come quickly. Amen.

October 16

Dreams and Visions about the Future — Part 4
Dancing on the Water

Following is a dream I had on September 29, 1977. It was so compelling that I felt I must record it.

I was outside and it was nighttime. As several others and I looked up toward the heavens, we saw all kinds of lights flashing, pictures and writings in the sky. I thought that this was some sign that the Lord was returning to earth, but I couldn't make sense out of any of the lettering or pictures at all and I was frustrated by this. I was condemning myself for my lack of understanding and discernment of the "signs of the times," that Jesus spoke about.

Then the Lord spoke to me, saying, "It will be more like *this*." At this point (within the dream) I was standing on the shore of the Pacific, looking out at the deep, green water. I saw a great tidal wave coming. There were several other Christians with me and they saw the same thing. It was terribly frightening and some turned and ran from the wave. I thought to myself, "Well, if this is God's plan that there is to be this wave and that those of us along the coast are to be destroyed by it, then I'll just go out and meet it." I was afraid, but I did it anyway. Several others came out with me. I was holding someone's hand. The wave was upon us when I said, "Well, this is the last breath I'll ever take," and I dove in.

However, instead of being sucked under, the wave was soft and warm and it lifted me up, so that I could take another breath and each time there was a swell, it lifted me higher and higher until I was standing on the water. I found I could walk on the water, and as I looked around there were several of my friends who were also walking around on the water with great joy. Next I discovered that I could slide — something similar to a cross between water skiing and ice-skating. We all started to dance with each other in three-quarter-waltz time.

Let them praise His name with the dance; Let them sing praises to Him with the timbrel and harp. For the Lord takes pleasure in His people; He will beautify the humble with salvation. Psalm 149:3,4 (NKJV)

Lord, help me to rejoice in your love with my whole body. I've heard of people dancing before you; teach me how to do that. Amen.

October 17

Dreams and Visions about the Future — Part 5
A Darker Sea

Years after I had the dancing-on-water dream, I had another dream about a similar subject. This second dream seems to put the other in balance. It came during a long juice fast and as a spiritual testing, I had an inward journey one night in which I was surrounded by what seemed to be a combination of my greatest fears and the horrors that will come upon the world in the last days — things I will live to see — sometimes so great, so fierce, so overwhelming, that they are all-encompassing, and through this great "shaking" all that I (we) will be able to cling to is the voice of God which says, not in words, but in a command directly to our spirits, "Do not be afraid." That one thing is what we have to cling to as we hang on to Him like a buoy on a storm-attacked ocean of gigantic waves.

So here again I had an ocean dream, but it was a dark and dreadful sea, yet one that we can overcome by listening and obeying that command and taking it into our spirits, "Don't be afraid."

For then there will be great tribulation, such as has not been since the beginning of the world until this time, no, nor ever shall be. Matthew 24:21 (NKJV)

Dear Lord, you have warned us in advance about difficulties that will come upon the Earth before you return. Indeed in many places on the earth, tribulation has already come. Help us to, no matter what happens in the world, not fear, but to share your peace and joy, strength and comfort with others. Amen.

October 18

Dreams and Visions about the Future — Part 6
What God Sees

I was in my later sixties when I had a most remarkable dream. I was standing in front of a large mirror and I looked up and saw Jesus standing behind me (only His misty reflected image). He spoke to me saying, "This is how I see you." I looked at myself. I had been transformed! I was young, with long dark brown hair (no longer gray). I had no wrinkles, no age spots, no scars and not a single blemish. I was pretty! But I was not beautiful. I was not yet dressed as a bride.

I woke up! What I realized is that God sees me already perfected (washed in the blood of the Lamb) but not yet *beautified*! I also realized that it was not just me that He sees this way. It is His bride — all of us who are His church, who are awaiting the return of our Bridegroom! We need to do whatever is necessary to be prepared for His coming!

> *You also must be ready all the time, for the Son of Man will come when least expected.* Matthew 24:44 (NLT)

Oh Lord God, I ask that you help your church to be equipped for your return to Earth! We long for that day! Please reveal to us what we need to do to "prepare the way of the Lord." Amen.

October 19

Would Jesus Be There?

As I sat down in St. David's Cathedral situated in a little valley near the southwest coast of Wales, I found that I was sobbing, tears streaming down my face. I don't know how to explain why. Perhaps it was the sense of history, the feeling that in the very building of this 12th century structure, there had been great sacrifice out of deep devotion to God, or that for hundreds of years, hundreds of worshipers had been in this very pew where I sat. A guide was speaking softly and his hushed tones suggested that *yes*, this was a place where Jesus Christ was known and worshipped. Again in the little Mwnt Chapel further up the coast — so simply designed, where the sweet aroma of bee's wax told of the careful polishing of the pews, we sat quietly and sensed the presence of the Lord. And then once more in Scotland at the magnificent St. Giles Cathedral in Edinburgh, a young man of God who preached the peace of Jesus Christ offered up noontime prayers.

At these places and in countless others, during our travels during the summer of 1999, including the Community Church in Richland, Washington, we found that the presence of the Lord and the knowledge of His love are there, in spite of myriad differences in the "packaging!" What faithless part of me even questioned that there would be true believers in any of these places, I don't know. I recall with joy the sense of God's presence in each sacred place — St. John in the Vale Church in Carlisle, England, Strata Florida Abbey in Wales, the charming Luss Parish Church close to the banks of Loch Lomond that offered a written blessing to all who visit. Whatever that source of lack of faith in me was, it faded as we traveled from place to place. In each chapel or church or cathedral or ancient abbey ruin, we found evidence that Jesus Christ was indeed Lord. So, my question, "Would Jesus be there?" was answered with a resounding, unequivocal *Yes*! The evidence that Jesus Christ was and is honored, loved and worshipped was there in each place, not only in the present, but down through the ages!

And some were persuaded by the things which were spoken...
Romans 28:24 (NKJV)

Lord, thank you that throughout the ages there have always been some who have been persuaded of the truth of the good news about your son, Jesus Christ. Amen.

October 20

Called to Do the Small Things

While going through a most difficult time — a period that lasted years, I felt I was doing absolutely nothing of value for God. Then a special friend, Karen, sent me a story that changed my attitude completely. It was about a man who heard the Lord speaking to him in the night and telling him to push the large rock in front of his home. He obeyed the Lord and from morning until night for days, then weeks, then years, pushed against the rock with all of his strength. The man was filled with discouragement at times because he could not move the rock, but he continued on in obedience. He questioned God, asking why he was such a failure, but the Lord spoke to him again, and reminded him that his job had not been to *move* the rock but to *push* against it, and in so doing, he had become incredibly strong, and now that he had obeyed all these years, it was the Lord who would move the rock!

Oh, this did my heart so much good. I had only pushed the rock, but that is all I was required to do! Sometimes our image of what God wants us to do for Him and what we want to do for God are completely in opposition!

> *And now, Israel, what does the Lord your God require of you, but to fear the Lord your God, to walk in all His ways and to love Him, to serve the Lord your God with all your heart and with all your soul, and to keep the commandments of the Lord and His statutes which I command you today for your good?*
> Deuteronomy 10:12, 13 (NKJV)

Lord, help me let go of my own great big ideas of what you want me to do for you, and help me to follow you in the small things, day by day. Amen.

October 21

The Choice While Looking Back

One morning as Don and I took our morning walk with Lucy, I told him that we have a choice. Life is either a string of one bad thing after another, or a string of one good thing after another with a lot of ordinary things in between. He laughed and said sarcastically, "Oh, for you, it's just one good thing after another, right? Especially coming to Arizona?" I said, "yes" and I meant it! For once, I meant it. Everybody's life includes the good and the bad but you can choose what you focus on as you look back. Yes, I've known grief, and in some ways the future is uncertain, but I've experienced so many wonderful things: I've had the best of husbands, the most wonderful sons, special daughters-in-law, amazing relatives, a series of great jobs, absolutely marvelous faithful friends and I've traveled in many different places in the United State and the world! And I think none of the good things would have happened, if I had chosen not to follow Jesus. So, when you know the Lord, in the midst of whatever life brings, tragedy or happiness, He is there with you, to put meaning into it.

> *...whatever things are true, whatever things are noble, whatever things are just, whatever things are pure, whatever things are lovely, whatever things are of good report, if there is any virtue and if there is anything praiseworthy — meditate on these things.* Philippians 4:8 (NKJV)

Lord, help me to trust you and you alone, day by day as good or ill unfolds and help me to think on those things that are good. Amen.

October 22

Out Damn Weed!

When I was in my teens I knew all about how to experience self-pity. It was easy to spend hours crying. But when I matured, I found that it was certainly not a very rewarding exercise and I also felt that it was not honoring to my Lord, so I made a point to extricate the practice from my life. I believe I did it fairly well, but there are those temptations and a new one — to become embittered. The "why me?" kinds of weed-like thoughts come once in a while and I know I must send them flying out from the garden of my mind before they are allowed to take hold and grow into roots of bitterness.

> *...lest any root of bitterness springing up cause trouble...*
> Hebrews 12:15b (NKJV)

Lord, help me to weed out my garden regularly, before seeds of bitterness take root. Amen.

October 23

A Special Birthday

When my son, Dan, turned 25, as I prepared for it I talked with God about him. Afterwards I recorded that conversation. Here is a portion of it:

> *Father, it's his twenty-fifth birthday. He said he wanted a pudding cake. I'm not really sure what that is. I wonder if he knows how much I cherish getting ready for his party. . .*
> *Lord, when I think of his birth, I wonder if he sensed the fears I felt when I went into false labor so many times—and the time in the hospital with the hormone injections when they were trying to stop the labor, did that effect him in anyway?*

Father, may Daniel know that you formed him in the womb and that he was exactly what and who you wanted him to be and that you welcomed him into the world and rejoiced at his birth. Be to him what and who I was not able to be as a parent. Be to him what and who his father was not able to be. Be his Mother God and His Father God, and bring others into his life who will be to him just what he needs. Oh, how many times I've said this prayer!

Oh Father, yesterday he was a baby. Today's he's a quarter of a century old — half my age. Lord, my greatest comfort is that you love him much more than I do. Help him to see how proud I am of him, know how much I love him, how I enjoy celebrating this day with him. What an emptiness would be in my heart if this boy had not been given to us. What a gift — this brand new life I was honored to give birth to. Lord, thank you for my son and the day on which you brought him into the world.

And Father, help the cake to turn out OK. Thank you. Amen.

For You have formed my inward parts; You have covered me in my mother's womb. I will praise You, for I am fearfully and wonderfully made; Marvelous are Your works, and that my souls knows very well. Psalm 139:13, 14 NKJV

Lord God, you knew each of us as we were being created in our mother's womb. Take us, our little human lives, and make us become not only children of the earth, but children of our Father in Heaven. Amen.

October 24

That Same Old Temptation

Dick and Irma (not their real names) are two of the most humble and honest servants of the Lord that I know. We've been friends since the early 1960s; that's long enough to make a sound judgment about character. Recently they were traveling and the last country they left before returning to the United States was Holland. Just before leaving they purchased some T-shirts for their grandsons. The T-shirts were placed in a yellow bag along with some apples for themselves. Dick ate his right away, but Irma saved hers for later.

On the plane coming back to the states, they were handed forms to fill out that asked if they had anything to declare; this would include any plant items, bulbs or seeds. Dick, remembering the apple, checked *yes* on the form. Irma thought that if he did this, they would have to relinquish the apple and she would not get to eat it, so she just happened to have some Liquid Paper™ in her purse; she used it, changing the declaration to *no*. But this wasn't the end of it. She began to feel guilty, but she was adamant! She wanted that apple!

When they arrived in the United States with a few carry-on items, they were told they would have to go through a special inspection; then another; with each one, they realized that they were being given "special" treatment. They were asked to stand aside. She was feeling more and more guilty, but still not willing to give up the apple and Dick was getting more and more nervous; had their lie been discovered?

Finally after almost two hours they found out why they were being detained. It seemed that the gifts they had purchased for their grandchildren had been placed in the yellow bag that is from a store that sells tulip bulbs. Many people try to bring bulbs into the United States, which is illegal, but when the only items discovered were T-shirts, they were allowed to enter without any more trouble.

The crisis passed, Irma sat down to eat the apple. Its fruit was not sweet. The distaste of having been dishonest marred its flavor. She explained what a difficult lesson this had been to learn. It was about being dishonest in even a small thing. When the conscience is tender in a godly person, you can't get away with "forbidden fruit!"

...she took of its fruit and ate. Genesis 3:6 (NKJV)

Lord, we ask that you deliver us from temptation, but when you allow temptations to come into our lives, may our consciences remain tender toward your Holy Spirit, who helps us recognize and gives us power to resist temptation. Amen.

October 25

The Little Affirmations

I remember the first time I was right. I must have been two or three years old. My grandmother and mother were there. It was breakfast time. Set before me was a bowl of oatmeal. I looked at it and saw that floating in the cereal were some ants. Not too many, just five or six perhaps. I knew the word "ants." I pointed at them and said, "Ants. Ants." They glanced at the bowl and said, "No, that's part of the cereal." I was steadfast. I don't remember getting impatient or angry. I just continued to point to the cereal and say, "Ants, ants." Finally they picked the bowl up and looked more closely. My grandmother then said, "Why she's right; those *are* ants!" I knew they had heard me and that they knew I was *right*! They took the bowl away and gave me something else to eat that morning. And I was satisfied. It gave me a sense of pride in the best sense of that word.

There are times that I know in my heart and spirit that I am right about something and yet no one else believes that I am. That's an uncomfortable feeling to have. But even when no one listens to me, I can go straight to the Lord and talk to Him and I know He hears me. He gives me a sense that what I have to say is important to Him. And if I'm important to Him, then I have a sense of being appreciated for who I am. It's not such a little thing; it's a big thing to me — to be acknowledged by my Lord.

> *But, LORD All-Powerful, you are a fair judge. You know how to test peoples' hearts and minds.* Jeremiah 11:20 (NCV)

Lord, I thank you for being there to listen to me and to encourage me and to judge me righteously. Amen.

October 26

Lucy's Perfect Day

Hello! I'm Lucy, Pat's and Don's dog. They are not sure what kind of dog I am. Some say Border collie. Some say sheltie. Some say Schipperke. I don't care, of course. I'm a dog, that's all I need to know, and I'm sure I'm the best of them all; at least that's what they tell me — super mutt par excellence. Today was my favorite day of all. In the morning, Pat said, "Walk." I know that word. It means time to smell a lot; as Don puts it, I "walk by smell and not by sight." I jumped up on the chair so that he could put my leash on and then off we went in the car to the smelling spot. It was extra special fun today because we went to a new place and there were new smells. I'm very good at this. I can tell you a lot of different things I smelled, but perhaps you'd rather not know; I can tell who and what has been around anywhere, any time! And this time there were not just other dogs either; there were cats, and lizards and moles. It was a time full of surprise odors.

And the ducks! I pretended to almost catch one this time. But, to be honest, my funnest time of all is to go to the high school football field. When I know it's time to go I just tremble all over with anticipation. Don throws the tennis ball. I run and catch it in my mouth. You should see me. Yes, as I said, today was a good day; I leaped in the air and caught the ball over and over. My eye/mouth coordination is truly remarkable. I tell you, being a dog is absolutely wonderful when you can do what you know you were made to do. I think humans would call this "a peak experience."

Oh yes, and how I love to prance — all four feet off the ground at once! What fun we had. Then to top it off we came home and I got a treat — bacon flavored, ah! My favorite. And I'm tired and happy as I roll over and get my tummy scratched, and they say to me, "I love Lucy." Joie de vivre is mine. Yes, it was a good dog day.

Let everything that hath breath praise the Lord. Psalm 150:6 (NKJV)

Thank you Lord of all earthly creatures, for the little friends you give us from the animal world that teach us about the joy of life! Amen.

October 27

Wonders of an Early Morning Walk

As I took an early morning walk on a brisk, fall day, I made a point to pay attention to everything I was experiencing, so that nothing would be lost. These are the things that I noticed:

- A healthy ache in my calves
- A cool breeze on my hot face
- The rustle and call of mourning doves and goldfinches rejoicing even before they leave the warmth of their nests to search for breakfast
- The satisfying crunch of dry magnolia leaves beneath my feet
- The fresh scent of dew on grass, dichondra, ferns and moss
- Lawn sprinklers impishly timed and unpredictably aimed
- A black and white tomcat meandering home after a rough night out
- The chilly dampness of the morning air embracing me with calm hope
- The lavender glow of the eastern sky dotted with soft white lace, moment by moment changing from one glory to the next
- A single bright green parrot, an alien in the land, speaking authoritatively in unknown tongues
- Ants, scripturally true, busily being a faithful little people
- Plump ladies barefoot in blue muumuus or rose robes tiptoeing across damp lawns for morning newspapers recently and imprecisely plopped down on brick sidewalks or quaint stone steps
- The smell of cinnamon rolls and coffee, freshly baked and brewed by loving hands
- A "rolly poley" on a sure path traversing mine in perfect and safe time between my nearly unnoticed strides
- A mocking bird's skilled pretense at being a crow
- Two squirrels rippling across the road and chasing each other around and up a tree trunk

- Walkers and runners, with steady gaits, and earphones, lost in their worlds of recorded music or airwave messages
- The big, beautiful, black beetle and I startling each other into changing directions
- The subtle, deceptive sweet scent of pink and white Oleander blossoms
- The song of praise that I sang yesterday greeting me in the same place this morning as though it hovered in the air, words and music not lost, but found, in the spiritual space it had created.
- And most wonderful, most humbling, most extraordinary of all, the presence, forever there, of the Word, by whom all wonders were created, my Lord, quietly walking with me, by my side to comfort and encourage and direct me as I begin this, a newborn day.

May I make a suggestion? If you are able, take a walk today and see what **you** can discover along the way.

I have no greater joy than to hear that my children walk in truth. 3 John, verse 4 (NKJV)

Lord, help me to walk not only physically but spiritually with you so that I will walk in truth. Amen.

October 28

Our Dream Car

In July of 1994 before my husband and I moved to Arizona, we decided to buy a "new" used car. We had our hearts set on a Buick and so we went to the Buick dealership in Cerritos, California. We looked around at the available autos and found a blue Buick — just what we wanted, except that it had automatically operated windows and I wanted manual controls. We told the salesperson that we would need to think about it overnight. He warned us that he couldn't guarantee it would be there the next day. After going home I said a short prayer about the whole thing and took a nap. While napping, I dreamed that I was standing behind a white Cutlass Ciera (Oldsmobile) and knowing without a doubt that this would/should be our new car. When I woke up my husband asked me, "Well, how do you feel about the Buick?" "Fine," I said, "but I had this dream about a white Cutlass Ciera. I think we should see if we can find it." He was skeptical, of course.

The next morning he called to tell the sales rep that we wanted the blue Buick. "Sorry," he said, "it's been sold, but I have another car I think you might be interested in. It's an Oldsmobile Cutlass Ciera." I was sitting near Don listening in on his side of the conversation. "Is it white?" My husband asked with a strange expression on his face. I saw my husband smile a little sheepishly as he said, "I think we want it. We'll be right over." When we arrived, there it was — the white car I had dreamed about with over 3,000 fewer miles than the blue Buick had and it was selling for $1,000 less. Maybe that was because it had manually controlled windows! "We'll take it," we told the salesman and it remained what we called our "dream car" until July of 1998, when God supplied us with another car.

And my God shall supply all your needs according to His riches in glory by Christ Jesus. Philippians 4:19 (NKJV)

Lord, thank you for caring about what we need in this physical world and for supplying us with the necessities of life. Amen.

October 29

The Kneeling Heart

We were meandering through a little antique store in Ojai, California, I saw an antique kneeling bench. I knelt there for a moment. In front of me was an old prayer book that was included in the price of $150; it was a marvelous bargain, but I did not buy it. I wish I had. Yet, both Don and I have rather bad knees and I fear it would not have insured that we would have prayed more often.

Do you kneel when you pray? Perhaps kneeling is just a cultural tradition — nothing wrong with it, but not a requirement for saying "proper" prayers! I find only a few times in which kneeling is mentioned in the scripture.

The Bible mentions stretching out before God, flat on your face! How often have you done that? Or lifting eyes and hands toward Heaven; is that your practice? St. Paul mentions bowing his knees before the Father (Ephesians 3:14). I often pray in bed in the night seasons. I have come to believe that no matter what physical position I take, it does not matter to God. You don't have to be in a certain physical posture to be taken seriously by Him; He sees the posture of the heart. If you call on the Lord, He will hear you, so you may be chopping onions in the kitchen, stuck in a traffic jam on I-10, or walking your dog through the park. God will hear and He will answer in His own way. He cares. He loves to have His children talk to Him, and the more often the better, physical stance, inconsequential.

> *Rejoice always, pray without ceasing, in everything give thanks; for this is the will of God in Christ Jesus for you.* 1 Thessalonians 5:16-18 (NKJV)

> *But the time is coming — indeed it's here now — when true worshipers will worship the Father in spirit and in truth. The Father is looking for those who will worship him that way. For God is Spirit, so those who worship him must worship in spirit and in truth.* John 4:23, 24 (NLT)

Lord God, help me to remember, no matter what I'm doing, to offer up little prayers to you throughout the day. Amen.

October 30

Another Restoration

Our high school did a production of the musical "Brigadoon" in 1957. I so wanted the lead role of Fiona and the audition song was, "The Heather on the Hill," which I thought I sang quite well. I did not get the role, but I was appointed student director. I loved this job and was excited as we enjoyed the opening night performance. It was a smash hit. However, the teacher and the choral director had heard some gossip about me (that I was living with a man); it wasn't true but they didn't know that. I was "fired" from my position as student director and was not welcomed at the rest of the performances. I was utterly devastated! It left me with a sense of shame and pain that lasted for a long time. We must forgive all such offenses, of course, but sometimes this is a process and takes a long time.

That process was completed when Don took me to Great Britain in 1999. One afternoon there we were —looking around us at the beauty of the "Heather on the Hill" in the Scottish highlands. I was washed over with the love of God as I knew He was telling me that here again He was restoring the years the locusts had eaten! I had the joy of being there in that place that was far more beautiful than the stage set had been. This was real and beautiful and bore witness to the glories of God's creation.

The grasslands of the wilderness become a lush pasture, and the hillsides blossom with joy. The meadows are clothed with flocks of sheep, and the valleys are carpeted with grain. They all shout and sing for joy! Psalm 65:12, 13 (NLT)

Oh dear Heavenly Father, thank you for the healing touches that you bring to our lives and thank you for the beauty of your world. Amen.

October 31

The God at Hand

I find it funny when I see people walking around everywhere talking on the phone as they bring their cell phones with them — to the park, to the airport (Well, that one really does make sense.), to the theater. Once in the middle of a play at the Pasadena Playhouse, a man who was seated right in front of us got a phone call. He picked up the phone, "Hello," he said, and then explained that he was in the middle of a performance and let them know he would call them back later. Meanwhile, of course, he disturbed everyone around him. Ah, the cell phones, boon and bane of the current technological age!

I read that in the Middle East that when a single man sees an attractive woman, he throws a cell phone at her feet and walks away, yelling back over his shoulder that he will be calling her. Later he keeps his promise, and if this new mode of meeting is appreciated, the couple set up a date!

So what's the point? Spiritually, though I don't want to continue the myth that God is a bellboy, He *is* there and available and closer than our newest, nearest state-of-the-art cell phone, dropped at our feet. He is the one we can trust to always be there to hear our pleas or our praises, or to calm or encourage us. No matter how long it's been since our last "call" to God, He will be thrilled to hear from you or from me today — no guilt trips, no nagging, just a welcoming heart filled with delight.

You are near, O Lord... Psalm 119:151a (NKJV)

Lord, I know you are near, so near that I sometimes take for granted that very nearness, but I truly want to keep in contact with you throughout my day, calling on you, not only as my Lord and King, but as my closest friend. Amen.

NOVEMBER

November 1

Lucy, Super Dog

Lucy has not only attacked mad dog, and the sky, but now has taken on Time itself. Perhaps it's just that she wants to stop the clock; she's not quite ready for the end of the year. At any rate she has discovered the large clock hanging on the outside wall of the house on our patio. It creates a challenge worthy of her skills. She is now, in fact, climbing the wall, to reach this clock. What she is after is what must appear to her to be a small lizard, the second hand, which is moving constantly. So up she goes, over and over again, trying and trying to get that thing, barking in between each attempt.

Life is full of challenges. I don't always like them, do you? And yet Lucy has made her most recent challenge into a game of never-ending delight! I would like that kind of attitude: go looking for challenges, just so I can have the fun of climbing a wall!

For by You I can run against a troop, and by my God I can leap over a wall. Psalm 18:29 (NKJV)

Lord, help me to see difficulties as challenging walls that you will help me to leap over. Amen.

November 2

Heaven's Manna

One night I dreamed about bread from Heaven. I was given a piece that was in the shape of a triangle. I knew, instinctively, that I was to tear off three corners and pass on the corners to three other people. I did so. Then I looked down and saw that the bread in my hand was the same size as it had been before, and the bread in the hands of the others was the same size as mine had originally been. Each of them was then tearing off three corners of their piece of bread, which always left a triangle of the same size, more for others and some remaining and I saw that this would go on indefinitely with no one going without. It was like a picture of the miracle of the feeding of the five thousand.

Many years later I read Evangelist Reinhard Bonnke's auto-biography, "Living a Life of Fire." In it he tells about a vision a woman had in a church service when he was still a child. She saw a very large crowd of black people. They were gathered in a semicircle around a little boy with a big loaf of bread. He was breaking it and sharing it and as he did so it began to increase. She then turned and pointed at Reinhard and said, "The little boy that I saw was this one." This was after he knew that God had called him to be an evangelist in Africa and it was a powerful confirmation to him! So, although my "bread" was shared with only a few and his was shared with what turned out to be millions, it is the same God who does the multiplying! Hallelujah!

But how do we do this sharing? It is surely by telling others about Jesus who is the Bread of Life. It is as though our own portion (knowledge of Him) becomes bread for others and that, in turn, multiplies, as it becomes bread for still others. It is like the ripples in a pool — each spreading farther and farther out, each piece of this divine bread dividing and multiplying. I believe that there is an innate Godly force that causes this creative miracle to happen in the spiritual realm as we share the "daily bread" that God gives to us.

And He took the five loaves and the two fish, and looking up to heaven, He blessed and broke and gave the loaves to the disciples; and the disciples gave to the multitudes. So they all ate and were filled... Matthew 14:19, 20 (NKJV)

I am the bread of life. Whoever comes to me will never be hungry again. John 6:35a (NLT)

Creator God, may I not just receive that bread from Heaven, your very life that you give to me, but may I give to others who will give it to others in their turn, that the Bread of Life may be divided and multiplied until the day of your return to Earth. Amen.

November 3

What Starts with A Small Thing...

In July of 1989 a United Airlines DC-10 crashed while landing with a disabled hydraulic system in Sioux City, Iowa. One hundred eleven people perished. The cause, after investigation, was found to be a tiny flaw in a piece of metal used in a fan. A series of occurrences followed, each building on the other, until the hydraulic system was damaged. But all it took was that small flaw which had gone unnoticed.

This made me think about character flaws, how they may seem small — at first, but how, unchecked they can grow and become destructive to the spiritual life of not only we as individuals, but to others with whom we relate — until severe damage is done. Think of it — the little lie, the little flirtation, the little income tax cheating! It's up to us to keep watch over our souls, to make sure that there is no area in which the Spirit of God has not become welcome. But this is a lifetime of work and we cannot do it without God's searchlight and without His giving us the power to overcome these "small" character flaws that we all have.

In your patience possess your souls. Luke 21:19 (NKJV)

Lord, help me to become aware of even the character flaws I consider small, so that I may allow you to correct and transform me in my inner person. Amen.

November 4

Failure?

Once again I had failed. Tried and failed. It didn't surprise God, of course. He had foreseen it all — my attempts at my own ideas about succeeding. This time I had just wanted everyone to like me and somehow, nice as I am, they didn't! I believe that it was said by someone wise that one sure formula for succeeding in failure is to try to try please everyone. Well, long time believing that one, I've been.

So my goal, (Yes, I know, I've said it before!) if I am wise, is to attempt not to please others, but to please God, who gives me realistic ways in which that can be done, and helps me set achievable goals day by day. And my goal now is to love (if not like) everyone, instead of the other way around. Since, by faith, I know that I have supernatural help, this is a realistic ambition.

Love never fails... 1 Corinthians 13:8 (NKJV)

Not by might, nor by power, but by my Spirit. . . Zechariah 4:6 (NLT)

Lord, teach me to love, and love through me. I acknowledge that I cannot do it on my own. Amen.

November 5

The Precious Gift of Time

Today is all there is, really. Yesterday will never return, and tomorrow is yet to exist. Today could be the last day of your life or mine. If it were so, would that make a difference? Would we do something differently? Would we tell someone we love him or her, confess a sin, write a poem, paint a picture, sing a song? It is God's gift that we do not, most of us, know the day and time of our death. I read somewhere that the last words of Queen Elizabeth I were, "All my possessions for a moment of time." How poignant — the acknowledgment of something that even by royalty cannot be bought. Jim Croce wrote the song, "Time in a Bottle" — the song about wishing time could be stored. But as the lyrics suggest, it cannot.

We have choices every day to do good or evil, speak kind words, or cruel, to be true or false. What do you choose to do today? If not today, choose someday soon to act as though it were your last on earth. Discover what a difference it would make. If it would make no difference whatsoever, you are a rare person indeed.

To everything there is a season, and a time to every purpose under the heaven. Ecclesiastes 3:1 (NKJV)

Dear God, as the Lord of both time and eternity, teach me to cherish every moment I have been allotted on earth. Amen.

November 6

The Gift of the Voice

The gift of speech is a wonderful gift, isn't it? I'm so grateful to be able to speak and to be able to sing. Once I was at the Caltech Athenaeum in Pasadena for lunch and someone wheeled the renowned scientist, Prof. Stephen Hawking, into the dining room. I was awed, but I realized, that even with all of his knowledge, he had to use a machine in order to be able to do something as simple as speaking. In 1998 the actor, Michael Lassen died. He had Lou Gehrig's Disease and had lost his voice and used the same kind of device. With its aid, he told the audience of how he missed his voice on a "Larry King Live" show. I was deeply moved and became aware of how thankful I am to be able to speak, but how easy it is to take it for granted.

I can use my voice in many different ways, I can use it to yell or nag or criticize or complain, or I can use it to encourage, praise, correct in love and comfort. The choice is always mine. What will be my choices in how I use my voice today? What will be yours?

From the same mouth come blessing and cursing. My brothers and sisters, this ought not to be so. James 3:10 (NRSVA)

...The words of the pure are pleasant. Proverbs 15:26 (NKJV)

Jesus, life is filled with so many choices, and many of them are mine just because I have a speaking voice. Help me to learn to use it with grace and wisdom. Amen.

November 7

Recorded Before

The Kingdom's gentle and it's bold,
The young believer and the old —
We're all in need of touch and sensing
Seeking for truth, and then dispensing
Out of wealth or out of need,
Planting faith which, like the seed,
Tiny, yet whose future was written in that grain
Before planted, warmed by sun, or watered by rain.

Lord, as we live out each moment of kindness,
May we be healed of our own inner blindness.
Help us cover with love, others' wrongs
With silence as well as with our songs,
Knowing our good deeds are written before
In some distant past beyond time's door.
May the seed of each spirit remember past seeing,
As our foreordained deeds come into being.

For we are His workmanship, created in Christ Jesus for good works, which God prepared beforehand that we should walk in them. Ephesians 2:10 (NKJV)

Lord, help me to trust you as you lead me into each good deed you have ordained I should perform. Amen.

November 8

In Search of Wisdom

St. Augustine wrote that the greatest good is wisdom, and Emanuel Swedenborg said that the divine essence itself is love and wisdom. So how about you? How is your WQ? Wisdom is not the same as knowledge. A scientist who has great knowledge but does not believe in God is, according to Scripture, a fool! Knowledge is a mixed potion; it can bring either joy or sorrow to the one who drinks, but wisdom — that is so godly a trait that it can only be a gift from God — accepted and increasing, or rejected and diminishing!

King Solomon was asked in a dream what he most wanted and he was praised for not asking for riches, or long life, but for an understanding heart (See 1 Kings 3.). If you had the choice of what you would want more than anything else, what would it be? To lose weight, win the lottery, take a trip into outer space, or would it be to, like King Solomon, receive an understanding heart?

For the Lord gives wisdom; From His mouth come knowledge and understanding; He stores up sound wisdom for the upright. Proverbs 2:6, 7 (NKJV)

Lord, please make me wise enough to know when I need to ask for your wisdom, not just in general, but specifically, and then give me the patience to stop and wait for an answer. Amen.

November 9

The Curse of Perfectionism

It was my first time to serve on jury duty and it was in downtown Los Angeles. I was nervous and afraid of making mistakes, and I made a bunch of them (i.e., parking in the wrong spot, emptying the change out of my purse before putting it on the conveyor belt to be x-rayed, and speaking to the judge about being excused from a case at the wrong moment). I felt miserable and stupid. But I learned something vitally important. I learned that nobody cared about all the mistakes I made. It was OK to be imperfect, to get lost, to wear the wrong thing, or not be selected to a panel. Everyone was there to do their jury duty job and/or to do something else while they waited. So if no one there cared, why should I? It was all part of the legal system, but I met not one Pharisee (legalist) there.

...but do not do according to their [Pharisee's] *works; for they say, and do not do. For they bind heavy burdens, hard to bear, and lay them on men's shoulders; but they themselves will not move them with one of their fingers.* Matthew 23:3b, 4 (NKJV)

Lord, thank you that you do not require of us to be neurotic perfectionists in our approach to life, so help us not to lay heavy, unrealistic burdens upon ourselves. Amen.

November 10

Learning to Swim

In her "Dear Abby" column on April 29, 1999 Abby reran what she considered a classic letter. It was from a woman who asked her husband, if she and his mother were in a canoe and it tipped over and he could save only one, which would it be — to which he responded that he would save his mother. Abby's advice to her was, "Learn to swim."

One day while walking around the small nearby lake, I saw some newborn ducklings standing lined up at the edge of the water. They didn't want to go in. A "parent" duck nearby, "encouraged" them in rather rough ways, until one-by-one, they plopped in, and found that they could (yes!) swim like ducks. One didn't want to go in, however. She just stood there (trembling?). The mother duck came up to her, gave her a good "kick" in the behind with her bill, and that little thing did a complete head-over-heal somersault nearly a foot in the air before plopping in with the rest of the ducklings.

Sometimes such rough treatment is the last thing we want to have happen to us. But sometimes "suck it up and live with it" is about as right on the mark as one can get! Life is tough, life isn't fair, and there are some mean people out there.

So, come on, jump into the midst of life's unpredictable "sea." You might as well, because if you don't somebody will come along and kick you in anyway!

Behold I send you out as sheep in the midst of wolves.
Therefore be wise as serpents and harmless as doves.
Matthew 10:16 (NKJV)

Lord, help me jump into the midst of life and all that is out there, dangers as well as joys, and also help me to be one who is as harmless as a dove. Amen.

November 11

Veterans Day

On the 11th hour of the 11th day of the 11th month of 1918, an armistice, or temporary cessation of hostilities, was declared between the Allied nations and Germany in the First World War (known as "the Great War"). This date was commemorated as Armistice Day beginning the following year. November 11th became a legal federal holiday in 1938. After World War II and the Korean War, Armistice Day became known as Veterans Day, a day to honor *all* who have served their country in the military. In many churches, including ours (Beaumont Presbyterian Church), there are special services (the Sunday prior to Nov. 11) honoring all the men and women in our congregation who have served in the armed services for the sake of the freedoms we have in this country. A portion of the theme song of each branch of the military is played and these brave men and women stand to applause. Following that, we sing together, "The Star Spangled Banner." Then the pastor prays for them and those who are serving currently anywhere in the world.

There is also the playing of taps and a flag folding ceremony. As the flag is folded a reader shares with us the symbolic meaning of each fold as follows: 1st Fold: The symbol of life; 2nd Fold: Our belief in eternal life; 3rd Fold: In honor of veterans departing the ranks who have given a portion of their lives for the defense of our country to attain peace throughout the world; 4th Fold: Represents our weaker nature, for as American citizens trusting in God, it is to Him we turn in times of peace as well as in times of war, for His divine guidance; 5th Fold: is a tribute to our country; 6th Fold: A reminder that as we pledge allegiance to the flag of the United States of America we need to do it from our hearts; 7th Fold: A tribute of our Armed Forces for protecting our country; 8th Fold: A tribute to the one who entered into the valley of the shadow of death, that we might see the light of day; 9th Fold: A tribute to women and mothers; 10th Fold: A tribute to fathers; 11th Fold: This represents the lower portion of the seal of King David and King Solomon, and glorifies in the Hebrews eyes, the God of Abraham, Isaac, and Jacob; 12th Fold: The emblem of eternity and glorifies in the Christian's eyes, God the Father, the Son and the Holy Spirit; 13th Fold: When the flag is completely folded, the stars are in the uppermost, reminding us of our nations motto, "In God We Trust."

I am so thankful to be a citizen of this country. I know we are not a perfect nation, but we are "one nation, under God," and I rejoice in the great privilege of being born in the land of the free and the home of the brave.

Let's remember to pray regularly for all those in the armed services wherever they may be serving. In the following verse replace the "me" with the name of anyone you know in the military.

Answer my prayers, O LORD for your unfailing love is wonderful. Take care of me, for your mercy is so plentiful. Psalm 69:16 (NLT)

Lord God of all the nations of the earth, we thank you for this nation, the United States of America, and for those of our armed services who have served and who are now serving anywhere in the world. May they know the wonder of your unfailing love. Please take care of them for your Name's sake. Amen.

November 12

The Holy Spirit's Work

In April 1999, the Associated Press reported that the man known as Duch (Kaing Guek Eav) confessed his part in the Khmer Rouge torture center where he took part in the Cambodian Genocide Program as a prison warden. He testified at his trial that he knew what was happening was wrong but that he was afraid to do anything about it for fear his family members would be killed. During what is now known as "the killing fields," 1.7 million Cambodians out of a population of 7.9 million, were murdered, tortured, starved or worked to death during the Khmer Rouge regime.

However, something amazing happened. Duch became a Christian and was deeply sorry for his actions. He was willing to face justice and he confessed his responsibility in this atrocity. He was found guilty on July 26, 2010 and given a sentence of 30 years but several years were deducted from that (for time served and for being illegally detained in one prison facility.) The total sentence came to 19 years.

Surely it is only through the prompting of the Holy Spirit that someone would come to such a courageous decision to confess such a crime. Conviction in our hearts of wrongdoing is the work of the Holy Spirit. We (our unredeemed selves) don't like that work. It points the finger at our own sins so that we might repent and confess, and though that part is difficult, how blessed we are after we've done so. When that still small voice of the Holy Spirit brings to mind something in our lives that we need to confess and from which we need to repent, it is time to listen and obey.

And when He [the Holy Spirit] *has come, He will convict the world of sin, and of righteousness, and of judgment...* John 16:8 (NKJV)

Dear God, thank you for sending your Holy Spirit into the world and into our lives. Help us to listen to Him as He reveals to us things we are doing that displease you so that we may confess, change, and be forgiven. Amen.

November 13

The Popularity of War

After Jimmy Carter left the presidency, he did more for the cause of peace than during his term in office. He and his wife founded the Carter Center and for years they both regularly find time to work for Habitat for Humanity. In April 1999, he and Rosalynn received the inaugural Delta Prize for Global Understanding, created by the University of Georgia with a grant from Delta Air Lines. "It is very difficult to wage peace," said Carter, whose center promotes human rights, democracy and health programs worldwide. It is slow, tedious, frustrating, often unsuccessful and rarely publicized. "War is very successful and very popular — disturbingly so." (quoted in *The Arizona Republic* April 29, 1999)

Yes, war is horrible, but it is here to stay, as Jesus warned us. Still, let us not use these words of Jesus as an excuse to wage it in the world, or in our personal lives. Let us, as Carter put it instead, "wage peace" whenever and wherever feasible and possible.

And you will hear of wars and rumors of wars. See that you are not troubled, for all these things must come to pass... Matthew 24:6 (NKJV)

Lord, help us to be your ambassadors for peace in the world. Amen.

November 14

A Modern Day Samaritan

When we were on the road on our way to Houston, Texas, I noticed the signs, "Drive Friendly" and "Don't Mess with Texas," a plea not to litter. Then our Chevrolet's alternator went out and the car died just as we were crossing a bridge. There we were, outside of Houston, due for a meeting, and no phone in sight. But, there was someone who saw us. Don noticed her turning around and going off the bridge. What he didn't know was that she had seen that we were in trouble and was on her way under the bridge and coming toward us. She drove around to our side of the road while we were scrambling down a hill trying to get to a distant farmhouse. She had a cell phone. She was delighted to help and was, as we told her "our angel." She was truly a veritable Good Samaritan.

We called AAA on her phone and a tow truck was there within half an hour, the car was taken to a dealership where the repair work was done in less than three hours and we were on our way. How good that there was someone who saw us and who was there to help. How often we need the help of others as we travel both physically and spiritually; how often others may need our help. We felt blessed when we were aided by that lovely lady, but she, our angel helper, was absolutely glowing; we could tell it made her feel delighted to be of help to this senior couple, so we weren't the only ones blessed.

> *Then a Samaritan traveling down the road came to where the hurt man was. When he saw the man, he felt very sorry for him.* Luke 10:33 (NCV)

Dear Lord, thank you for taking care of us through human angels that you send to us. Please use us to be angels in the lives of others. Amen.

November 15

Reunions

I'm a real softy when it comes to TV shows about family reunions. I know the endings are not always tied up in a neat bow, but when I see a mother reunited with a son she had to have adopted 25 years ago, or a father with a daughter who had looked and looked and almost given up finding him, I'm so terribly moved. I'm sitting there blurry-eyed with my tissue box reveling in every tear — whether theirs or mine! It just feels *so* good!

What is there that is so gripping, so intense about seeing these reunions? I can think of one possibility: There is something about this that reminds us of "HOME" — the way it *should* be. And there is something in us that longs for that "HOME" — it is a little bit of heaven on earth, then, to see these reunions, almost prophetic of what's to come.

Can you imagine it? — All of your loved ones, who have gone before you, are waiting to see you, and rushing to meet you when you go "over Jordan" — and there, the dearest of all, waiting with open arms to welcome you, the Lord Jesus himself. Or, should the Lord Jesus Christ return to Earth before we die, He will be bringing with

Him those who have gone before and so our hearts are comforted. Whatever the future, it is going to be inexpressibly marvelous.

For if we believe that Jesus died and rose again, even so God will bring with Him those who sleep in Jesus. 1 Thessalonians 4:14 (NKJV)

Thank you Lord that we can look forward to a Heavenly reunion that is more wonderful than we can possibly imagine. Amen.

November 16

Things Almost Lost

I play the piano and as a teenager my favorite composers were Debussy, Ravel and McDowell. I often played a short piece by Edvard McDowell entitled, "To a Wild Rose." My piano teacher told me this story: When McDowell finished that particular composition, he decided he didn't like it so he threw it in a waste basket. His wife, however, having heard it played and loving it, retrieved it from the trash, and saved it — saved it for the world. What a beautiful, sweet melody it is and to think it could have been lost forever.

But our God is the God of the "lost" and He doesn't throw people away. He doesn't give up on anyone, not even the worst of sinners, not the mentally challenged man on the street, not the bag lady, not the drug addict, not the murderer, not your run-away daughter, or your tattooed, tongue pierced son, not the clever, lying politician, nor the hate-filled racist, nor "ordinary" sinners. And this list is including only those in our society. What about the little ones who live in the slums outlying the capital of Lima, Peru? What about those of the Romani (Gypsy) community? What about the Songhai people of Sub-Saharan African? God knows about each one. He sees. He cares. He is just waiting for any and all to respond to his love, waiting for someone to draw near, for the lost sons and daughters to come back home, waiting at the door for someone to come answer His knocking, knocking on the entryways of the hearts of everyone, including you and me.

Do you sometimes feel that life has thrown you into the trash? It's not too late for you. From your heart, ask God to retrieve you and redeem you. He will hear you. He will come.

Looking for the blessed hope and glorious appearing of our great God and Savior Jesus Christ, who gave Himself for us that He might redeem us from every lawless deed and purify for Himself His own special people. Titus 2:13, 14 (NKJV)

Lord, thank you for hearing our call to you and for redeeming us and making us your own. Amen.

November 17

An Answered Prayer

There are times when I feel I'm having to wait such a long time for God to answer my prayers that I'm almost tempted to give up. For years we prayed that our sons would come to the Lord. Though they seemed to know Him when young they drifted away. We kept praying. Then in the fall of 2009 our son, Michael, realized, partly through a dream in which his life was threatened, that He needed God. He found a church, was baptized, attends a Bible study and has regular visits with His pastor! What a joy it was to see our son baptized and to make an open confession of His faith in Jesus Christ as his Savior and Lord. We can see the changes that his newfound faith has made in His life. There is a new joy and a lightness of heart, and the fruit of the Spirit is already visible.

Yes! God had heard our heart-felt prayers all along. Such answers to our petitions give us all hope and encourages us to keep on praying, especially for the salvation of our loved ones.

Ask and it will be given to you; seek, and you will find; knock, and it will be opened to you. Matthew 7:7 (NKJV)

Lord, I praise you for answered prayer! We know that you are not willing that any should perish, but that all should come to eternal life in You, so we will keep on praying! Amen.

November 18

Wanted: More Laughs

My father's hometown was Waurika, Oklahoma. For years, while living in California, he subscribed to the *Waurika News Democrat*, a weekly newspaper. I don't have the date of publication but it would have been in the 1950s that this humorous item appeared, one that Daddy liked so much that he framed it and hung it on the wall near the cash register in "Harper's House", his antique/junk store.

Monday:
For sale, a used sewing machine. Call Mr. Tom Kelly at 555-3455 after seven o'clock and ask for Mrs. Perkins who lives with him cheap.

Tuesday:
Correction: — An error appeared in Mr. Tom Kelly's classified advertisement yesterday. It should have read, For sale, a used sewing machine cheap. Call Mr. Tom Kelly at 555-3455 and ask for Mrs. Perkins who lives with him after seven o'clock.

Wednesday:
Mr. Tom Kelly has reported several annoying telephone calls as a result of a classified advertisement in this newspaper yesterday. The ad stands corrected: For sale, a used sewing machine, cheap. Call Mr. Tom Kelly after seven o'clock at 555-3455 and ask for Mrs. Perkins who loves with him.

Thursday:
Notice: I, Tom Kelly, no longer have a used sewing machine for sale. I took an ax and smashed it. I also no longer have a housekeeper. Mrs. Perkins resigned yesterday.

§

I like this because it reminds me of my Dad's sense of humor. Ah yes! How important it is to be able to laugh. He had lots of physical ailments, but never complained; he just kind of accepted things that happened in his life. I don't remember him ever questioning, "Why me?" or feeling sorry for himself. One of the best things about my Dad was his ability to laugh at life. So let's make this our goal: Have fun and laugh more!

> *He will yet fill your mouth with laughing, And your lips with rejoicing.* Job 8:21 (NKJV)

God of Joy, sometimes I take life and myself and my old body too seriously. Help me to get a sense of humor about it all and learn to laugh more. Amen.

November 19

The Case of the Missing Salad

The table was spread with all the usual Thanksgiving fare — turkey, mashed potatoes, stuffing, etc. Mother (Don's mother), Joe, her husband, Dan, our son, and Don and I were all laughing and talking. Sometimes Mother interrupted with a, "What did you say?" because of her hearing problem. Don had made a big salad that was placed in the center of the table, but as usual, on a feast day, the salad seems to be the last to be served. Small saucers in lieu of salad plates were at each place setting. I didn't use the little plate for myself because I wanted a lot of greens and so I served my own salad on the dinner plate, and then asked Mother if I could serve her. She said, "Yes, but just a little bit of each thing." I did as she requested. I then asked her if she wanted some salad dressing, "Yes," she said, "but just a very little bit." I carefully drizzled some thousand island dressing on her salad.

The next thing I remember is that I heard myself saying, "Mmmm, that salad was really good." I suddenly felt a kind of awful sinking jar as I looked at my plate: There was my own salad uneaten. I looked at Mother's place setting; her salad plate with salad was missing. I looked down. Her salad plate was empty and in front of me. I had eaten her salad entirely up without realizing it! I didn't even remember doing it. I blushed and said, "Oh, no! How embarrassing! I've eaten Mother's salad. I'll dish you another, Mother." She was oblivious! No one else had noticed either. I could have gotten away with serving another salad and kept my mouth shut, but I had now given everyone a chance to laugh at me! I dished up, carefully once again, Mother's second salad and then ate my own. It was good! But not as trance inducing as having eaten someone else's!

Stolen water is sweet, and bread eaten in secret is pleasant. Proverbs 9:17 (NKJV)

Lord, thank you for laughter. Amen.

November 20

To Give Thanks or Not — That is the Question

Years ago our Sunday school teacher, "Terry," explained to us why he did not believe in thanking God for food. He described how he felt one Thanksgiving as he looked at the fare that so completely covered the table that he couldn't see the tablecloth. He found himself unable to thank God because he thought of all those who do not have food. "If I thank God for giving this food to me," he said, "then I am in turn saying that God has denied food to someone in Africa or China. I am saying that when He loves, He blesses and when He does not love, He withholds." Therefore, Terry could not, in all honesty, thank God for the food set before him.

I gave a lot of thought to this. First I felt a bit guilty, because I try to remember to thank God for food often. *Maybe I've been wrong.* But then as I considered Terry's logic and took it to its extreme, the more absurd I found it to be. Perhaps, for instance, I then should not thank God that I can hear because there are those who are deaf, or thank Him that I can see, because there are those who are blind. And perhaps I should not thank God for my husband; after all, there are so many who do not have a mate. In fact, I should not even thank God for the gift of life, because there are so many who are no longer living.

So, having given much thought to this deep and philosophical problem of whether one should indeed give thanks to God or not, I decided that: Since Jesus broke bread and gave thanks without bringing to mind those who have not; since in my Nave's Topical Bible, I find that there are ten columns of verses in which thanksgiving is mentioned; and since I believe God is the Creator of such a wonderful and varied array of food, I find that I *must* thank Him. The best part of this is that the more I thank God for whatever good is in my life — the senses, the sunset, the flowers, the people or the food, I find myself a happier and more joyful person because the very thanking creates in me a thankful heart. I told Terry about my conclusion and it was satisfying to hear him say, after a moment's hesitation, that I was right — that we should continue to offer thanks and so together, though at different tables on Thanksgiving Day, we would both believe and practice offering heartfelt and shameless thanksgiving to the Lord our God.

It is good to give thanks unto the Lord. Psalm 92:1 (NKJV)

Lord, help me to remember to give thanks to you every single day of my life. Give me a thankful heart and help me to see all the blessings that you have given to me, especially the invisible things that are of the greatest value. Amen.

November 21

To Rise Above

One of Mom's most mysterious words of advice was: "Rise above it." Whatever *it* was, no matter how difficult, could be risen above according to her. This brief and cryptic bit of wisdom has gone through several levels of analysis throughout my lifetime. The first was something like a magical floating above and out of reach of human reality. Later it became an absurd and ideal myth, something not possible to achieve at all. Last, it became a rewording of Jesus' words about overcoming! That, I think, is what she meant. I know it was something she could achieve and yet she was a real person, not one given to fantasy. I know that though she seldom spoke about her relationship to the Lord, she had lived out the Christian life in beautiful and godly ways. Now when I think about "rising above it" and am challenged to do so, the "rising above it" is a shared reality empowered by the One who himself overcame the world! It is not a fantasy, but a glorious reality because I can enter into the victory of Jesus Christ himself.

> *I have told you all this so that you may have peace in me. Here on earth you will have many trials and sorrows. But take heart, because I have overcome the world.* John 16:33 (NLT)

Dear Lord Jesus, in those times when I feel overcome by the terrors or pain or duties of the world, help me to be lifted up to a new perspective of my circumstances, so that I may be free and at peace and in a place of joy with you. Amen.

November 22

Who's Keeper?

"Sally" saw the birds flying across the road in front of her. But she was a psychologist and was attempting to learn the lessons about not having to take care of everyone else; she wanted to learn to take care of herself. So to herself she said, "They can take care of themselves" about the finches that tried to escape the grate of her Honda Civic. But one little bird didn't make it. And she saw it (in her rearview mirror) just lying in the street, obviously dead with its neck broken. She says that she cried out, "Oh no!" and burst into tears. She pulled the car over to the side of the road and sat there for a long time. She re-evaluated her newfound freedom about not having to take care of others. It was at least a year later that she told me about the bird she had killed with tears streaming down her face. "I was wrong," she said, "Sometimes we are supposed to look out for others. I don't mean just birds, or animals. I mean, sometimes people really do need extra help from those who are stronger. I won't let this happen again. I *am* my brother's keeper."

Am I my brother's keeper? Genesis 4:9 (NKJV)

Father God, I know there are times when you have called me to be your hands or feet or voice, times to come alongside and protect and help, whether animals or humans. Give me the grace and wisdom to know when you are leading me to do something or say something! I will obey. Amen.

November 23

Being Specific in Thanksgiving

Five-year old David was naturally musical. When asked to say grace at the dinner table one evening he soberly bowed his head and prayed, "Dear God, Thank you for the meat, thank you for the peas, thank you for the rice..." At this point he burst into song with the commercial jingle: "Rice-a-Roni, the San Francisco Treat!" And then he continued without losing a beat, "Thank you for the salad, thank you for the pie. Amen."

Now that's being specific. Remember, "Name your blessings, count them one by one?" That old song had the secret and so did little David. It's in the looking at each special thing and thanking God for it, that we learn the secret of Thanksgiving, not just in November, but all year through, because in focusing on all the good things, we fill our minds with the joy of all that life has to offer.

Offer to God thanksgiving. Psalm 50:14 (NKJV)

Lord, for all things, small and great, I give you thanks. My cup overflows! Amen.

November 24

The Silent Comforter

There are so many different kinds of mental illness. Depression alone includes: SAD (seasonal affective disorder), hormonally caused, situational, the depressive side of bi-polar personality disorder, etc. When I've shared this problem with others, I've found that the world seems to be divided into three kinds of listeners: 1. Those who don't want to hear about my problem at all. 2. Those who want to fix me and give me all kinds of simplistic advice, and 3. Those who will just listen and say, "I'm sorry." The first person seems to be in denial about suffering. The second wants to do something to make *themselves* feel better. But the third will just be with you without judgment and without offering unasked for advice. Often it is the silent listener who holds a hand that is the most needed in this sometimes sad world of ours.

If, in our unhappy moments Jesus seems silent, it is because He is being this third kind of listener and it is a sweet intimacy that He offers us; no words need be spoken. When we give Him a chance to be there with us He won't let us down by forcing us to be anything or anyone other than who we are at that very moment. Oh, what a precious companion He is!

> *He will not quarrel nor cry out, Nor will anyone hear His voice in the streets. A bruised reed he will not break...*
> Matthew 12:19, 20 (NKJV)

Dear Jesus, thank you for coming to us silently in our times of feeling like bruised reeds and let us receive your gentle, silent, comforting presence. Amen.

November 25

The History of the Cross

I once read a story from a source I don't recall, but I can remember the essence of the account. It was said to be written by a warrior who supposedly lived centuries before Christ and this man had a dream in which he saw a wondrous tree that spoke to him of its history on the earth. The tree told how it was cut down, formed into an instrument of death for the "The King of Heaven," who was placed upon it to die. The tree spoke of sharing the suffering, the reviling that it bore with the wounds of piercing and the blood that spilled upon it. It spoke of how darkness covered the corpse and how all nature wept.

Whether it was truly written as a prophetic dream I don't know, but the truth was in it for there was a tree that was formed into a cross on which suffered and died the King of Heaven. What became of that cross?

We look for the Holy Grail, but has the Cross itself been sought? Some have claimed to have pieces of the Cross. But surely it is not the physical cross that we need to find; it is the meaning of that Cross in history. For the sake of our very souls, each of us must come face-to-face with the historical Cross and decide its place in our life on earth. What we decide now will determine what will happen to us in the hereafter.

For the message of the cross is foolishness to those who are perishing, but to us who are being saved it is the power of God. 1 Corinthians 1:18 (NKJV)

Father, we thank you for the simple message of the Gospel. In your wisdom and by grace you have given us your son Jesus Christ and Him crucified. As those who are being saved, we acknowledge the message of the Cross as the essence of your power and grace. Amen.

November 26

Goodbye to Lucy and Hello to Pixie

Months before it was time to say goodbye to our precious dog, Lucy, I had a dream that two angels came to give me a white envelope. In it, I was told, was the description of our next dog. I backed off and refused to open it or even take it and started crying. I feared that if I took it Lucy would die. The angels were very understanding and didn't force it on me. But when I woke up I knew that this dream meant that we would have another dog and that it would be white.

In jest one day, I told the Lord, "Well, OK, if we are to have another dog then I want one about the size of a cat that is smart and loves to sit in my lap." Later that year we found out that our son, Michael and his wife, Karen, were going to breed their Maltese with a miniature poodle and that our Christmas gift that year (2009) would be a puppy from this litter. They knew that Lucy would not be with us too much longer and they didn't want us to be without a dog.

We got our new doggie, Pixie, a Malti-poo, months before we had to say goodbye to our Lucy. Lucy taught Pixie some important things (such as not barking at other dogs on our walks) before she left us and she even tried to play with Pixie on a few occasions. When it was time to say goody-bye, Lucy went peacefully as we held her and told her how much we loved her.

Now Pixie did not take Lucy's place because no dog could ever do that; she was too special, and we will always cherish the memories of our years together.

But let me describe Pixie: She is small, very smart and loves to sit in my lap. She is an utter delight and loves everyone and us! Her greatest fault is that she kisses too much, but we've learned to live with that.

Never let loyalty and kindness leave you. Proverbs 3:3a (NLT)

Lord, Maker of all creatures on the Earth, thank you for the precious doggies that you have given to the human race. They are living demonstrations of your love and loyalty and kindness. Amen.

November 27

Sweet Talking Yourself

At one time in my life I took a class that taught the use of affirmations to change your life. It was all pretty self-centered stuff, but, according to the teacher, if you kept reading these little cards every day, it would really help you!

I had forgotten the lessons from that class until recently when I listened in on how I was talking to myself. I found, to my shock, that I had taken on the terrible habit of bad-mouthing myself, putting myself down, calling myself an idiot, weakling, and a failure. The part of me that somehow believed such discouraging words would motivate me to change, had obviously been dead wrong.

Now I'm doing something new; I'm replacing those negative words with some positive words like: *God loves you! God rejoiced on the day you were born! You are dear to God! You look great for your age! I am of great value to the Lord! The Good Shepherd is a faithful friend and is with me all the time! God wants to help me right now! You accomplished a lot today! I am truly blessed in so many ways.*

I do this at any time, but sometimes in front of the mirror, smiling and giving myself a thumbs up. And you know what? It's working. I feel better! Somewhere inside of me, the downtrodden, demoralized little Patty, believes what these happy, positive words are saying. And why not? They are true.

Try it. You'll like it!

Don't use foul or abusive language. Let everything you say be good and helpful, so that your words will be an encourage-ment to those who hear them. Ephesians 4:29 (NLT)

Lord, set a watch on my lips so that I will speak nothing but helpful things to myself and others. Amen.

November 28

Oysters and Pearls

Do you know that you can purchase little cans that hold an oyster? When you open it, inside you discover your own cultured pearl. There it is! — Pink, or cream or even lavender in color! — all your very own, something beautiful and precious that no one on earth as ever seen or touched before.

But think about that little piece of sand that is placed there and the building up over time of a protection around it, so that it will not irritate. What in your life is like that? What bothers you, again and again, over and over so that you repeatedly must, over time, cover it with love and forgiveness until it is smooth and beautiful — a new creation, something gritty and irritating is now something lustrous and beautiful — a treasure forever, commonly known as: HOPE. Such may the irritations of life become if we continue to allow God's transforming work to take place.

> *...We also glory in tribulations, knowing that tribulation produces perseverance; and perseverance, character; and character, hope.* Romans 5:3 (NKJV)

Father, there are things in my life that irritate me, things that cause pain and suffering in my heart. Please teach me, by your grace, how to use them to produce character and hope in me. Amen.

November 29

A Friend from the Past

Don Houser was my piano teacher. I went for my first lesson when I was eleven or twelve. He treated me with respect and caring and although he was only 18 at the time, he was to me the perfect image of what a man should be. His likeness still appears in my dreams when I'm in need of inner strength. He gave me something precious and indefinable and taught me something far more important than music. I am deeply indebted to him.

If I could find him, I would thank him for several things: First of all, for giving me an experience of a good man in my life — he was, even at such a young age, honorable, patient, kind and generous. He made me feel valued and helped me gain self-esteem. He implanted within me an image of what a virtuous man can be. I'm certain, without his influence, I never would have chosen such a good man to be my husband.

I would also thank him for teaching me about health. Because of his words of warning, I never became a smoker (like the rest of my family). I seldom drink (and good thing, what with all the alcoholism in my family) and I've always enjoyed a healthy diet, all because of his guidance.

And, of course, I am forever grateful to him for the music! Music has been an integral and healing part of my life.

I would thank him too for helping me spiritually by sharing with me how God saw him through a difficult time in his life. He truly cared about me.

I've attempted through a search agency to find him, but without success. Now, I try to remember to thank those who have meant so much to me while we are still in touch. It is difficult not to be able to give love and appreciation where it is so richly deserved.

Perhaps you can think of someone in your life that you truly appreciate and can let him or her know by a phone call or a note today. I believe that when we take the time to express our appreciation it will bless us as much as it blesses that special person.

Cast your bread upon the waters, for you will find it after many days. Ecclesiastes 11:1 (NKJV)

Dear Lord, you have brought so many people into my life for which I am deeply grateful. Help me to find ways to express my gratitude. Amen.

November 30

The Faux Case of the Missing Bells

It was a lovely Sunday morning. Before strolling through the gardens at Descanso in LaCanada-Flintridge, California, I visited the gift shop. The scents of spice scented candles greeted me as I opened the door. The air was filled with the sweetest bird song I've ever heard, offered for all to enjoy, by a golden canary named Sunshine. Tears filled my eyes as I walked by her cage and whispered a "thank you" to her. On a table toward the back of the shop, I found a little brown basket full of brass bells with red cords attached. There were several different kinds and I decided to purchase four for my bell collection. At a price of only 95 cents each I had found a real bargain. I asked the clerk if I could leave them on the counter and come back and purchase them later. She granted my request, and I saw her push them to the right of the cash register.

I went on my way for two lovely hours, walking and sitting, in shade or sun. I talked to God and meditated in sweet silence. I then returned to the gift shop and retrieved the bells.

When I got home, I wanted to add them to my collection. I hesitated for a moment. "Let's see," I thought, "where do I keep my bells? They must be in the cabinet with..." I opened the cabinet door and looked in on my collection of birds and little boxes. But, there were no bells! My mouth dropped open. It was then, and only then, that I realized with chagrin, that I don't collect bells, never have, well not, that is, until then.

I was so shocked that I found I was laughing out loud at myself! (I've heard that one of the things that make us laugh is the element of the unexpected.) Well the Lord knows that my bell collection wasn't really missing because there never had been any bells. When we forget something that was there in our minds and it's gone, it's a matter of memory loss; but what is it called when you forget something that was never in your memory banks to begin with? It's a few something else that's missing, I fear.

A time to weep and a time to laugh. Ecclesiastes 3:4 (NKJV)

Heavenly Father, I thank you for the kinds of surprises that make me chuckle, even at myself! Help me to be a good sport, and when the joke's on me, let me be the first to laugh. Amen.

DECEMBER

December 1

The Joy of Tears

I believe in tears.
They make me feel soft,
Remind me I am a still a child.
I feel tears when I
See
A rose just opening
The Grand Canyon
A work of art that keeps on giving
An old lady stopping to look at a fern leaf.
I feel tears when I
Smell
"Joy" perfume mixed with memories
Frankincense
Lemon meringue pie like Grandma used to bake
Night Blooming Jasmine in the evening
I feel tears when I
Hear
A Chopin Prelude
Warm wind through palm trees
A mocking bird in the middle of the night
A child calling me to come share a sunset
I feel tears when I
Touch
Someone's forehead with my lips
A trembling, new born kitten
The cool petal of a Japanese Magnolia against my cheek
That tender spot at the back of a baby's neck.
I feel tears when I
Taste
Fresh, fresh strawberries, shared with a special friend
A leathery egg cooked by my children on my birthday
My favorite wine in candlelight

My husband's lips, after we've been apart
In all these things and
many, many more
I let life reach me with the joy of tears.

I've heard it said, and I believe it: Happiness comes from things that happen to us; joy comes from something on the inside. But surely the appreciation of things on the outside comes from appreciation that is springing up from something in our spirits. We can teach ourselves to truly look about and receive from the world around us, remembering and rejoicing in the One who has created the wonders of this unique planet called Earth and the One who holds everything together by the word of His power.

I will greatly rejoice in the Lord, My soul shall be joyful in my God... Isaiah 61:10 (NKJV)

The heavens are yours, and the earth is yours; everything in the world is yours —you created it all. Psalm 89:11 (NLT)

Spirit of Jesus, give us open hearts so that we may receive with thanksgiving all that you have created for us to enjoy on the earth and in the heavens. Amen.

December 2

The Thorns

I believe it was on "Animal Planet" that I saw her. She was just a little kitten and she had fallen into a cactus plant and gotten stuck, crying out and unable to extricate herself. She was covered with thorny spines that had pierced her body, dozens of them. When the helpers came they couldn't even see her because she was so covered with thorns that she looked like part of the cactus. When they discovered exactly where she was they couldn't get her out without wrapping her in blankets to protect themselves as well as her. I couldn't turn off the TV. I had to see what was going to happen to her. I knew she couldn't possibly survive, but what if I was wrong?

She was taken to a veterinarian clinic and they anesthetized her while several aides worked over her for three hours, plucking out each spine with tweezers, one at a time. Finally she was free of every thorn that her pierced her tiny body. They let her sleep. She began to heal, and very quickly at that! Within a week she was completely well! I was so happy I saw the end to this story!

As I thought about her later that day, the Lord spoke to me. He said, "Some people are like that kitten, full of spines, and when you try to get close, they are prickly." The next day the Lord spoke to me again about that kitten. He named a friend of mine and said, "She is like that." I quickly agreed! The day following that, while I was driving to a prayer meeting, the Lord spoke to me again. He lovingly said, "**You** are like that." "Oh." I said.

Then Nathan said to David, 'You are that man!' 2 Samuel 12:7 (NLT)

Omniscient God, I know it is true, but at this age? And after all the inner healing you've done in my life, there's still more? Then teach me how to rest in your healing presence and allow you to remove these thorns from me, so that I will no longer be so "touchy." Amen.

December 3

Fantasy or Reality?

We all have hopes and dreams. Sometimes they come true. Sometimes they do not. Only God knows which are those that are part of His plan for us.

Of Dreams and Hopes

The Music of Dreams,
Healing
Moves like a cool lavender mist

Along corridors of my soul
Under great, locked doors,
Wanders through long-forgotten halls
Between columns, anciently familiar
And following, I'm led gently through
Tears of lost
Desires
Hopes
Memories
That I might forgive myself for deserting them
And reclaim them
For my own.

Dreams! No, not night, but the daydream kinds. Hopes. Things we wish for. As we live our lives, we find that some of our dreams for ourselves and our loved ones will need to be let go of, sad as that may be for us. But, some, some are placed in our souls by the Holy Spirit and they will "come true." May the Lord reveal to us the difference.

The hope of the righteous shall be gladness... Proverbs 10:28 (NKJV)

Lord, be the author of my hopes and dreams that I might not become disheartened but have faith to believe. Amen.

December 4

The Phantom Critics

For so much of my life I have sought to please others. It's an ongoing challenge. I wrote the following in 1964, and I'm still in the process of learning how to be a pleaser of my Lord rather than looking to please others.

They were there forever, it seems:
The audience of one and sometimes more,
The judges who applauded or offered their critiques

Just always, always there
Somewhere behind the wings of this black stage inside my head
Their jeering, ghostly faces wagged
Body-less, forever haunting me on my endless performing pilgrimage
I know who you are now:
Farcical puppets inspirited by my mind's ventriloquist
I want to be alone now
To sing, to dance, to play
To an audience of two — Just you and me, Lord.
I want to learn to believe that we are enough, just the two of us.
I want to find the simplicity to answer the myth of all I once feared
Worthless, silly, inconsequential about myself.
Oh my Lord, deliver me from those wretched critics
Help me say good-bye to those tired grotesque masks.
Help me let them fade away, those sad, intruding spies.
Help me to believe that the way you created me is enough,
And that you will complete the work that you've begun in me,
and that, *that is* sufficient.

The Lord is the one we need to please, not others. If you have suffered the fear of what others think, including a demanding part of yourself that I express in this poem, pray that God will release you from that tyranny in your own life. It's really up to each of us to find out what God's will is so that we will aim to please only Him in all that we do. As we aspire to that, I believe we will find that to do His will alone is the most satisfying accomplishment of all.

> *...be filled with the knowledge of His will in all wisdom and spiritual understanding; that you may have a walk worthy of the Lord, fully pleasing Him, being fruitful in every good work and increasing in the knowledge of God; strengthened with all might, according to His glorious power...* Colossians 1:9b-11 (NKJV)

Lord, so often I've craved the praise of others, and yet, the praise that I want more than any other is yours. Help me find your will, and enable me to accomplish it by your power and grace and to the praise of your glory. Amen.

December 5

The Prayers of Strangers

In April of 2000 I was present at a horrible scene. It is indelibly etched on my heart. I saw a mother and child standing on the southwest corner of an intersection in Phoenix, waiting for the light to change. Suddenly, a loud crash! The mother grabbed her daughter and tried to turn away, tried to step back, but it was too late. A pickup truck was aiming at them, jumping the curb, rolling over them, all within a second's time. Then silence. Both were pinned under the truck. I was screaming out loud in my own car just a few feet away, "No! No!" I pulled into a parking lot and made a 911 call. Thankfully, someone else had already done so.

Still in my car, I started praying for the child and the mother, knowing that there was nothing else I could do. I saw, to my wonder, that the mother was conscious, talking. I heard no cries from the child. Emergency help arrived. The fire department paramedics and crew appeared — quick, skilled, and competent. They would do what had to be done.

When I finally quit shaking, I left the scene. I had been on my way to a Christian bookstore to buy my husband a card for our 40th wedding anniversary. I went to the store anyway, and while there, I began to cry and explained my tears, describing to the clerk at the checkout counter what I had witnessed. Store patrons standing nearby overheard. Soon a lady came up, took my hand and said, "Let's all pray." She then offered up a powerful prayer as the rest of us agreed with her for the lives of the mother and child to be spared. When she said "amen" I looked behind me and saw that at least seven more people had joined us in prayer. The store clerk gave me a caring, assuring hug and called me "sis." When I left that place, instead of feeling that I was in the midst of a horrible study in helplessness, I had a sense of deep peace.

The next day the local newspaper reported that the mother and child had survived! The mother had received burns and suffered pelvic injuries, but her daughter, 4 years old, had been treated and released from the hospital.

At first I was upset that God had "arranged" my day so that I would be there to witness this horrible scene. Later I saw how selfish I was to think that way. It was obvious that God wanted me to be there and to find the others so that we could all pray together. Those prayers were answered! So, I learned that sometimes when we think we are in the wrong place at the wrong time, we are actually in the right place at the right time, even though it doesn't *feel* that way at the moment.

Be anxious for nothing, but in everything by prayer and supplication, with thanksgiving, let your requests be made known to God; and the peace of God, which surpasses all understanding, will guard your hearts and minds through Christ Jesus. Philippians 4:6, 7 (NKJV)

Dear God, when we find ourselves in situations where things seem hopeless, help us to remember to pray and invite you, by our prayers, to intervene in what is happening around us. Amen.

December 6

Favorite Places

My bedroom window sans glasses

Looking up through the window screen
One may see an impressionist scene
In myriad shades of green on green
With dawn's golden blue sparkling in between.

Of all the homes in which I lived there is one favorite. For 19 years we lived on Mission Street in South Pasadena, California. I cherished those days and still hold dear the memories of our family of four all together. There will never be a home like that for us again, so big and roomy and full of light, old, filled with memories, not just our own, and the windows looking out on our avocado tree here, or the silver fir there, or the oleander that surrounded us, or the reds and pinks of the patches of azaleas. Ah, it was a little bit of paradise.

In Goodyear, Arizona, we looked out our windows and saw a Palo Verde, palm trees, an ocotillo, Yucca, and a prickly pear cactus, a different kind of beauty spoke to me there.

In Beaumont, California, where we now live in the San Gorgonio Pass, my favorite view is from our living and dining room windows when the sun is setting. Our view faces west so we can see golden sunsets, tinged with a hint of pink almost every evening. And just a few steps away from our condo, we can enjoy views of San Gorgonio Mountain to the north (highest mountain in Southern California) and San Jacinto Mountain to the Southeast — Both snowcapped during the winter months! How beautiful it is here!

Maybe I've finally learned that I don't have to look back any more and risk turning into pillar of salt! God is teaching me how to appreciate each new place, each new world where He has placed us, and to just keep on following Him. There will always be beautiful views!

But his [Lot's] *wife looked back behind him, and she became a pillar of salt.* Genesis 19:26 (NKJV)

Lord, help us to be thankful for what was past, but also thankful for what is now, and help us to make every place our "favorite" until we find ourselves in Heaven itself. Amen.

December 7

About the Green Peas

If we are honest, we will admit that once in a while we truly want someone to anticipate our needs. It must be the child in us, looking for the perfect parent. But how rarely anyone does read our minds? So, when they don't, we are brave, aren't we? We've learned how to say, "Me? Oh, I'm fine." Or we may think that we have learned to ask "properly," and pride ourselves that we know how to communicate our needs in mature, healthy, non-controlling ways.

Well, here's a story about someone who knew how to ask and get exactly what he wanted. It was one of those large Cummings family dinners, probably a Christmas day feast. At the table were seated Mother and Dad Cummings, Don's brothers and his sister, aunts and uncles, and nephews. One of them, six-year old Steven suddenly burst into vociferous, heart-felt sobs. Everyone turned to him, asking, "Steven, what's wrong?" He choked out, with trembling lower lip and eyes flooded with tears, "Nobody passed me the peas."

Everybody knew [knows] the feeling! Everybody simultaneously reached for the peas. Could it be that Steven knew something we've forgotten?

Of course, there is One who has anticipated our genuine needs even before the foundation of the world. And He has said that He will answer even before we ask. The deepest longings of our innermost beings have already been provided for because He has foreseen our deprivation and has placed within us the God-shaped vacuum, which only He can fill. He has given us **Himself** as Savior and Lord; He has sent to us the **Holy Spirit**, the One who is a teacher, a guide and a comforter, as well as the One who makes us aware of our sin; and added to all this, God has provided community for us in **one another**.

It will come to pass that before they call, I will answer; And while they are still speaking, I will hear. Isaiah 65:24 (NKJV)

Thank you, Lord for being the Perfect Parent who knows what we truly need, and thank you for revealing to us that our greatest need is for you to become our all in all. Amen.

December 8

A Bird Shower

I've seen many a bird take many a bath, but one day I saw a bird taking a shower. I was at a strip mall in Goodyear. It was a hot summer day. There was a ground level fountain there that had 16 holes out of which a spray of water would spring at any time. Sometimes, one might continue to splash forth for a number of minutes. A dove found this to be so. He waddled up to one of the active fountains, lifted his left wing and held it there for the water to thoroughly cleanse, then he turned around and held up his right wing beneath it as well, as the water continued to rain down with its refreshing, cleansing flow! He alternated arms, uh, I mean wings, several times and then walked off and plopped his wet body in a warm sunny spot to dry off.

Now what's the point? The point is that the world of God's creatures is full of fun and funny things. Just look for them. And laugh.

And Sarah said, 'God has made me laugh, so that all who hear will laugh with me.' Gen. 21:6 (NKJV)

Lord, help me to look around today and see the humor in your world. Amen.

December 9

The Gift of Parenthood

Michael

In the dark
Stumble over a can (used coffee)
and a stuffed tiger (not quite as stuffed as it used to be)
and walk through some papers and over a blanket
sit down on a narrow bunk bed
listen to gentle breathing
feel a very smooth, very soft cheek
Meet for just a moment
a kind of quiet peacefulness and warmth and contentment
And give some love through a touch to that small form.
Thrill in a moment of subconscious
Unhindered reception.
His name is Michael,
And he is our first born son.

The gift of parenthood is one of God's greatest gifts. To sense the miracle of a life growing within you and then to see that life come forth and grow and develop his or her own personality — what a wonder! I am thankful for those first years of being a mother. My son, Michael, is one of my heroes. He struggled with reading disabilities and overcame them; he now loves to read. He was a theater arts major and had to take singing lessons even though he is tone deaf! How he did it, I don't know, but by sheer will power and practicing over and over and over, he learned to sing the required song, a musical number from the musical "Oliver."

As I shared earlier, he came to the realization that he needs a Savior not too long ago and he has found a fine church very close to his home, reads the Bible regularly and attends a Bible study. We've been greatly gifted to have Michael as a son, but now he is a brother in Christ as well.

Children are a gift from the LORD; babies are a reward.
Psalm 127:3 (NCV)

Lord, thank you for the gift of our precious children. Amen.

December 10

Twinkle Toes

There were three of them — boys, jaywalking across the street in front of my car. They looked a little guilty, but I smiled at them as I put my foot on the brake. The third one, brown skinned with deep blue eyes and straight black hair smiled back at me, and then rewarded my patience by gracefully dancing, prancing, twirling across the road before me. The joy, the playfulness, the exuberant energy that he shared swirled up inside of me in response. Whenever was a street so much a happy stage, or a jaywalker so entertaining a joy dancer?

This happened years ago and I'll never forget that boy. He was a blessing sent from God.

They send forth their little ones like a flock, And their children dance. Job 21:11 (NKJV)

Lord, bless that boy, now a man, wherever he is; may he continue in the joy of life and spread it around just like he did that day. And as for the rest of us, teach us to do the same. Amen.

December 11

Spiritual Gifts — Part 1
Wisdom and Knowledge

The gifts of the Spirit of God, what an important difference they have made in my life. That's why I want to share with you some of the things I've learned about them. I choose December because it is a month of gifts and this is the best of times to thankfully consider what God has given to us to aid us in our day-by-day lives.

Let me begin by explaining one thing: God gives to *every* believer the Holy Spirit. Having stated that, know that the Spirit of God will enable us, each one, to have at least one spiritual gift that we will be able to use regularly to help us in whatever ministry to which God has called us. I believe that we may experience any of these gifts at any time because we have within us the presence of God's Spirit who is actually the One who is acting out the demonstration of the gift or gifts. However, there is usually one gift that we will find being manifested repeatedly for the benefit of others.

We are not given a choice as to the gift we will receive, but the Scripture does make it clear that we will not all be given the same gift or gifts. What are these gifts? How do we even recognize them when we have received them? The gifts that are listed in 1 Corinthians 12 are in the context of mentioning different ministries and activities and just before one of the most famous chapters in the Bible, the "Love Chapter."

The gifts mentioned in the 1 Corinthians passage are: (1) word of wisdom; (2) word of knowledge; (3) faith; (4) healings; (5) miracles; (6) prophecy; (7) discerning of spirits; (8) tongues, and (9), interpretation of tongues. In the next few days, we will be looking at each of these.

For today, let's look at the word of wisdom and the word of knowledge, most often paired. The gift of wisdom is basically what you need to help you properly use the gift of knowledge that you receive. I may learn through the gift of knowledge that a friend has started drinking again. The gift of wisdom will tell me what to do with that knowledge. This recently happened to me and the answer was not to tell the person I knew, but to pray for her.

It's important to know that the gift of knowledge is one of the most common of all of the gifts. Many Christians I've spoken with have experienced this gift and not recognized it for what it is. It may manifest itself at any time, but is most likely to come during prayer. It will come in one of several forms, but will always be something that you do not already know from personal knowledge. Some of the forms it may take are: You will *hear* a word or words in your mind; you will *see* something in your mind's eye; you will, in short, know something that you didn't know before and it is coming to you from the Spirit of the Lord. (An example of this gift is mentioned in the March 28 entry about finding my lost sapphire or the entry on October 28 about our "dream car.")

> *To one is given the word of wisdom through the Spirit; to another the word of knowledge through the same Spirit.* I Corinthians 12:8 (NKJV)

Lord, I trust you to give me the knowledge and wisdom I need for today. Amen.

December 12

Spiritual Gifts — Part 2
Faith

Those with this special gift of faith are visionaries and may see something clearly that has not occurred yet — a way of seeing how God is going to work in a situation that appears impossible from the human vantage point. This gift gives one a great sense of courage to go ahead with plans in spite of all external appearances. (Note: This is not the general gift of faith in Jesus Christ.) It has to do with knowing, without a shadow of doubt, what God is going to do in regard to something before there is any evidence whatsoever. In my experience, this gift is rarely exhibited. Bob Pierce, the founder of World Vision, Milliard Fuller, the founder of Habitat for Humanity, and Evangelist Reinhard Bonnke, founder of Christ for All Nations have all displayed this gift as they brought forth the ministries to which God called them.

I have experienced it in more personal, less astounding ways too. One example is the occasion when I knew that God was going to heal a marriage. I agreed to pray with a dear friend about her marriage because I knew that He was going to reunite this couple. I just *knew*! And He did, after a year of prayers. In another case, a friend who almost died knew that she was going to live; she just *knew*! She lived! We all need to ask God to give us wisdom to know what is truly of Him, and to ask Him for a confirmation from Scripture and/or from at least one other Christian if we believe we have been given the gift of faith.

[Jesus speaking of the Roman centurion] *I say to you, I have not found such great faith, not even in Israel!* Luke 7:9 (NKJV)

Lord, I trust that you will give me the gift of faith when I need it. Amen.

December 13

Spiritual Gifts — Part 3
Healing

All of us have a measure of healing to offer others. However, the Lord does seem to more often use certain people for the healing ministry, whether ministering physical healing or inner healing. Both are included in the gift of healings as mentioned in Scripture. When we have spent time with someone through whom the Lord manifests the gift of inner healing, we will sense some healing occurring on the inside.

In a workshop I took on the gift of physical healing, the teacher said that in his personal experience, he found that God did supernaturally heal in about 30% of cases; these were occasions when there was no doubt about it; they were pure, clear healings. In praying for those who are sick, I believe that there is usually a mixture of natural (medical community) and supernatural (God's direct intervention), sometimes clearly more one than the other. However, since all healing comes from God, God is still the one who deserves the glory!

> *...and the power of the Lord was present to heal them.* Luke 5:17 (NKJV)

Lord, you are the God of healing. Heal us in our minds, in our souls, in our spirits and in our bodies, we pray, and give us gifts of healing for others, and may the glory be yours. Amen.

December 14

Spiritual Gifts — Part 4
Miracles

I suspect that people experience this gift occasionally but don't recognize when it happens. I almost missed this one small miracle in my life:

One Saturday morning when I was going to minister on the Diakonos Prayer Team at an inner healing seminar, I had a most remarkable experience. I still can't believe it, and yet I do, because of the way that the whole episode transpired. Everyone attending was to bring a salad. I often brought some form of protein to these luncheons, because that's one dish that is usually missing and I need the protein as I have a tendency toward low blood sugar. This time I decided on a tuna and egg salad.

After preparing it, and as I was cleaning up, I decided to take the eggs that were in the egg carton and put them into the refrigerator door containers. There were quite a few left in the box, and there were some eggs in the refrigerator tray already. I didn't want to do a partial job, so, wanting to make sure that they would all fit, I counted the eggs in the carton and the empty egg "holes" in the door tray. There were 16 holes.

There were ten eggs already in the tray. There were six eggs in the carton. *Good, they'll fit,* I said to myself. I stood in front of the refrigerator door and emptied the egg carton of all eggs. Did you get that? I emptied it of *all* the eggs. No more eggs, right?

Wrong! As I started to throw the carton into the trash I felt a heaviness in the carton. I opened it again. There, inside, as clean and fresh as you can imagine, was — you guessed it! An egg! I thought at first, *Well, I must have just not seen that egg. But how strange. How could I have missed it — especially with all of that careful counting? Oh, well.* At this point I recognized that there was something else happening here: I had an overwhelming urge to eat it. In fact, I felt led, yes, *led* to eat the egg. Though I had planned to have only a light breakfast that morning I prepared and ate this special egg as well, and I might add, it was delicious.

Later in the day, when the meeting broke for lunch, I was approached by someone who needed a lot of my time and energy. When I walked over to the salad bar to get my tuna salad, I was shocked to see that it was all gone! But, then I remembered the egg — the egg that I had eaten earlier that was now going to help me get through the rest of the meeting without being too weak to pray and minister to others. That was a miracle egg. Since then, when I hear stories of God miraculously supplying food I fully believe it. God *does* still work creative miracles. I've seen one myself!

> *He blessed and broke and gave the loaves to the disciples; and the disciples gave to the multitudes.* Matthew 14:19 (NKJV)

Lord, we believe that you still perform creative miracles. Help us to trust you for more of them. Amen.

December 15

Spiritual Gifts — Part 5
Prophecy

Let's look at the gift of prophecy. We are most likely to receive a personal word from the Lord in a charismatic setting, but this isn't always the case. For instance, if we were to receive a personal prophecy from someone ministering to us, this would be the Lord speaking directly to us through that person. It is *forthtelling*, a word of affirmation that is uplifting (usually not *foretelling*). Here is an example: "My child, know that I have seen your tears and am acquainted with your suffering. Don't be afraid; I will go with you through this valley." This is a healing and comforting word, but all such prophecies should be judged carefully by your own sense of what God is doing in your life and then, of course, should be scriptural, and, if possible, confirmed by others present though this is not always possible.

No prophecy is ever absolutely perfect, for in this world no one is privy to the complete truth. Scripture says that we *"know in part and we prophecy in part"* (I Cor. 13:12). If the word you are given does not seem to apply to you now, but seems a good, life-giving word, store it in your heart and wait and see; time may bring out the meaning. If it does not seem life-giving, reject it; it is probably someone's personal idea about you or even a word brought forth out of envy or wrong motives, rather than a word from God.

Therefore, brethren, desire earnestly to prophesy... 1 Corinthians 14:39 (NKJV)

Father, help me to be open to receive these personal words from you, and give me the help I need to discern them properly. Amen.

December 16

Spiritual Gifts — Part 6
Discernment

The gift of discernment has many different manifestations. It helps us determine whether something is: 1. Of the Spirit of God; 2. Of human origin; 3. Of satanic origin, 4. Of angelic origin; and 5. Of the truth or a lie. It helps us to discern, for instance, if the spirit of fear we are sensing, is from the person we are praying for, or is demonic. Some with this gift will sense evil or good in a particular location. Others may sense the certain presence of heavenly angels. Some have a keen sense of whether something is true or false. All these are ways in which the gift of discernment may be manifested. This is an incredibly valuable gift but for some reason it is rare. I think it is a gift that we need more and more.

> *But the natural man does not receive the things of the Spirit of God, for they are foolishness to him; nor can he know them, because they are spiritually discerned.* 1 Corinthians 2:14 (NKJV)

Lord, I pray for those who are reading about this gift today, that you will give this charisma of discernment to anyone who is willing to receive it. Amen.

December 17

Spiritual Gifts — Part 7
Tongues and Interpretation of Tongues

The gift of tongues is without a doubt the most divisive of the spiritual gifts. It has caused churches to split and certain denominations have sent home missionaries when they discover they have this gift. It should be used with great caution and only in settings where it is understood and accepted. It is also a greatly misunderstood gift. It is not, for instance, a gift in which the person speaking goes into a trance! As it is one of my own gifts, I can tell you that it's just right there, on the "tip of your tongue" when you need it. As Herald Bredesen told us when we met him in Taiwan in 1963, "Tongues don't go through the bottleneck of your mind." What I believe he meant is that this supernatural spiritual language bypasses the limitations of our intellects.

There are two separate uses of the gifts of tongues that need to be clarified. One is a speaking out in an assembly of believers in another language that calls for an interpretation. In this case, such interpretation would take a form similar to that of a prophecy (i.e., a specific, personal word from the Lord such as "Fear not. I am the good shepherd..."). Sometimes the interpretation may be praises to the Lord, such as a personal psalm.

The second use of tongues is for prayer purposes. This is a private prayer language, which does not call for an interpretation. This is usually a quiet petitioning, but it may involve weeping or moaning. When a believer prays this way, she or he is allowing the Holy Spirit to pray through him or her so that the petition offered may be considered the "perfect prayer."

> *...do not forbid to speak with tongues.* 1 Corinthians 14:39 (NKJV)

Lord, endow some of your servants somewhere in the world with this unique gift today and may they use it faithfully. Amen.

December 18

Spiritual Gifts — Part 8
The Principal Spiritual Gift

As I mentioned in Part I, I believe that all Christians possess the greatest gift — that of the Holy Spirit — and can expect to be given any of the gifts of the Spirit at any time. I also believe that believers will consistently exhibit gifts that are of special use for whatever ministry into which God has called them. Some of these gifts are quite common in the church, such as service or mercy. Other gifts are more obviously what would be called "charismatic" such as those you have read about these past days.

I believe that during Christ's ministry on Earth he exhibited all but two of the gifts — those of tongues and interpretation. Think about it: Wisdom, knowledge, faith, healings, miracles, and prophesying — Jesus practiced them all.

As for you, dear believer, why not make a point to discover what your gifts are if you have not already done so. You may find out in several ways but the best is to ask other Christians what they see your gifts to be; they can confirm those gifts for you. Our gifts will help determine what our ministry should be (All believers are called to some form of ministry.) When we are using our God-given supernatural gifts, it feels "just right" — as though that's what we were made for, what we are *supposed* to be doing. Surely, there is little else that could be more satisfying.

And God has appointed these in the church: first apostles, second prophets, third teachers, after that miracles, then gifts of healing, helps, administration, varieties of tongues. Are all apostles? Are all prophets? Are all teachers? Are all workers of miracles? Do all have gifts of healings? Do all speak with tongues? Do all interpret? 1 Corinthians 12:28-30 (NKJV)

God, make us good stewards of the spiritual gifts that you have given to us. Help us to be willing to work on their proper use, that we might be your servants and the servants of others. Amen.

December 19

When There is No Santa Claus

When Mom was around seven years old, she had one doll. She loved this doll, one of her very few toys. One year when Christmas was nearing Grandma took her aside and told her that since they had no gift for her little sister, four-year old Elizabeth (my Aunt Didi), she would have to take Mama's doll and clean it up and make new clothes for it so Elizabeth would have a nice Christmas gift from Santa. Grandma thought Mama wouldn't mind because she was too old to believe in Santa anymore. But that was the first time Mama had heard there was no Santa Claus, so she ended up with no real doll and no fantasy Santa either.

It made mama sad. She told me this story when I was a little girl after I had discovered the truth, that Santa is a myth; and it made me sad too. I didn't know then that there is one who was there beside me to comfort me. Later I would learn His name; it's Jesus and He is the One who came to bind up those whose hearts have been broken in some way.

The Spirit of the Sovereign LORD is on me, because the LORD has anointed me to preach good news to the poor. He has sent me to bind up the brokenhearted, to proclaim freedom for the captives and release from darkness for the prisoners... Isaiah 61:1 (NIV)

Dear Father in Heaven, it is sometimes hard to admit that a part of us is still a child. Other adults don't see the child and we have to pretend that we are grown up when we don't always feel that way. There are the disappointed, broken hearted places within us that need your comfort. Please touch us in those places so that they may be comforted and healed and, in turn, reach out and comfort and heal others. Amen.

December 20

God's Christmas Tree

We were at a church retreat at Forest Home in the San Bernardino Mountains. I was not feeling well and regretted that I was not able to go to the Saturday morning meeting. I stayed in our cabin by myself and opened the drapes to look out on the beautiful grounds. It had rained all night long, but in the morning the sky was clear. As I looked out my window I was given my own little vision of the Lord's glory. What I saw made me gasp! It was a pine tree ablaze with light. About nine feet tall, it looked for all the world like a supernatural vision of a Christmas tree, laden with tiny little rainbow colored lights, thousands of them. These shimmering and dancing drops hung from all the branches as a full spectrum of morning sunlight was captured in each one! What a wonder! What a sight! What a special gift the Lord had prepared for me so that I too might be cheered and blessed at this retreat, which was indeed meant to restore and equip us for the weeks ahead! Had I not been barefoot already, I would have taken the shoes from off my feet!

> *...the bush burned with fire, but the bush was not consumed...take your sandals off your feet, for the place where you stand is holy ground.* Exodus 3:5 (NKJV)

Lord God, thank you for special displays of beauty that bring a sense of your glory to us. Amen.

December 21

What Size Was That?

I just checked out a web site that allows you to punch in your body measurements, creates a model to your exact proportions, and then you can try clothes on it, to see how they will look on you! It's fun, like playing paper dolls! Some of you will remember those little cardboard dolls that we could dress with paper clothes!

I told a friend of mine about this web site and she said her daughter had given her a software program that would do the same thing. She and her daughter were doing it together, and her husband was in the same room. She didn't want him to know her true measurements, so she punched in some more flattering figures. Upon doing this, a message popped up on the screen that said something like this: "If you are not honest about the measurements that you gave us, we can't help you." She and her daughter burst out laughing.

So what does that remind you of? Do you, like me, sometimes cheat on your inner life's "measurements," telling God that things are better than they really are? Perhaps God would say to us something like, "If you aren't honest with me and don't ask for what you really need, how can I help you?" God knows it all, there's no use cheating. We need to tell it the way it is! You know the kinds of things I mean — even things like, *I don't like my husband right now*; or *I'm too fat*; or *I stole a stamp from work yesterday*; or *I don't want to go on*, or *God, You disappoint me because I you didn't answer my prayer request*. Since God already knows how we feel, we may as well level with Him. And what a wonderful God we have, one who wants us to be authentic with Him.

> *Therefore I will not restrain my mouth; I will speak in the anguish of my spirit; I will complain in the bitterness of my soul.* Job 7:11

> *My heart is breaking. . . Why am I discouraged? Why is my heart so sad?* (Psalm 42:4 & 5)

Dear God, Help me, like Job and like David, to be real with you and to share with you what I'm really thinking and feeling. Amen.

December 22

Friends Together

There is something I must share with you all before this book is completed and that is the vital importance of special small groups. These are not just social groups, but loving Christian communities of friends. I've had the great privilege and joy and comfort of being in many such groups, some which met for years.

How wonderful these times of sharing are! What a difference these small groups have made in our lives with the support and love we received from these precious friends. In my heart, these are mini churches — assemblies of fellow believers.

But why do I share this? Even though I am an introvert, it's been vitally important for me to have these groups throughout my life. I think most people can benefit deeply from such meeting of friends. So I share this to encourage you to pray about starting your own group or finding one to join. It could change your life and the lives of many others for the better forever!

And let us consider one another in order to stir up love and good works, not forsaking the assembling of ourselves together... Hebrews 10:25 (NKJV)

Lord, help us to remember to meet together with others so that we may encourage and help one another and, in turn, receive the blessings of friendship. Amen.

December 23

A Praying Heart

Is God good? Does God listen? Does He really care? Does He really answer prayers? Why don't my prayers get answered the way I want? How could God let this happen?

Do you ever ask any of these questions? I do. It's a natural part of an authentic relationship with our Father God. When it comes to going to Him in prayer, I'm convinced that though there are no magic formulas, there may be secrets to having our prayers answered.

One is that we are to start with faith. We are to believe that God loves us — He cares. We are to believe that God hears us. We are to believe that God wants the best for us. We are to believe that if we will learn to "listen" in on what God is doing and pray toward that end, that our prayers will be answered. We are to believe that if we ask for advice He will give us wisdom, that if we ask for direction, He will lead the way. Once we pray like this, expecting that our good Heavenly Father will hear and answer, we ask and the asking will bring into reality on Earth, what was once only a vision of the future in the mind of God. His purpose will be done on earth as it is in Heaven. We are to believe that God wants to give us the desires of our hearts, not the desires of hardened hearts, but desires of the new hearts of flesh that He has promised to give us!

Then I will give them one heart, and I will put a new spirit within them, and take the stony heart out of their flesh, and give them a heart of flesh. Ezekiel 11:19 (NKJV)

Dear Father, give us hearts that are pure and believing, soft and pliable in your hands, so that when we come to you in prayer, we will know that in one way or another, you always answer our requests. Amen.

December 24

A Reading for Christmas Eve
In the Words of a Witness to the Night of Nights

I don't know why I know it but this, *this*, is a special night. There's a sweetness in the air, a sense of wonder and expectation all around the inn, but especially over near the stable. I'm waiting for — well, I don't really know what. But the suspense is beyond words, a sense of awe, a sense of — a key turning, a door opening, something new.

I feel that I'm somehow, by chance, in the center of the history of humankind. I've had this feeling all evening and it's not going away. It's as though deep in my spirit I sense that something, something that is about to happen — will change the world forever. Yes, that's it; something is going to happen *tonight*. The feeling is almost over-whelming; more than I can take in, yet I know it is true — the hush in the atmosphere (even the crickets have stopped their chirping), the clarity of the stars, the purity and the freshness of the air.

Wait! Wait a moment! Listen! Can't you hear it? What is that? That sound — I've never heard anything like it. Where is...? Oh! Yes! It's coming from the hills over there, and look! There's a light shining in the sky too, shining where the shepherds are watching their sheep. Listen! It's the sound of voices, voices singing, no, not human voices, not earthly voices. What glorious music — like I've never heard before. It can't be from this world. It just can't be. It's as though a gap between Heaven and Earth is being bridged.

But wait, I hear something else. Oh! Oh my!

Can't you hear it? That sound, it's so familiar and yet, that's the most incredible sound I've ever heard! Oh! — Even more wonderful than the voices of those angels singing. Somehow I know — I *know* that that is the sound that will alter all that has ever happened in the past and change all that will ever happen in the future. I'm telling you the truth; there's never been a night like this before, and there will never be a night like this again. No! The world will never be the same after tonight.

Oh, you can't hear it can you? Oh dear, then you won't understand how I feel. No, I've got to caution you that it doesn't make sense, this awe, this sense of wonder about that sound. When I tell you, I can hear you asking, "Is that all? What could be so special about that?" Oh, but it *is*, believe me, it *is* special; I assure you it is wonderfully, marvelously special. I just can't believe that I, it can't be that I, the poor wife of an innkeeper, am allowed to be in on this mystery, this secret wonder of the ages.

You see, it's the sound — it's the sound of a Baby crying.

I have made you hear new things from this time, Even hidden things, and you did not know them. They are created now and not from the beginning. Isaiah 48:6, 7

And suddenly there was with the angel a multitude of the heavenly host praising God and saying: 'Glory to God in the highest, And on earth peace, good will toward men!' Luke 2:13, 14 (NKJV)

Dear Jesus, Lord and Savior, thank you for loving us so much that you left your heavenly home and came to Earth as a human being — as a baby who cried, as a boy who got lost, as a man who worked as a carpenter. You were one who walked among us, lived among us, and then took on the death of the Cross, dying for us so that we might have life Eternal in You. Amen.

December 25

Christmas Day is Here!

The day so full of things to do! The day that children love. The day of gifts. The day of remembering. The day of missing loved ones gone before. And for some, the day of sadness because it's the day in which we're "supposed" to be happy. Whatever today means to you, just know this: God loves you. Jesus came into the world, the exact date unknown. But the important part is: He came! And He came for you and for me. Between everything else that happens today, remember, "Jesus loves me, this I know."

> *Therefore the Lord Himself will give you a sign: Behold, the virgin shall conceive and bear a Son, and shall call His name Immanuel* [God with us]. ' Isaiah 7:14 (NKJV)

Lord, give us inner peace this day as we remember the day you were sent to Earth. Amen.

December 26

Here Comes the Train

It's hard to admit it, but for many years Christmas was a difficult holiday for me. During that time in my life I experienced not only the usually stress of the season, but also an inexplicable sadness that increased as the date came closer. I have read that many people feel sad or depressed at Christmas but they also feel pressure to be "happy" and "merry," which, of course, makes them feel even worse. For me, it helped just a bit to write the following poem that expressed, with just a tad of humor, what I was feeling.

The Christmas Express

Here it comes! It's the Christmas Express
Loaded with baggage of headaches and stress.
I can hear it now; I dare not look back.
I've got to keep running, keep on the track.

The chimney needs fixing, the rugs are a mess.
Once past Thanksgiving, there goes thankfulness!
Time to buy the cards now but how many to send?
Or should I be asking, *How much can I spend?*

The Express comes closer! I know, I can hear
Its insistent rumbling sounding in my ear.
And there goes that whistle — a warning so clear
That I've got to run faster; it's getting too near.

And still it comes nearer; I can feel the ground,
Its trembling and quaking added to the sound.
Oh! The children's Christmas play — how could I forget?
Did I pick up the costumes from the cleaners yet?

And the Christmas tree, big or small, live or dead?
How to keep a warm smile, yet have a cool head?
And there's that noise and that vibration at my heel —
The Christmas Express! It's causing me to reel.

It's just about now. It happens each year.
It comes upon me — the thing I most fear:
Everything and me! Are out of control
But the Christmas Express continues to roll.

Running over and past and I'm left in its wake,
Feeling as flat as a Christmas pancake.
I don't remember much about the big day.
Denial and repression seem to keep it that way.

But potatoes were mashed and the cranberries sauced.
And though no one ate it, the salad was tossed.
A nephew cried — no one passed him the peas.
It seems he forgot he was supposed to 'please.'

Well, it's all over now and yet I won't try
To finally fit in the time to just cry.
In fact, it's so quiet, I can hear myself sigh
"Never again," but I know that's a lie.

God decided to let his people know this rich and glorious
secret which he has for all people. This secret is Christ
himself, who is in you. He is our only hope for glory.
Colossians 1:27 (NCV)

Jesus, you are the hope of the ages and however I celebrate your birth, whether with crowds, or in solitude, I praise and honor you and give you glory forever and forever. Amen.

December 27

Unwanted?

She was supposed to be born on this date in 1938. Instead, she had already been in the world for two months, having come as a 3-½ pound preemie. Some months earlier her mother had stood in front of a mirror and looked at herself crying out, "Oh, no."

You see, this "thing" had happened to her: She was not married and she was pregnant. At one point she decided to end the pregnancy, not by abortion, but by falling and hopefully causing a miscarriage. It didn't work. That baby stayed in the womb until she had been in there for seven months. When she was born, her mother could hold her in one hand. She found out this "thing" was a little person, a little girl, the only girl born in the hospital in Little Rock, Arkansas that week (all the rest were "big" boys). A nurse came by and announced, "That little thing ain't gonna live; she's just like a little bird." But the "little thing" did, and the father who had by that time married the mother, proudly carried her home once she weighed five pounds. She was wanted after all.

You've probably guessed who she is — me. I've been on this blue planet for 72 years now! How amazing is that!

> *You have covered me in my mother's womb...My frame was not hidden from you when I was made in secret...Your eyes saw my substance, being yet unformed. And in Your book they all were written, The days fashioned for me, When as yet there were none of them.* Psalm 139:13-16 (NKJV)

My Father in Heaven, thank you for allowing me to born! I am so happy to be here! Amen.

December 28

Newspaper Prayers

One of my favorite lessons about prayer was learned at a religious retreat sponsored by Hollywood Presbyterian Church. The conference leader, the Rev. Ralph Osborn, passed out newspapers to the participants. He told us to pray through the paper. What did he mean? Well, basically we were to turn the pages, and be aware that prayer is needed everywhere, and so as we read, we were to pray for the people and situations that filled those pages.

The most important lesson I learned from this experience was that even as reading the paper can be distressing, it can also be the time when we cast the cares of the world onto God where they belong. Rarely there is anything one can do about the bad news, but always one can pray. Then instead of leaving the newspaper, full of the heaviness of all the sin, suffering, and sorrow that we've encountered there, we can leave each person or situation in God's hands — that boy in critical condition after a car accident, that family whose home was burned down, the unrest in war-torn countries, and so forth.

Sometimes the Lord may ask us to *do* something (i.e., send a note, give to a cause), but always, it is good to pray. Then we can put the paper down, get up, and leave those worries with our sovereign God.

Casting all your care upon Him, for He cares for you. 1 Peter 5:7 (NKJV)

Lord God, help me to learn to leave things in your hands. I trust that you will hear my prayer daily for those about whom I read. Amen.

December 29

Creation's Ongoing Mysteries

Science. I have fancied myself a frustrated scientist my entire life. I do not have a place in my brain that does mathematics, though I did try a course in astronomy once (big mistake!). I loved working at Cal-Tech in the 60s because I was surrounded by scientists — teaching staff and students — all in search of "truth." Of course the truth they were after was only that which could be proven! That was the key for them. Their paradigm considered no God as fact or Divine Designer.

But as I look at what scientists have discovered in even the last few years, I see that "truth" is changing, it is unfolding, it is a continual revelation in every scientific field. What a wonder the creation of God is. Scientists who believe in God say there is a pattern, a design, therefore there must be a Designer! Yes, and what a Designer — no matter how or where we look, there are things in earth or sky that are larger, or further, or smaller or, in some way, different, than once thought. There are more things to be discovered; the answers only bring on more questions! The world is a wonder! And I know the One who did it all! What a delight. Our God is so great that He has made Himself known to the little ones, the little human beings living on the little blue ball in this Milky Way galaxy, in the vastness of space —Earthlings, all of us, visited once by God in the flesh!

Ah, but there are other dimensions; I know because my God came from a place beyond time and space to be in time and space! And that's the greatest wonder of all, the strangest miracle in the history of the world.

In the beginning God created the heavens and the earth. Genesis 1:1

And the word became flesh and dwelt among us. John 1:14 (NKJV)

Lord God, maker of the universes, we honor and praise you for your design of incomprehensible complexity and beauty and we praise and bless you for coming to dwell for a time on the earth that you created so that we might come to know you as more than Creator, but also as friend and Savior. Amen.

December 30

A Key — Forgiveness

Of all the things in my life that I have learned to do through a function of the will, it is to forgive. I am still learning. And now I'm suggesting that if you haven't already done so, make a *habit* of it. As someone has said, "When you become a Christian, you relinquish your right to get even." I'm not suggesting that we can do this on our own. Without God we can do nothing, and we need His power and grace to forgive others but we can start with our wills, telling God that we are willing to do so, and then ask for His help.

So forgive! Do it all the time, day-by-day, moment-by-moment. Let it go, the memories, the bitterness, the hatred, the need for revenge — just let it go. For me, this is the hardest and yet it is the best thing I'm learning to do. It sets me free. In a sense it will also sets God free to do what He wants to do in my life and the life of that person who needs forgiveness.

Think about it; meditate on it. Who is it that you need to forgive? Ask God to show you. Then start the process. And that's what it is — a process — some times one of a lifetime. Remember this: forgiveness is a prerequisite for being forgiven by God. Some things are trivial and easy to forgive like the woman at the cash register who was rude to you. Other things, like sexual abuse by a parent, will take a long, long time. But keep at it.

I pray that you, my dear reader, will, if you do not already, practice this key to spiritual freedom: Learn how to forgive, make it a habit! I promise you it will change your life from the inside out.

> *...if you have anything against anyone, forgive him, that your Father in heaven may also forgive you your trespasses, But if you do not forgive, neither will your Father in heaven forgive your trespasses.* Mark 11:25, 26 (NKJV)

Father, show me those I need to forgive and I promise I will start the process of that forgiveness now and keep it going until there is no more anger, or pain, or fear or need for revenge left in me. Amen.

December 31

The Principal Thing

In my life, since knowing Jesus, there is one thing that I have longed to do above all else, and that is to love. God commands that we love Him with all our hearts, minds, souls and strength, and that we are to love our neighbors as ourselves. Love is considered one of the main fruits of the Spirit. Some believe that the scripture verse in Galatians 5:22 that describes the fruit of the Spirit uses the word "love" and the following words, not as a list of equal qualities, but as descriptions of the fruit (singular) of love itself — its many manifestations. Next month, I'm going to start out the New Year by reading "love chapter" (1 Corinthians 13); will you join me? Love is without doubt, the most important thing for each of us to learn — to be a loving human being toward God and others. The way to learn better how to do that is to choose the better part — like Mary in the Bible did — spending time with Jesus.

Learning how to love is a lifetime lesson. How do I do it? What is the most loving thing I can do in this situation? How can I best love this person? What do I do? What do I say? What do I *not* say? Some people are using the, "What-Would-Jesus-Do?" motto to help them. That's a good thing, but unless we know Him, I mean *really* know Him intimately, we won't know what He would do; we are only guessing. Until and unless we know Him truly, in everyday conversation, regular Bible reading, intimate contacts, times of receiving, times of giving praise and offering up worship, times of just resting peacefully in His presence, until then, we won't know how to love because we won't know what He is showing us in each situation or how to allow His love to flow through us as we become one with Him. We are to be united in heart and soul and spirit with Him, the One who is LOVE.

A few weeks ago I was going to go shopping and I asked God to reveal me how He sees the people around me. This is what He showed me: He loved each one with compassion and caring and concern, and as I felt His love for them, I found that I loved them too! I blessed them or I prayed little prayers for them. I discovered anew that God loves each individual. What a wonder!

Yes, our God is love. Love is the ultimate definition of God and Jesus was the ultimate expression of God's love in action when He came to Earth. Without God we can do nothing and without Him teaching us and loving through us, no matter how much we want to, we won't be able to do it, because we can't do it on our own. That simply means asking for help to be a loving person. Let's make that our aim every day in this coming year.

> *But the fruit of the Spirit is love, joy, peace, longsuffering, kindness, goodness, faithfulness, gentleness, self-control. Against such there is no law.* Galatians 5:22, 23 (NKJV) *Let all that you do be done with love.* 1 Corinthians 16:14 (NKJV)

Lord God, help me to be **one with you** so that I will love with your love, and may all the glory be yours. Amen.

In Times of Death

When my grandmother died, I remember walking into the funeral parlor to view her body. That's when I knew that the person — who she was — had gone, her spirit had left. That was just a frame, empty, no longer needed. She, the essence of her being, was with God.

Hattie was my mother's roommate at the hospital where she spent her last months. When Hattie died, I didn't know it had happened. However, on my way to visit my mother, I was suddenly surrounded with a cloud of glory! I felt the angels, I felt Heaven, I felt God. I thought to myself, "Mama must have died and gone to be with the Lord." But no, when I arrived, I found that it wasn't her time yet, it was Hattie's. She had gone to be with her dear Jesus! And I got a sneak preview of what it must be like to be welcomed Home.

When Birgitta's little grandma died, she was with her in Sweden. She was looking at her and then turned away and looked at the red amaryllis in the window. She watched as before her eyes, it gently as though filmed with a stop action camera, wilted, and hung its head in melancholy. It was as though suddenly all life had gone out of it. She turned to look at her grandmother again, and realized her spirit had gone at the same moment the flower had wilted. What a lovely, sweet picture of one's final going away that was—a flower gently fading. That is the best illustration of what death is about I've ever heard, but yet the mystery remains.

The grass withers, the flower fades, But the word of our God stands forever. Isaiah 40:7

Lord God, you hold the keys of death and Hades, help us to deal with the death of our loved ones by your supernatural power and sustain us with your comfort. Amen.

CPSIA information can be obtained at www.ICGtesting.com
260640BV00001B/105/P